Piagetian Dimensions
of Clinical Relevance

Piagetian Dimensions
of Clinical Relevance

HUGH ROSEN

Columbia University Press
New York 1985

Library of Congress Cataloging in Publication Data

Rosen, Hugh.
Piagetian dimensions of clinical relevance.

Rev. ed. of: Pathway to Piaget. 1st ed. c1977.
Bibliography: p.
Includes index.
1. Cognition in children. 2. Piaget, Jean, 1896–
3. Child psychotherapy. I. Rosen, Hugh. Pathway to
Piaget. II. Title. [DNLM: 1. Piaget, Jean, 1896–
2. Child Development. 3. Cognition–in infancy & child-
hood. 4. Psychotherapy–in infancy & childhood.
WS 105.5.C7 R813p]
BF723.C5R67 1985   155.4'13   85-2608
ISBN 0-231-06076-9

Columbia University Press
New York Guildford, Surrey
Copyright © 1985 Columbia University Press

Printed in the United States of America

Clothbound editions of Columbia University Press books are
Smyth-sewn and printed on permanent and durable acid-free paper.

Book design by Ken Venezio.

To
Evan Gist
for making the theories come alive

Contents

Preface

I have often been approached by colleagues and students in the mental health field who profess an interest in knowing more about the work of Jean Piaget, for certainly they sense the significance of it for anyone seriously interested in human growth and behavior. However, they find the prospect of ranging through his vast and difficult material dismaying. Yet none of the extant introductory texts on Piaget's work, some of which are excellent, have been written expressly to address the special interests of clinicians. Most books on Piaget's theories and research focus upon the normal development of logical thought in the individual and the construction of knowledge about the physical world. If they address a sphere of application at all, it is generally to the field of education. While the present volume offers a thorough exposition of Piaget's standard works, it goes beyond that to explore implications of the Piagetian paradigm for such domains as affectivity, interpersonal relationships, social reasoning, moral judgment, adaptive communication, developmental psychopathology, and clinical interventions. In formulating this material, I have made a generous use of theoretical and research efforts by others who have adopted Piaget's work as a point of departure. The credit for any errors in this book, however, should unequivocably be accorded to me.

The first edition of this book was published in 1977 under the title *Pathway to Piaget: A Guide for Clinicians, Educators, and Developmentalists.* Although it is likely to continue to be of interest and value to educators and even more so to developmentalists, it has undergone a major revision with the special interests of the clinician in mind. The first chapter has been greatly expanded to encompass some of

Piaget's more recent work on such topics as consciousness, memory, causality, reflected abstraction, and equilibration. In addition, the description of formal operations has been extended considerably. Four other chapters from the first edition have been reorganized and integrated into a single chapter under the unifying theme of social-cognitive development. New material reflecting the current positions of such developmentalists as Damon, Gilligan, and Turiel in the areas of sociomoral knowledge has been incorporated into the chapter, as has been Kohlberg's revised statement on his moral stage theory.

The chapter on conservation that appeared in the first edition has been deleted in the second. It was decided that it contained much more material than the clinician would ever want to know about the subject, while the essentials of conservation are amply presented in other parts of the book. In general, an attempt has been made throughout the book to update material wherever indicated.

A completely new chapter has been added to this revised edition, in which the Piagetian paradigm is examined from the standpoint of its relevance to psychotherapy and other clinical interventions. Although not a system of psychotherapy itself, Piaget's genetic epistemology does offer a point of view from which to reconceptualize psychotherapeutic models and, in some instances, to generate new approaches to clinical assessment and intervention.

Piaget's work is comprised of a set of interlocking concepts and postulates, each component being difficult to understand without grasping the whole; while at the same time the total gestalt cannot be comprehended without a knowledge of its parts. It is in the very nature of the material that a careful exposition of it will warrant a certain amount of repetition. Yet it is hoped that each repetition will impart a slightly different perspective and a moderately novel insight to an aspect of the material. As dreams were said by Freud to be a royal road to the unconscious, I hope this book will prove to be an enlightening pathway to Piaget.

Sadly, since the publication of the first edition of this work, Piaget has died. Despite the extinction of his physical being, the spirit of Piaget most certainly will be conserved here on Earth. He was and continues to be an inspiration to many around the world through his recognized intellectual genius and consummate sense of humanity. His lifelong devotion and ceaseless efforts to developing the science of genetic epistemology have produced a paradigm shift of epic proportions in the way we now conceive of child development and adult cognition.

I would like to acknowledge the assistance I have received from several sources. I am indebted to Dr. William Adamson, chief of Child and Adolescent Psychiatry, Education and Training in the Department of Mental Health Sciences at Hahnemann University. His continued interest in this material and constructive comments have been helpful. The persistent enthusiasm, curiosity, and questions of my students have been an impetus without which this book may never have been written. Sally Sylk, the typist of the newly revised manuscript, has my gratitude for her diligence, fortitude, and competence. It is a pleasure to know someone who does not stop thinking upon entering into the role of typist. My thanks go to Dr. Wilbert R. Sykes for calling me, a total stranger to him, from another city one day to urge that I pursue a second printing of the book. His call was the impetus that led to the present volume. Also, my appreciation is extended to Susan Koscielniak, executive editor at Columbia University Press, and Joan McQuary, managing editor, for their guidance in bringing this project to fruition. Finally, I wish to cite the contribution of my friend Kevin Kuehlwein, whose moral support and intellectual stimulation throughout the writing of the current revision were invaluable.

Piagetian Dimensions
of Clinical Relevance

CHAPTER I

Genetic Epistemology:
Basic Concepts and Overview

Clinicians in the helping professions are invariably familiar with the field of human development. Nevertheless, their grasp of psychosexual and social development is rarely matched by an equal understanding of the evolution of cognitive competencies. Much interest mixed with awe is often expressed concerning the formidable work of Jean Piaget (1896–1980), who was undisputably this century's most productive and prominent developmental psychologist. His work comprises a highly complex and interdependent system which is difficult to comprehend in depth and, therefore, keeps many motivated but busy practitioners from studying it. The purpose of this chapter is to provide a theoretical foundation for the remainder of this book and to facilitate the process of comprehension in the more ambitious reader who may wish to turn to original Piagetian sources.

The ultimate goal of all Piaget's professional efforts has been to advance a science of genetic epistemology. The realm of epistemology embraces an examination of the nature of knowledge and the manner in which it is acquired. The qualifying term "genetic" is not a reference to the hereditary transmission of cognitive characteristics, but refers to the individual's own historical process in the acquisition of knowledge. The "genesis of knowledge" is perhaps a phrase which aptly captures the appropriate meaning. Epistemology is a well-established discipline in the tradition of Western philosophy. However, Piaget has gone far beyond the unvalidated speculations of philosophers and has rooted his pursuit of this science in empirical studies.

Piaget's epistemological focus is upon the relationship between knower and known.

At age ten Piaget published his first paper, a one-page description of a partly albino sparrow which he had observed in the park. During adolescence he published many papers on the subject of malacology, a branch of zoology. Born in 1896, Piaget was awarded a doctorate in 1918 at the University of Neuchâtel for his studies in the natural sciences and his thesis on mollusks. Previous baccalaureate work had already exposed him to such significant areas as psychology, logic, and the scientific method. All of these subjects, including his biological studies, were later to merge in a vast interrelated network of theory and research which was to become the Piagetian system. Postdoctorate studies involved Piaget in two psychological laboratories and Bleuler's psychiatric clinic in Zurich. Following a one-year experience in Zurich, he attended the Sorbonne for two years, where he pursued courses in such subjects as psychopathology, logic, and the philosophy of science. All of this eventuated with an experience standardizing Burt's reasoning tests in work with Parisian children at a grade school which was host to one of Binet's laboratories. Although he was interested in the correct answers given by the children, Piaget was fascinated by their mistakes. Discerning that the wrong answers were possibly governed by a developmental pattern, Piaget embarked upon the science of genetic epistemology. In brief, he sought to discover the reasoning behind the answers rather than to focus merely on the answers themselves. Evans (1973) contains Piaget's autobiography and expands upon these comments.

A summary statement of Piaget's work, to be elaborated upon in the balance of this book, is as follows. Development can be viewed as a series of cognitive transformations that liberate the growing person from embeddedness in environmental content. At the sensorimotor level the infant experiences the world as an extension of himself, and his knowledge of things is contingent on his overt actions upon them. There is no notion of past or future. With progression toward and especially into the preoperational period, there emerges a sense of the present in relation to past and future. Things in the world become known to have a continuing existence independent of the child's actions upon them. The child is now, however, perceptually grounded, and hence, the most salient perceptual features of what he observes become the basis for rules through which he processes information. It is in the concrete operational period that the perceptual is transcended by the construction of a logically coherent conceptual system. Yet the conceptual organization of the concrete operational period is limited by embeddedness in what is already known and familiar to the child. Concrete operations can perform only upon the real or actual. The cognitive reorganization that comes with the formal operational period frees the child from content or embeddedness in the real and liberates him to roam the realm of the possible and hypothetical. The capacity to generate new knowledge for himself and possibly even knowledge that is new to society is now his. Piaget states, "The proper function of cognitive processes . . . is to construct forms, then forms of forms, and so on. These constructs will be ever more abstract, and freer or more detached from all content" (1974/ 1980a:99).[1] With the advance from each cognitive stage to the next, the child acquires the capacity to think about the prior stage, in which he had been formerly embedded. Each advance offers a new perspective to the child on his old way of knowing-in-the-world.

METHODOLOGY

The Piagetian methodology has varied over the years. A consistent thread has been its reliance upon direct work with children in contrast to Freudian methodology. As is well known, Freud's developmental psychology was based primarily on reconctructions from the verbalization of his adult patients, relying heavily upon fantasy, dreams, associations, and memory. Both giants of psychology, however, utilized a clinical method. Piaget's first five books primarily center on discussions between the investigator and the children, the former posing questions which the latter attempt to answer. A standardized approach is deliberately avoided as the questioner is prepared to delve further into the child's line of reasoning, being sure to follow the cues of the child. Applying the method properly is the key to fruitful results, and Piaget maintains that at least a year of training is necessary to acquire proficiency in its use.

1. First date refers to original version in non-English; second date refers to English source utilized by the author. References at the end of this book are arranged by English date in chronological order.

The following period of Piaget's studies concentrated mainly upon the growth of intelligence during infancy and was based heavily upon direct obvservation, embellished by the ingenious use of objects placed in the environment for the child to manipulate. Piaget's approach to observing infants is akin to Darwin's meticulous accumulation of minute bits of data which were integrated to produce a theory of evolution. The richness of detail captured by Piaget is extraordinary, and one must read the original source material to fully appreciate it (Piaget 1936/1963, 1936/1971a, 1946/1962a). It has become commonplace to criticize Piaget's infancy studies because he employed a sample of only three babies, all of whom happened to be his own offspring. Significantly, however, there have been replicated studies, one of which utilizes a sample of ninety babies, essentially validating Piaget's own findings (Décarie 1965).

A third period of Piaget's work introduced an experimental method in which the child is presented with materials and assigned a problem-solving task. The child's subsequent actions are observed, and, in addition, he is asked to provide explanations for what he is doing. Studies utilizing this method have led to the formulation of highly complex logico-mathematical models. Piaget has never been interested in assigning quantitative measurements to intellectual attainment. He has consistently concentrated upon a qualitative assessment of the mental mechanisms underlying developing cognitive competencies. Furthermore, he has not sought to overwhelm with massive statistical data. Instead, his qualitative findings have served to generate innumerable hypotheses which have been experimented with cross-culturally around the world. The frequency with which replicated studies have confirmed his findings has been great. Criteria for a good theory embrace its potential for a fertile production of hypotheses. In this respect, Piaget's theories meet the test with consummate vigor.

In the final phase of his life's work, Piaget returned to several central themes to which he proceeded to apply his refined methodology. These themes are his biological orientation to cognition (Piaget 1974/1980a), physical causality (Piaget with Garcia 1971/1974), and the equilibration theory as an explanation of the developmental process (Piaget 1974/1980b, 1975/1977). Another subject of major significance, the relationship between action and thought, was covered in two volumes (Piaget 1974/1976a, 1974/1978) during this period.

FUNCTION AND STRUCTURE

In Piaget's view, intelligence is not an entity of the mind set apart from the body. It is an integral part of the person and is subject to some of the same biological processes governing the material aspects of all human and other organisims. These processes, specifically adaptation and organization, are known as functional invariants. They are called invariant because they continue to function in the same manner throughout the developmental stages, in contrast to cognitive structures which undergo qualitative changes over time. Before clarifying the functional invariants further, it will be useful, indeed necessary, to expand upon the nature of structures, as the two are so interrelated that one set cannot exist without the other. Although Piaget has shown great inventiveness in postulating theories about structures, he is actually part of a much broader contemporary movement known as structuralism. Prominent among the structuralists are Noam Chomsky, a world renowned linguist, and Claude Lévi-Strauss, a towering figure among anthropologists. Gardner, in speaking of all three researchers, Chomsky, Lévi-Strauss, and Piaget, has stated the following:

Each of these scholars focuses particularly on Man, seeing him as a constructive organism, with generative capacities, who nonetheless is preordained to follow certain paths in his intellectual development and achievement because of the structure of his own brain and the regulating forces in the human environment. (1972:242)

In another chapter he makes the following concise and illuminating statement:

In short the structuralists sought underlying arrangements of elements which determined overt forms of behavior and thought, could be expressed in logical formal language, and reflected the biological attributes of human beings. (p. 40)

Despite the immense similarity of their thought, Piaget differs significantly from both Chomsky and Lévi-Strauss in at least one major area. Piaget is a radical constructivist. Unlike the other two scholars, he does not believe that structures are innate. Chomsky, for example, points to the existence of inborn, linguistic structures which enable a child of even only average intelligence to exercise a set of universal

rules for dealing creatively with and learning relatively quickly any
language his environment exposes him to. Although these structures
permit the child to creatively generate an infinite variety of sentences
with his newly acquired language, they are static in the sense that
their essential character is not modified as the child develops. In sharp
contrast, Piaget asserts that cognitive structures are not innate. At
the beginning of infancy there exist only primitive reflexes, such as
sucking and grasping. Gradually the reflex behavior becomes refined
and coordinated and the child, through continued interaction with
his environment, constructs a progressively more complex network of
structures which provides cognitive competencies enabling increasingly more successful problem solving and adaptation. Before identifying the major periods of development, it will be necessary to elaborate
upon the functional invariants.

Adaptation and Organization. Adaptation is basically the organism's
relation to the external world, and organization is essentially an internal matter. Assimilation and accommodation are the twin processes
which interact together to form adaptation. The former is conservative
as it is a process in which the cognitive structure does not change.
What occurs is that the external stimulus, input from the outside, is
received and interpreted from the standpoint of the existing structure.
The external world is not received as a mere copy of reality. Instead,
what is "out there" is modified to conform to the present character of
the mental structures at the time of the interaction between organism
and environment. For example, in the case of a very young child
whose contact with four-legged, furry creatures has been confined to
small dogs, a drive in the country exposing him to cows and horses
may lead to exclamations about the extra large "dogs." The classificatory scheme (structure) for four-legged, furry creatures is presently
simple and globular. However, in the course of interacting with the
environment over time, the child will attempt to alter the existing
scheme to conform to the unique or differentiating features of the
new stimuli. Continued exposure to horses will lead to the recognition
that they have their own way of running and that they are capable of
kicking strongly. Since dogs neither gallop nor kick, the child will
modify his mental structure in order to differentiate between horses
and dogs. Eventually his classification schemes will become suffi-

ciently sophisticated so that he will not only be able to differentiate among four-legged, furry creatures, but will be able to deal with them in a hierarchical and inclusive relationship. In other words, he will recognize that horses and dogs are two of many types of creatures, all of which may be classified as animals.

The emergence of new mental structures and the modification of preexisting ones are brought about by attempts to accommodate the existing structures to the contours of the external reality. Because it involves change, accommodation is viewed as progressive, in contrast to assimilation which is conservative, since in the latter there is no alteration of structure. These twin processes are of singular importance as reflected in the following comment by Flavell: "Assimilation and accommodation constitute the most fundamental ingredients of intellectual functioning. Both functions are present in every intellectual act, of whatever type, and developmental level" (1963:58). Nevertheless, the relationship between these two processes will vary throughout development. Generally, when intelligent functioning is present there will be an equilibrium, a balance, between assimilation and accommodation. On the one hand, equilibrium avoids an excessive and slavish conformity to the external and surface appearance of reality, while on the other, it avoids constantly fitting external stimuli into one's own subjective schemes, regardless of the new features of the stimuli which do not appear to fit. Hence, the complex events in a child's life do not simply make an imprint upon a passive mind, but are actively construed by him through an internal meaning system which continuously develops into a rich, highly organized, and interlocking network of cognitive structures. Commenting on what he sees as Piaget's main epistemological thesis, Flavell states: "The cognizing organism is at all levels a very, very active agent who always meets the environment well over halfway, who actually *constructs* his world by assimilating it to schemas while accommodating these schemas to its constraints" (1963:71).

Organization, one of the two functional invariants, plays a vital role in the internal meaning system of the human organism. Examples of this can be observed as early as during infancy. At first the baby will suck reflexively. If the hand happens to fall into the mouth, sucking will be activated. But shortly after birth the infant begins to coordinate the placement of his thumb into his mouth with the sucking behavior. Within a few months such separate schemas as looking and grasping are organized into a single scheme manifesting such behavior as grasping an object which then is brought closer and visually examined. The term "scheme" does not stand simply for a single act; it refers primarily to an abstract structure which covers a whole class of similar behaviors. It is, in a sense, an internal design for action. Advanced and more complex structures are no longer called schemes, but operations. An operation is an internalized action. By its nature it supposes some conservation, has the characteristic of reversibility, and is always related to a larger system of operations. To study the essentials of Piaget's work is to study the construction of operations. An example of organization at a later developmental period may be enlightening. Movement into the concrete operational period is usually initiated by the emergence of classificatory and seriating operations. Classification at this point involves not only the ability to arrange objects in a proper hierarchy, but also the competence to recognize and understand the inclusion relationships obtaining. Seriation is the capacity to place a group of different-sized objects in appropriate order, without trial and error, ranging in a progressive series from the smallest to the largest, or vice versa.

Classificatory and seriation structures always precede the cognitive competence for dealing properly with number tasks; the reverse order never occurs. Piaget's explanation (Piaget 1941/1965a) for this empirical fact is that the two earlier operations are organized to form a number operation. In other words, the ability to grasp number depends upon classification and seriation because by its very nature it is made up of these operations. For example, to grasp the nature of the number five, it is necessary to understand that it is inclusive of a particular group of individual units each treated alike, regardless of other differences (i.e., color, shape, weight), much as when one assigns individual items to a class. In this instance, the class is the cardinal number five. In addition, to truly grasp the nature of five it must be understood that five is simultaneously greater than four and less than six. The capacity manifested here to see the relational nature of five in either direction is one form of reversibility, a cornerstone of intellectual attainment, and it is precisely this ability that enables seriation to emerge. Explained in this way, it is possible to see that an ability to fully comprehend numbers will never precede the development of classificatory and seriation structures, as the logic of the situation dictates the inevitable sequence. Not surprisingly, independent research continues to find the same sequence of development discovered earlier by Piaget in this and other areas.

DEVELOPMENTAL PERIODS

The thought processes of children differ substantially from those of adults, just as they do between very young children and older children. These differences are not simply a matter of having less intelligence when younger and more when older. Rather, they are qualitative and are attributable to the mental structures which change over time through adaptation and organization. Piaget's research has revealed four major developmental periods, each one made up of numerous stages and substages.

Sensorimotor Period. The sensorimotor period extends from the beginning of life to approximately eighteen to twenty-four months of age. At the beginning of this period the infant is characterized by a profound egocentrism. Egocentrism is the inability to differentiate between subject and object. It does not imply selfishness, but is a term used by Piaget mainly to denote a particular type of cognitive deficit. Each period witnesses a decline of the form of egocentrism specific to it as intellectual progress occurs, but as the child enters the next period he experiences a new level of egocentrism.

During infancy the child does not differentiate between his sensations and their external referents. Even more broadly, he does not differentiate between himself and the outside world. Piaget is willing to allow that this is narcissism, but it is such without a Narcissus (Piaget 1924/1969a). The point is that at this earliest phase of development there is no differentiated sense of self to be experienced as separate from nonself. Nevertheless, throughout infancy there is a gradual construction of schemes which enables the child to undergo a miniature "Copernican revolution." Hence, by the close of the sensorimotor period, the child experiences himself as only one object existing among innumerable others, each enjoying spatial positions relative to one another.

In the earlier phases of the period, the child's actions tend to be body centered, but there occurs a progressive decentering as the child's actions increasingly display a differentiation between his own body and other objects. A hallmark of intelligent behavior, the adaptation of a means to achieve an end, evolves throughout this process. Goals obtained earlier only by trial and error are eventually achieved more economically, eliminating the inefficiency of such procedures. By the end of this period, the goal itself can be held in mind from the beginning of a planned sequence of actions, whereas earlier a goal would first be obtained as the result of an accidental manipulation upon the environment and subsequently, sought deliberately (Piaget 1936/1963). Keeping pace with these accomplishments, the infant is also acquiring cognitive competencies in object permanence, causality, space, and time (Piaget 1936/1971a). All of these developments are significant both in themselves and as precursors to more advanced intellectual achievements. Although symbolic activity does not appear until the sixth and final stage of the sensorimotor period, Piaget views this period as the foundation of intelligence because the child's overt actions so clearly manifest intelligent behavior. Further, he cites this period as sound proof for his controversial stand that language acquisition is not a necessary condition for intelligence. In fact, he believes that the development of cognitive structures are necessary to language acquisition. A growing body of research has been providing support to Piaget's position on the language-cognition controversy (Furth 1966; Sinclair-de-Zwart 1969; Cromer 1974).

The sensorimotor period is also important because it illustrates the roots of Piaget's view that all intelligence is action. (Note that he does not maintain that all action is intelligent.) It is of course more difficult to appreciate this outlook beyond the sensorimotor period. However, Piaget insists that overt, intelligent behavior during the first period of intellectual development subsequently becomes interiorized, and the solutions to problems are worked out through mental actions.

The reader interested in a comparison between Piaget's sensorimotor period and psychoanalytic theory might wish to consult Wolff (1960).

Preoperational Period. The crowning achievement of the sensorimotor period is the use of the symbol. The major attainments in goal-directed behavior, object permanence, causality, space, and time are all contingent upon the use of the symnbol. The sixth stage of sensorimotor period heralds the beginning of the preoperational period, which covers the child's life from approximately eighteen to twenty-four months through six or seven years of age. The first phase of the preoperational period is characterized by the development of the semiotic function (called the symbolic function in Piaget's earlier work). It is at this point in development that representational thought arrives, allowing the child to mentally leap into the past and future. He is no longer destined to be grounded within the field of the immediate present. The semiotic function is made up of two components: signs and symbols. Signs are words and symbols like those utilized in mathematics and science. They are arbitrary in that they bear no necessary or intrinsic relationship to that which they signify, and public in that they are an agreed-upon convention and socially shared. Symbols (other than those employed in mathematics and science) are such elements as dream symbols, mental images, symbolic play, and deferred imitation (Piaget (1946/1962a). Both symbols and signs are called signifiers, which means that they can represent objects not present to the the perceptual apparatus. However, unlike signs, symbols are motivated, tend to be ego-involved, and are private. Also, symbols resemble that which is signified. For example, a mental image can represent an absent object, but to do so it must resemble that object in some way. Conversely, a word (sign) can stand for an absent object but need not resemble it at all. In interpreting Piaget, Furth (1966) points out that he uses the term "symbolic" in a more Freudian sense than in the sense of symbolic-logic. Hence, there is an element of egocentrism about it, for it does not reflect the objective comprehension which one would look for in refined logical thinking. But it is precisely the development of logical thinking that has been the primary focus of Piagetian investigations.

The preoperational period may prove to be of exceptional interest to many clinicians. Much of Piaget's early work is devoted to this period of the child's development, although not confined to it, and covers such areas as language and thought (Piaget 1923/1955), modes of reasoning (Piaget 1924/1969a), the child's view of the world and causality (Piaget 1926/1960a, 1927/1969b), and the development of the child's moral judgment (Piaget 1932/1965b). On the whole, Piaget stresses the limitations rather than the achievements of this period.

Nevertheless, it is quite a fascinating period of growth. During this period the child centers his thinking, which means that he attends to one aspect of an object or event rather than decentering and thereby taking into account two or more aspects simultaneously. For example, if two sticks of the same size are placed side by side horizontally, with the left and right ends aligned evenly, the child can recognize that they are the same length. However, if the top stick is moved to the left, the young child will no longer recognize the identity of length. He will usually center on the observable fact that the top stick is farther to the left and will consider it as the longer of the two. He fails to recognize that while the stick is longer at the left end, it is shorter at the right end. In brief, he is not decentering, as he is not taking into account simultaneously both the left and right sides of the arrangement. Although the child is now able to represent absent objects in his mind, his actual reasoning tends to be perceptually rooted in that, by centering on only one aspect of what he sees, he distorts information and draws false conclusions. Later he will develop the ability to decenter and will have constructed appropriate mental mechanisms for penetrating beyond misleading visual cues. This will enable him to process information in a more accurate and adaptive fashion.

A second major limitation of the preoperational period is irreversibility. The child is unable to follow a process from beginning to end and retrace the steps back to the starting point. A very complex or even a simple procedure may be involved. In the elementary example of the two sticks given above, the preoperational child does not yet have the capacity to grasp mentally that the procedure could be reversed, and the sticks brought back into alignment. When he becomes capable of reversible thinking he reasons that were the sticks to be realigned they would again be the same size; therefore, they must now be the same size even though they are not evenly aligned. The child's irreversible thinking subjects him to contradictory and unsystematic thinking.

A third major limiting aspect of the preoperational period is the static character of the child's thinking. He is not attuned to transformations, but instead centers on separate states. For example, when two beakers of the same size are established as containing an equal amount of water, he believes that there is more water in a third, narrower but taller beaker after the water from one of the first two vessels is poured into it. He centers on the height of the third vessel, failing to recognize the nature of the dynamic change which he has observed occurring. He lacks the operational structures which develop in the next period and enable him to deal with tasks involving transformations.

During the latter part of the preoperational period the child undergoes a transition during which he moves from centering on states toward comprehending transformations. His thinking becomes semireversible and his capacity for conceptualizing becomes more mature. At the opening of the period he functions only at a preconceptual stage. He does not have the capacity to identify a single defining common characteristic of a class and to consistently apply it to the total range of objects to which it is applicable. Instead, for example, he will start to group objects according to color (he may place together a blue circle and a blue triangle) and then shift to using shape as a defining characteristic (possibly adding a red triangle next to the blue triangle). The thinking reflected in this illustration proceeds from particular to particular and is called transductive reasoning. It is neither inductive nor deductive. Numerous instances of children's statements exemplifying transductive reasoning are provided in the book by Piaget on this subject. One of these is the child stating, "I haven't had my nap so it isn't afternoon" (1924/1969a:232). Another is "Daddy's getting hot water, so he's going to shave" (p. 231). Of course, it is possible for the conclusions arrived at this way to be correct, but they will not necessarily be so, and when they are it will not be for the right reason. The preconcept lacks genuine individuality and genuine generality. We are all familiar with the young child who mistakes any man who walks down the street, perhaps puffing a pipe as his father usually does, to be his father. The child does not have a true concept of his father as a single individual, nor does he have a true general concept of all men forming a class, in which his father is only one member. The preconcept exists on a plane halfway between the individual and the general and is responsible for fostering transductive reasoning. Piaget comments, "In other words, transduction is reasoning without reversible nestings of a hierarchy of classes and relations" (1946/1962a:234). A little further he remarks, "To sum up, it is clear that transduction, which is co-ordination without a hierarchy of nestings, remains half-way between practical reasoning, which is a continuation of sensorimotor co-ordinations, and truly logical reasoning" (p. 237). In the latter phase of the preoperational period the child is able to properly arrange concrete materials in true hierarchies. However, when questioned about these his answers reveal that he does not as yet have a genuine comprehension of inclusion in the classification systems. As an example, a child dealing with twelve wooden beads, ten of which are brown and two of which are white, would persist in thinking that there are more brown beads than wooden beads. He would continue to do this even after clearly establishing that there are a total of twelve wooden beads and that the brown beads, as well as the white beads, are indeed wooden. He lacks the ability to simultaneously consider the subclass (brown beads) and the general class (wooden beads). Once separating the part from the whole, he loses sight of the fact that the subclass is nested or included within the more general class.

Egocentrism in the preoperational period offers a fascinating topic for study. Its remnants when persisting into the adult life of an individual may explain some of the irrational behavior encountered, and may account for interpersonal problems and perhaps even psychopathology (Odier 1956; Lidz 1973; Serban 1982). Because he does not have the ability to differentiate between his own point of view and that of others, the preoperational child cannot take the role of another. He assumes that what he thinks and feels is a predominant view shared by all. This has a far-reaching effect on his speech and social interaction (Piaget 1923/1955). The child does not bother to construct sentences which will provide the information which the listener needs for comprehension. He uses pronouns without explanatory referents, he leaves out necessary causal connections, and he does not offer logical proof of his assertions. He appears to be under the impression that he is understood regardless of these shortcomings which, of course, he is unaware of. In brief, the child is not aware of the listener's informational needs and, therefore, makes no attempt to adapt to them. The situation is rendered even more complicated when the listener is a peer, for he, too, is locked into his own egocentrism. The listener often believes he has understood the speaker, when actually he has only assimilated what he has heard into his own meaning system. Communication of this sort rarely achieves the satisfactory results sought by the speaker. Consequently, there will be frustration and friction. It is out of the crucible of social interaction, with its increasing challenges and demands for clarification and proof, that genuinely socialized speech begins to emerge. Egocentric speech, in turn, begins to decline.

There are other quite interesting and important preoperational phenomena, such as animism, realism, and artificialism, which Piaget has investigated and explains by once again invoking the concept of an underlying egocentrism. These, along with the child's tendency to see chance events in the world as motivated (psychological causality), reveal a great deal about the cosmology of the child. Piaget cautions the reader against interpreting these findings as suggesting that the child has a highly integrated and systematic worldview. The verbal responses of the child reflect spontaneous thoughts to questions he had never before considered. Indeed, the unsystematic character of the preoperational child's thinking is one of its most striking features.

Despite the earlier emphasis upon the limiting characteristics of the preoperational period, Piaget's recent work (Piaget 1976b) highlights the growth of knowledge that takes place during that period. Two significant capabilities are known as identities and functions. These both constitute knowledge that is qualitative in nature, rather than quantitative, as will appear when concrete operations emerge. For example, in the case of conservation of liquid, younger children believe that when water is poured from a short, wide container to a higher, thinner container, there is more in the latter. Yet, although they think the amount has been changed, they recognize that it is still basically the same water that has been transferred from one container to another. Hence, while preschool children do not conserve quantity, they do maintain qualitative identity throughout the transfer that occurs. Just prior to exhibiting qualitative identity, the children do pass through a stage in which they actually believe that the water poured into the second container is not even the same water as that which had been in the first container. Qualitative identity is thus seen to be an acquisition of the late preoperational period.

The logic of functions during the preoperational period is given special attention by Piaget. Here we are dealing with a semilogic involving covariations between two variables. The child's capability enables him to know that a change in one variable corresponds to a change in another variable. This is expressed in the formula $y = f(x)$, which represents a functional relationship. What it means is that a change in y is a function of a change in x. For example, if we were to observe a string placed over a pulley, we would see that segment A would become longer if it were pulled at that end, while at the same time the corresponding segment B on the other end of the pulley would become shorter. The child of four or five years of age recognizes this covariation and that the string is the same string as before the action was taken. What he does not yet recognize is that segment A + segment B before the action is equal to segment A + segment B after the action. Conservation of length, a quantitative competence, is a concrete operational acquisition. Qualitative invariance, however, appears in the late preoperational period.

In brief, Piaget divides the preoperational period into two phases, which are the preconceptual phase (two to four years) and the intuitive phase (four to seven years). Although logical errors characteristic of transductive reasoning may be found even in adult populations, such reasoning is a distinguishing characteristic of the preconceptual phase of development. During the intuitive phase the child's mode of knowing remains governed by perceptual input, but his increasing mastery of imagery proves a significant aid in the acquisition of knowledge. Decisive advances are made during the latter part of the preoperational period in areas known as qualitative conservations or identities and functions.

Concrete Operational Period. The third major epoch of intellectual development is the period of concrete operations. Much of what has occurred during the previous period has been preparatory for the achievements of the concrete plane. Marking the arrival of the concrete operational period is a systematic network of cognitive structures. Each operation, which is an internalized mental action, is an integral part of this newly emerging cognitive-structural system. The period generally starts at about six or seven years of age and continues until about eleven or twelve. The growing child is now capable of consistent and logical thought processes which take place internally. Flavell, in comparing the previous period and the one now under consideration, has stated the following:

In the preoperational period the child does possess, of course, representational actions in various states of internalization. But these preoperational actions, which Piaget sometimes labels *intuitions,* are sporadic and isolated cognitive expressions which do not coalesce into the tight ensembles we have been discussing. (1963:166)

The operations of this period are called concrete because they apply to objects rather than purely abstract concepts or verbal hypotheses. Weight, for example, will not be conceived of as an abstract concept in itself, but is tied to thinking about this heavy ball of clay or that light ball of clay. Any assumptions or premises from which the child proceeds to reason to a conclusion must be based on reality as he knows it. A wide range of physical materials has been utilized to test children in the Piagetian tasks of this period. The tasks include classification, seriation, one-to-one correspondences, and conservation of many kinds. Possibly because of the heavy emphasis on these materials, a notion has arisen in which it is believed that concrete operations can only be applied to objects which are visible and present in the environment. Lewis suggests a broader interpretation as found in the remarks which follow:

In saying that all this thinking still tends to be concrete in nature, Piaget does not mean that the child's reasoning is necessarily confined to what is present to his senses. In memory and in imagination the child can transport himself in time and space. But his thinking remains concrete so long as it is bound to the actual features of a situation—present or absent—rather than free to explore and deal with new and abstract relationships or to entertain a hypothesis and reason from it. (1963:169)

The logical structures of the concrete operational period are called groupings and involve both the logic of relations and the logic of class inclusion. The former has already been alluded to in the discussion on seriation, or ordering. It entails a type of reversible thinking known as reciprocity. In other words, if A is greater than B, then reciprocally B is less than A. Reciprocal thought in seriation is also seen in the school-age child's ability to recognize that in a set of ten different-sized sticks, B is larger than A and smaller than all of the remaining sticks. In other words, his thinking is reversible in that he can think in both directions. Transitivity is still another operation which the child has constructed and which applies here. It is the ability to draw conclusions about two elements through comparison with an intermediary element. For example, if A equals B and B equals C, then it follows that A equals C. At the concrete operational period, transitivity can be applied to real objects, but it is not until the formal operational period that it can be performed on a purely verbal level.

The logic of class inclusion entails reversible thinking known as negation or inversion. For example, in the grouping referred to as additive composition, the child can combine elements into a nesting of hierarchies and separate them by subtraction, thereby restoring the original position. For example, boys plus girls equal children. Children plus adults equal human beings. These additive compositions can be reversed. Adults removed from human beings leave children. Girls removed from children leave boys. In algebraic terms, $A + A^1 = B$. Negating the process, $B - A^1 = A$ (Pulaski 1971). The initial operation carried out in one direction is canceled by reversing the operation to restore the original position. Multiple classification is also a cognitive competency arrived at in this period. Formerly only able to attend to one feature of an object at a time, the child can now attend to two features of an object simultaneously. A banana, for example, can be viewed as both yellow and long. Class multiplication of this type is called bi-univocal and constitutes another of what Piaget calls groupings. There is a total of nine groupings of logical classes and relations which actually are quite complicated. The reader who seeks to grapple with these may wish to consult Flavell (1963) or Inhelder and Piaget (1955/1958, 1959/1969).

The characteristics of preoperational thinking which have been cited as limitations are eliminated with the development of concrete operations. The child is no longer misled by perceptual cues. He does not mistake appearance for reality. The ability to decenter, or attend to several aspects of a situation simultaneously, replaces centration. Thinking is no longer static but relates to transformations. Irreversibility gives way to reversibility of thought. All of these changes signifying more adaptive thinking are beautifully illustrated in conservation, a Piagetian task of singular import. Paiget's position is that all rational activity is necessarily contingent upon conservation. Conservation is the capacity to grasp that, despite certain changes in an object or set of objects, there are particular properties which remain unchanged. For example, given two balls of clay of equal amounts, reshaping one so that it is elongated will change the shape, but the two objects will still possess the same amount of clay. As another example, suppose that there is one row of ten pennies spread out evenly on a flat surface. Visibly below each penny in a one-to-one correspondence is a button. Will condensing one of the two rows change the equivalence of the sets? The preoperational child thinks that it will, even though he realizes that originally there were ten objects in that set. On the other hand, the concrete operational child will conserve number, knowing that changing the arrangement does not alter the actual number in either of the two rows.

Conservation studies are numerous and apply to a wide range of fields including substance, weight, volume, number, length, distance, area, time, and speed. A great deal of cross-cultural research has been done utilizing conservation tasks, most of which has confirmed Piaget's findings. It has been of considerable interest to note that the conservation of substance, weight, and volume does not emerge all at once, but is found to develop sequentially over a span of years. Conservaton of substance first appears at seven or eight years of age, weight at eight or nine years, and volume at eleven or twelve. In general, one should not conceive of concrete operational competence as emerging fully developed in all tasks at the threshold of this period. The development of cognitive competence in concrete operational tasks continues and is consolidated throughout the entire period and possibly even into the formal operational period.

What exactly does the concrete operational child disclose during a cognitive probe that accounts for his capacity to conserve; to utilize thought that is decentered, reversible, and transformational? Piaget believes that this newly emerging ability is based on several operations which have been constructed through the child's interaction with the environment and his own self-regulating mechanisms. Methodologically, Piaget poses questions to the child so that he can ascertain the line of reasoning which enables the child to conclude that conservation has taken place. The conserving child generally offers one or more of several explanations. He may say that the elongated piece of clay contains the same amount as the remaining ball of clay, because nothing has been added and nothing has been subtracted. Piaget calls this the identity operation. An alternative explanation often presented is the assertion that the sausage-shaped piece of clay could be compressed back into its original form, and, therefore, it must possess the same amount it had at the outset of the experiment. The reader will perhaps recognize this as the type of reversible thinking known as negation or inversion. Lastly, the child will sometimes use an operation called compensation, which enables him to recognize that what has been gained in length is lost in width; hence, there has been no overall change in amount. In other words, although the sausage-shaped clay is now longer than it was originally, it has become narrower, which compensates for the gain in length. Piaget also refers to this operation as reciprocity, another form of reversible thinking.

What if there were no cognitive competencies allowing for conservation in the many areas cited earlier? Science and modern technology as we know them could hardly exist. Indeed, everyday life would most likely be a chaotic affair, as the order and consistency necessary for civilization would not be possible. Yet somehow children all over the world do develop these cognitive capacities, in the same invariable sequence, even though they are rarely taught conservation directly. Conservation arrived at through natural interaction between the child and his environment has two outstanding characteristics. The first is its stability. It is not likely that the child will regress to a preconservation stage once he progresses beyond the initial phase of the preliminary acquisition of the relevant operations. The second is the logical certitude upon which the recognition of conservation is predicated. A child who has arrived at conservation competencies through the development of operational structures is unlikely to be misled by perceptual cues. He knows as a logical necessity that the mere reshaping of one of two objects, previously established as equal in substance, weight, and volume, will not alter the equality in those dimensions (Smedslund 1961 a-f).

Another component of the concrete operational period which develops alongside the logico-mathematical operations discussed above is known as infralogical operations. They address a different level of reality and are not considered inferior despite the use of the term "infralogical." While logico-mathematical operations deal with discrete discontinuous objects, such as the separate members constituting any class of objects, infralogical operations deal with continuous wholes, such as a single line or a block of space (Piaget and Inhelder 1966/1969). When members of a class are combined to form a higher order class, the members retain their distinctive and separate character. When separated from other members, they do not lose their discreteness. In contradistinction, in infralogical operations when a part is removed from a continuous whole, its integrity is not maintained. The whole object requires spatiotemporal proximity to maintain its integrity. Each of the groupings of the logical operations has a structural analogue in the form of an infralogical grouping (Flavell 1963). The major works covering infralogic are those on space (Piaget and Inhelder 1948/1967) and geometry (Piaget, Inhelder, and Szeminska 1948/1960).

Formal Operational Period. The period of formal operations is the last major cognitive epoch to evolve. An initial phase first appears at about twelve years of age and continues to about age fifteen. A second phase through the latter part of adolescence is one of consolidation and strengthening of the newly developed structures. Although Piaget does not posit a developmental period beyond this one, formal operations can be utilized to continuously deepen one's understanding of any body of knowledge, and they may be extended to achieve mastery over an increasingly wider range of knowledge domains throughout a lifetime. Formal operations are generative of new knowledge and, hence, promote novelty, invention, and creative thought of the highest order. Even so, it should be recognized that for Piaget, each individual's own process of intellectual development at *each* stage is a creative one.

The formal operational period is distinguished by the young person's cognitive ability to pursue the form of an argument apart from its content. For example, the statement "From if A, then B, it follows that if not B, then not A" is true (Flavell 1977). In other words, if given the presence of A it is always the case that B will be present, then in the absence of B, it will always be the case that A will be absent. This a logically valid line of reasoning regardless of whatever content A and B symbolize. It is not even necessary to know what they symbolize in order to derive a correct conclusion. This procedure is known as interpropositional reasoning and is more advanced than the intrapropositional reasoning of the concrete operational period, during which reasoning is confined to propositional statements about reality. The formal operational thinker is capable of symbolic reasoning, whereas the concrete operational thinker is content bound. Further, the formal operational thinker does not simply have theories about reality, but he also thinks about his own theories; he does not simply employ strategies of reasoning, but he thinks about and analyzes those strategies. This characteristic feature of formal operational thought is known as meta-thought.

Upon the arrival of the formal operational period, reality becomes subsumed by the realm of the possible. Inhelder and Piaget state the following:

In other words, formal thinking is essentially hypothetico-deductive. By this we mean that the deduction no longer refers directly to perceived realities but to hypothetical statements, i.e., it refers to propositions which are formulations or hypotheses or which formulate facts or events independently of whether or not they actually occur. (1955/1958:251)

Operations of the concrete operational period involve real objects and, therefore, are first-degree operatons. On the other hand, formal operations are second-degree operations. They go beyond the actual and the known object to employ hypothetico-deductive reasoning. Inhelder and Piaget observe that "the connection indicated by the words 'if . . . then' (inferential implication) links a required logical consequence to an assertion whose truth is merely a possibility" (1955/1958:257).

The young adolescent has now become capable of pursuing hypothetico-deductive reasoning by successfully designing and executing a scientific experiment. He can assess a situation, isolate single variables while holding all other variables constant, and proceed to draw logical conclusions based upon accurate observation of what takes place. Further, he has acquired the ability to successfully solve some problems through the use of combinatorial analysis. Given a range of elements and a task of discovering which particular combinations produce a specifically desired effect, he can arrange the elements in such a way as to systematically and exhaustively test all possible combinations.

An illustration from the work of Inhelder and Piaget (1955/1958) on what has been under discussion will be useful here. In this particular experiment children were asked to discover what it was that caused the bending of rods which were riveted over a basin of water. Several variables came into play, such as length of rod, material it was made of, whether it was thick or thin, and its shape such as round or square. Another variable was a set of differing weights which were available to place at the end of the horizontal rods. Children of varying ages participated in this experiment. Their problem-solving strategies became increasingly more efficient with age. However, it was only the adolescent subjects who evidenced hypothetico-deductive reasoning in applying the scientific method. They discovered that a long rod would cause bending, but that the presence of bending did not necessarily indicate that there was a long rod. This was due to the fact that bending could also be caused by a heavy weight being placed on a short rod. Such a relationship between length and bending constitutes a sufficient, but not necessary, condition. It is a logical relationship referred to quite simply as that of implication. Comprehending this invokes interpropositional reasoning, which can be stated symbolically as: if x, then y; but if y, then not necessarily x. A variation of this example is reciprocal implication, a causal relationship in which it follows that if x, then y, and if y, then x. In a separate experiment formal operational thinkers effectively discovered precisely this relationship when attempting to determine the cause of rapid oscillation of a pendulum. Among the several variables involved, only a short string on the pendulum would cause rapid movement. Therefore, it would follow that whenever such movement is said to obtain, it could logically be inferred that there must be a short string, as only that variable could cause such an effect. This constitutes a necessary and sufficient condition. Stated symbolically: if x, then y; if y, then x.

Implication and reciprocal implication together with fourteen other types of causal relationships constitute what Piaget and Inhelder call the sixteen binary operations model. The model depicts the way in which two propositions can be variously interrelated to produce sixteen posssible causal relationships. To illustrate, in symbolic terms let P and Q represent the two propositions. The negation or falsity of these propositions is represented by placing a horizontal sign above them, as follows: $\bar{P}$ and $\bar{Q}$. In modern logic the sixteen possibilities are rendered into truth tables. The general form of a truth table looks like example 1.1.

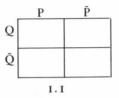

1.1

Of the four possibilities in this four-celled truth table, there are sixteen possible combinations, ranging from all four cells marked true (T) to all four cells marked false (F). To illustrate, two truth tables, one representing implication and the other reciprocal implication, are presented in example 1.2.

	P	P̄				P	P̄	
Q	T	T	P = long		Q	T	F	P = short
Q̄	F	T	Q = bending		Q̄	F	T	Q = fast

Implication   Reciprocal Implication
(Rod Experiment)   1.2   (Pendulum Experiment)

The way to read a truth table is to note whether the combined propositions may logically be verified in reality or not. For example, in the pendulum experiment it will never be that one will discover a short string and a not fast or slow movement. Stated more generally, the causal connection of reciprocal relationship does not ever include an instance in which propositions P and Q̄ are true. Hence, an F for false has been placed in the lower left quadrant. To cite another example, in the rod experiment it is possible to have a not long or short rod and still have bending. In formal terms, it is possible in the causal relationship of implication to verify an instance of P̄ and Q. Therefore, a T for true has been placed in the upper right quadrant.

Particularly pertinent to the above material is a comment by Gruber and Vonèche in which they state:

The point of this combinatorial system is that the operations in question form a closely knit system in which passage from one element of the structure to another is always possible. . . . Thanks to this closed system of transformations the preadolescent becomes capable of inserting real cases in the set of all possible cases that can be generated logically. Reality has become a special case of possibility. The system of all possible combinations forms the logic of propositions. (1977:395)

By "preadolescent," Gruber and Vonèche mean the child on the threshold of formal operations.

In addition to the sixteen binary operations model, Piaget has identified one other powerful model that is characteristic of the formal operational period of development. It is known as the INRC structure and can be brought to bear to explain a variety of phenomena in the physical world. An attempt will be made here to present a simplified version of Piaget's specific application to the equilibrium problem. In this structure I = identity, N = negation, R = reciprocity, and C = correlation. A balance and a set of weights are used in this experiment. The point of the problem is to see if the child understands the set of relationships which obtain between the weights on both sides of the balance and the distance of the weights on each side from the center. Involved in dealing effectively with this problem is proportionality and the integration of both forms of reversibility. These constitute formal operational structures offering a high range of power. Their conceptual sophistication is especially apparent when compared with the strategy of the young preoperational child who attempts to restore an imbalance of the scale by pushing down with his hand the end that is tipped upward. The identity is affected by adding weight to one side of the scale. Since this disrupts the balance, the problem is to restore it. The action can be negated by simply removing the weight that had been added. This, of course, restores the original balance. Reciprocity is an action that will restore the balance by compensating for the added weight rather than by negating it. Reciprocity neutralizes the effect of adding weight. By definition, the correlation is the inverse of the reciprocal. It has the same effect as would the adding of weight, but does not involve actually adding weight. If weight is added to one side, the effect can be neutralized by moving the weight on the opposite side outward from the center of the balance. The inverse or correlation of this reciprocal action would be to move the same weight inward rather than outward. This correlation action has the same effect as adding weight on the opposite side would have had. An alternate way of achieving a reciprocal effect is to move the weight that has been added closer to the center. This neutralizes the effect of having added the weight. The inverse or correlation would be to move the original weight outward from the center without adding any more weight. In doing so an imbalance will be effected as would have been the case had weight been added. Conversely, the correlation of removing weight from the original amount would be to move the original weight closer to the center instead of actually removing any weight. A simple reciprocal operation to adding weight on one side would be to add the same amount on the other side at an equal distance from the center. The inversion or correlation to that operation would be to remove weight from the opposite side from which one might have added the weight to create an imbalance. Either adding weight on one side or removing it from the other will produce the same type of imbalance.

What can be seen from this analysis is that I and C will produce the same result. Applied to the scale problem, there will be an imbalance created whether one adds weight or performs the inverse of the reciprocal. On the other hand, N and R will also produce the same effect as one another. Whether one removes the added weight or performs an operation that neutralizes it, the balance that has been disrupted by adding weight would be restored. In the concrete operational period the two reversible operations are applied separately; negation to the classification task and reciprocity to the seriation task. In the formal operational period negation and reciprocity are integrated into one unified system. For example, the adolescent thinker in resolving the equilibrium problem realizes that he can remove some of the added weight *and* move the remaining weight somewhat closer to the center. There is a recognition of the proportionate relationship that an increase in weight and decrease in distance is equal to a decrease in weight and an increase in distance. In the INRC structure each of the operations is defined in relation to the others. It is only at the formal operational period that the young person fully understands the subtlety and multiplicity of these interrelated connections and is able to apply this comprehension across a wide range of problems.

The INRC structure is actually a very abstract model of operational thought, even though its application here has been to a tangible illustration. In fact, Piaget construes it as being isomorphic in structure with the sixteen binary operations model. The two models are organized to form a superordinate structure at the formal operational period.[2] These two powerful models of logical operations which Piaget uses to explain the higher order thinking of formal operations are part of a cognitive unconscious. The complex and systematic network of mental structures which enable formal operational thought is not known to the thinker as such, however. (For further discussion of the cognitive unconscious, see page 198.) Weiner (1975) has advanced a model of psychotherapy based upon Piaget's conception of a cognitive unconscious.

A major advance of the formal operational period is the capacity to generate second order concepts and relationships. First order concepts are derived directly from objects in the real world, such as weight and volume. The concept of density ($W \div V$), however, is a second order concept because it is not directly abstracted from the real world, but is a relationship between two first order concepts. Extending this further, a comparison between two second order concepts provides a second order relationship. The ability to think at this level of development, for example, would facilitate the resolution of problems about whether an object would float on water. If the object is more dense than the water, it will sink, and if it is less dense, it will float. Speed or velocity would be another example of a second order concept, as it is derived by dividing distance by time, two first order concepts. Comparing the speed of one object to another is, once again, dealing with a second order relationship.

The achievement of formal operations is not predetermined, and it does not follow that all people will attain them. In an extensive study, Kuhn, Langer, Kohlherg, and Haan (1977) concluded that most adults maintain a developmental position between the concrete and formal operational periods. Approximately 30 percent go beyond this transitional state to achieve a consolidated formal operational level. About 15 percent of their subjects evidenced that they had attained no formal operational thought whatsoever. As adolescence is the period during which development of formal operations is occurring, one would expect to find a gradual progression toward a higher incidence with the passing of each of the teen years. While the subjects of Kuhn et al. were from an industrialized society, observations of some primitive

2. See Cowan (1978) for an elaboration upon how the INRC structure and the sixteen binary operations are interrelated.

tribes suggest that adult members of the entire group may not have reached the formal operational period. However, this is a debatable issue and it is entirely possible that while formal operations are theoretically independent of the content to which they are applied, in actual practice an individual may appear to utilize them in some areas and not in others. Piaget's comments on this are suggestive:

In brief, our . . . hypothesis would state that all normal subjects attain the stage of formal operations or structuring if not between 11–12 to 14–15 years, in any case between 15 and 20 years. However, they reach this stage in different areas according to their aptitudes and their professional specializations (advanced studies or different types of apprenticeship for the various trades): the way in which these formal structures are used, however, is not necessarily the same in all cases.

A formal structure seems . . . generalizable as it deals with hypotheses. However, it is one thing to dissociate the form from the content in a field which is of interest to the subject and within which he can apply his curiosity and initiative, and it is another to be able to generalize this same spontaneity of research and comprehension to a field foreign to the subject's career and interest. 1972a:9–10).

Thus it can be seen that despite the theoretical purity of disengaging form from content in the formal operational period, Piaget freely acknowledges in his later work that interest and aptitude contribute significantly to the actual performance of formal operational thought.

Egocentrism in the concrete operational period is seen in the child's inability to differentiate between the newly achieved structures and the actual object or content to which they are applied. As stated earlier, in the formal operational period the newly constructed logical structures enable thinking logically within the wider realm of the possible encompassing reality as merely one subset of what is possible. The adolescent arriving at the final period of cognitive development begins to look to the future and to experiment mentally with adult roles. He generates a multitude of abstract theories about the way society ought to be and is unmindful of the point of view which characterizes those who have been living and struggling for a much longer time in the society he hopes to reform. Highly speculative philosophical and political ventures are typical at this time in development. Inhelder and Piaget comment as follows:

The indefinite extension of powers of thought made possible by the new instruments of propositional logic at first is conducive to a failure to distinguish between the ego's new and unpredicted capacities and the social or cosmic universe to which they are applied. In other words, the adolescent goes through a phase in which he attributes an unlimited power to his own thoughts so that the dream of a glorious future or of transforming the world through Ideas (even if this idealism takes a materialistic form) seems to be not only fantasy but also an effective action which in itself modifies the empirical world. This is obviously a form of cognitive egocentrism. (1955/1958:345–346)

Decentration from this egocentrism of adolescence is facilitated largely by the establishment of peer groups in which ideas are expressed and tested out on one another. It is within this social context that the adolescent may discover the vulnerability of his ideas. Of even greater significance in fostering the decline of egocentrism in this period is passage into an occupation or professional training. Taking a job places the adolescent in an adult role, and in doing so he undergoes a transition from idealistic reformer to achiever. However, the transition is a slow one, as the adolescent's belief in the omnipotence of thought persists for some time to come. Nevertheless, the ultimate decline of egocentrism when achieved liberates the individual's thinking so that it is characterized by objectivity and reciprocity. He can now differentiate between his own thought and reality, between his own point of view and society's; in brief, he entertains multiple perspectives simultaneously and coordinates these many viewpoints in his own mind. If there is ever to be a universal and prolonged epoch of peace, it will be forged and maintained by people who have rid themselves of cognitive egocentrism.

FORMS OF ABSTRACTION

Piaget (1974/1980a) makes a conceptual distinction of considerable import pertaining to the abstracting process. One form of this activity is empirical abstraction, which is charactierized as exogenous knowledge. Put simply, it is the intellectual process leading to information about attributes that are inherent to objects within the external environment. For instance, anyone handling an object may derive a sense of its weight. Observing the same object will provide information about such variables as shape, color, or texture. Endogenous knowledge, known as reflecting or reflexive abstraction, is derived from the individual's coordination of actions or of operations. Knowledge of this kind is called endogenous because the focal point is the knowing subject and not the external object.

The term "reflecting" has two aspects as Piaget conceives of it. One is that of a projection of "reflecting" from a lower to a higher level. For example, an action from the sensorimotor period may be projected onto the representational plane once it has been interiorized. Eventually, at a later stage of development, operations once used to understand the environment are projected to a still higher plane where they, themselves, become the object of thought. The second is that it involves a mental reorganization or reconstruction. As Vuyk states, "The essential point is that the reconstruction leads to a new structure, that is to say, a qualitative change is made" (1981:119). Piaget emphasizes that exogenous and endogenous knowledge are not independent of one another. Exogenous knowledge provides the content which can only be understood by assimilation to structures that are endogenous constructions.

There is a classic example of reflecting abstraction which Piaget (1964) started writing about years ago and which he has frequently cited. It is that of a young child under seven years of age conting ten pebbles aligned in a row before him. He counts from left to right and from right to left. There are ten pebbles either way. He then goes through several sequences in which he keeps realigning the pebbles in different ways, such as in the shape of a circle. With each new realignment he recounts the pebbles from different directions, never failing to find that there are always exactly ten. In Piaget's view, the child has discovered not a property of the pebbles, but a property of his own actions: regardless of the order that the pebbles are cast in, the sum does not change. Eventually, upon reflecting on his own activity, the child will construct logico-mathematical knowledge which enables him to comprehend that the sum of *any* array of objects is independent of the way in which they are arranged. This endogenous contruction can then be generalized to all objects in any context. It has become for him a general rule which transcends his spatio-temporal actions upon the specific objects.

The term "reflected abstraction" is reserved for the formal operational period, usually beginning to appear at around eleven or twelve years of age. The terms "reflecting" or "reflective abstraction" are used variously, sometimes referring to abstraction anywhere along the span of development and sometimes confined in usage to the construction of logico-mathematical knowledge prior to formal operational thought. Reflected abstraction, specific to formal operations, is defined succinctly by Piaget as "conscious products of the reflexive abstractions" (1974/1976a:352). Piaget (1974/1976a) has investigated young people's increasing ability to conceptualize and verbalize the very nature of their own thinking strategies; the child's ability to achieve cognizance or consciousness of his own thought processes. It is this ability to render the cognitive unconscious conscious which constitutes reflected abstraction. In these studies the younger child can be observed successfully coming up with solutions to action-oriented problems before the time that he can successfully explain how he performed. The logico-mathematical structures necessary for successful behavioral performance would seem to be present before the child's cognizance or consciousness of his own reasoning strategies is evident. It is with the advent of formal operations that the capacity for cognizance emerges. This, of course, is not a new theme to Piaget's work and has its analogue in the sensorimotor period. It should be noted that although the formal operational adolescent achieves consciousness of his own actions and structures, he does not formalize this reconstructed knowledge into the logico-mathematical systems or models as Piaget and other philosopher-scientists have done (Vuyk 1981).

STAGES AND TRANSITIONS

In the foregoing exposition of Piaget's work there have been many references to the concept of stages. A review and refinement of the implications of this aspect of the system is now in order. The exquisitely detailed empirical validation of the innumerable and complex facets of human cognitive development will not be discussed here, but can be found throughout the books and articles which Piaget has authored over a lifetime of dedicated professional work. What becomes evident, however, in examining these detailed observations is that there is an invariable sequence to each stage of development. For example, if a particular competency is observed to develop in the

sequence ABC, it would be predicted that it will always develop in
that order, and it would not be predicted that an alternate order such
as ACB would be observed. Piaget has discovered that conservation
of substance, weight, and volume always appears in exactly that
sequence, spanning the concrete operational period and with an in-
terim of approximately two years between each stage. The early roots
of conservation can be observed in the development of object permanence, which occures in six invariably ordered stages during the
sensorimotor period. Familiarity with these stages reveals an internal
logic which makes the invariable character of their development not
at all surprising.

An approach to studying Piaget that will facilitate comprehension
is to examine each stage of cognitive competency in relation to its
preceding and subsequent stages. The principle to bear in mind is
that a given stage represents an advance over the former stage and a
limitation in relation to the following one. This applies to the broader
periods (sometimes called stages themselves) as well. For example, as
already noted, the concrete operational period is characterized by a
systematic and well-integrated network of logical structures in contrast to the preoperational period, which is unsystematic, not well-
integrated, and lacking in the ability to apply consistently logical
operations. Nevertheless, the concrete operational child can only
apply logical operations to real or familiar events and lacks the ability
to perform hypothetico-deductive reasoning or to engage in systematic
combinatorial analysis.

Piaget's views are often misunderstood to mean that arriving at a
particular level of development signifies that all cognitive functioning
is characterized by that level. It is more accurate to recognize that a
child, or even an adult, who has arrived at a certain level of development possesses the underlying structures needed for the type of performances typical of that level, and at times demonstrates behavior
governed by those structures, but does not necessarily do so in all of
his cognitive functioning. The brilliant scientist who exercises his
formal operational thinking constantly in the laboratory may not evidence the same high level of cognitive functioning in his personal life
and decision making. In fact, many everyday problem situations can
adequately be resolved through the use of concrete operations. Furthermore, certain rudiments of primitive stages of development may
persist into adulthood. For example, the earliest stages of development

during infancy show the child behaving in the causal sphere as if spatial contact were not necessary to produce certain effects upon objects. The infant may kick his foot in the air repeatedly as if to duplicate a pervious effect of moving a rattle dangling on a string which the infant's foot had fortuitously hit a few moments before. Rudiments of this early magical stage can be seen in adults who seek to change a red light by snapping their fingers, influence the weather by carrying an umbrella on a clear day, or affect the outcome of a ball game they may be observing, by their own body movements (Pulaski 1971).

The stage concept is often confused with the various ages that are so frequently cited in Piagetian literature. It has never been Piaget's intention to assert that specific cognitive competencies appear automatically at given ages. Such a viewpoint would be more in keeping with a maturational position. Although Piaget fully recognizes the necessity for neurophysiological maturation to occur, he does not believe that such maturation is a sufficient condition to produce the various stages which the developing child undergoes. Piaget is an interactionist and, therefore, places considerable emphasis upon the facilitative nature of the child interacting with people, objects, and events in the environment. As a result, contrary to what one would predict from a maturational view, there may be great differences in rate of development from individual to individual and perhaps even more so from culture to culture. The invariable sequence of the stages is what is universal and does not differ. When Piaget cites a certain age as the time when a problem is solved, he is utilizing a statistical convention, signifying that three-fourths of the children of that age have supplied the correct answer. More fully, if a problem is said to be solved at age seven, then it also follows that one-half of the children at age six can solve it, and one-third of the children at age five.

The progression from stage to stage is not really a simple matter, but is actually a complex one based on the countinuing organization and integration of preceding structures. Thus each new structure, while qualitatively different from its predecessors, subsumes the previous ones into a more highly organized network of structures. Piaget states as follows:

Inhelder and I, when considering the development of structures and of thought, speak of stages only in connexion with the formation of total structures. We include as special cases all structures observable during a given stage which integrate with the structures of the preceding stage as necessary sub-structures. (1960b:11)

Not all developmentalists subscribe to a view of stages as being quite so coherent, systematic, and organized as does Piaget himself. This question is presently a matter of some dispute, with insufficient evidence to arrive at a definitive conclusion thus far. However, even many of those who do not embrace Piaget's precise description of stages as "the formation of total structures" do give credence to the general direction of cognitive development he suggests and to the notion of essentially different strategies of reasoning emerging with age progression.

A discussion of cognitive development through stages inevitably gives rise to the question of what the mechanism is which accounts for the transition from one stage to the next. Piaget identifies four factors influencing development, which are heredity and the maturation of the nervous system, interaction with the physical environment involving the manipulation of objects, social transmission, and equilibration. It is the last of these which is most strongly emphasized in the Piagetian framework and which actually coordinates development in the other three spheres. The concepts of disequilibrium, equilibration, and equilibrium are not especially easy to grasp. Frequent exposure to them in a variety of contexts will undoubtedly increase one's familiarity with and comprehension of them. They are vital to Piaget's system and have far-reaching implications for the fields of education and psycotherapy. Langer, in commenting upon the probabilistic model which Piaget adopts to explain the equilibration process, states succinctly:

The thesis is that, when the child is in a structural state of disequilibrium, his assimilatory and accommodatory functions act to establish greater equilibrium. This can only come about by the performance of those actions that compensate for the perturbation and then feedback of the information obtained by these acts to the operative mental system. In this way the child changes his mental actions and develops. (1969:24)

In Piaget's own words:

An apparatus which solves problems by a succession of approximations based on a series of feedbacks shows in the most decisive manner the part played by the concepts of disequilibrium and of progressive equilibration. As long as there is disequilibrium, i.e., while the problem still remains unsolved, a new negative feedback is set off, whereas the attainment of the correct solution is marked by the production of a state of equilibrium. (1960b:9)

In the same context, Piaget (see also Flavell 1963) elaborates an example dealing with the development of the conservation of substance. He cites the study of a child six or seven years old who, at the outset, denies the existence of the conservation of substances. A ball of clay is elongated and the child adopts the strategy that there is more substance in state B (sausage shaped) than in state A (ball shaped) because it is longer. Note that he is centering on one aspect (length) only, from which he reasons. Further elongation leads the child to the same conclusion, namely that there is even more in state C because it is "still longer." However, in the next phase the error is corrected by negative feedback, for as the clay continues to be lengthened the quality of thinness, until now disregarded, becomes prominent. In fact, during this intermediary phase, the child will now say there is less clay, since he observes that it has become "too thin."Of course, he is actually still in error as he has merely substituted one centration, length, for another, thinness.

There then follows a stage of oscillation during which the child hesitatingly goes back and forth between saying first that there is more clay and then that there is less. At this time he lacks the coordination of actions which reversibility imparts. In the fourth phase, however, his strategy shifts and he attends not exclusively to one aspect of the phenomenon or another, but instead to the transformation itself. In so doing, he recognizes that what is gained in length is lost in width and, hence, through this compensatory mechasnism grasps that there is no overall change in the amount. In other words, the coordination of actions now takes place through a self-regulating process known as equilibration, which leads to the achievement of conservation of substance.

It is noteworthy that this has taken place with a child, age six or seven, who is already at the brink of acquiring the conservation of substance. If this procedure were to be attempted with a much younger child, it is not likely that the same outcome would occur. Similarly, if it were to be attempted with children of the same age, but using conservation of weight or volume, it would again be unlikely that there would have been the same outcome. Briefly, the developmental level of the child will determine whether or not he can mean-ingfully utilize new factors introduced into his environment. This gives rise to the principle of moderate novelty, which urges that to stimulate further development the new stimuli (cognitive aliment) should be neither monotonously what the child is already familiar with, nor too dissimilar from what he is presently familiar with. Inhelder, Sinclair, and Bovet in a recent work on the subject under discussion conclude their book by remarking:

> It is no less erroneous to assume that cognitive learning consists in the activation of already existing structures than to suppose that it consists in a substitution of new modes of reasoning for old. Learning is a constantly renewed process of synthesis between continuity and novelty. (1974:271–272)

Their work, reflecting years of research based on a Piagetian theoret-ical model, is a major breakthrough in the field of training studies designed to assist the passage of the subject from one stage of cognitive development to the next. Relatively primitive and uncoordinated schemes are not viewed as imparting mistaken or false information which must be eliminated by training or coercion. Such schemes are regarded as indicative of necessary stages which the developing child must undergo, and, however inadequate at the time, they provide the "foundation for further constructions" (p. 25).

Concepts of cognitive conflict, incongruity, and subjective dissat-isfaction are all relevant to Piaget's view of mental development. Inhelder, Sinclair, and Bovet (1974) have focused specifically on these areas. Their studies emphasize the kindling of the child's curiosity followed by the cognitive conflict introduced when his predictions are not matched by the events to follow in an experiment or when the schemes of two separate subsystems are brought into opposition. In this connection, it is essential to keep in mind, as suggested previously, that contradiction is not a property of a thing, but is a function of the subject-object relation, as influenced by the subject's level of cognitive development. In Piaget's words, "A device is not a disturber in itself, but, on the contrary, is conceived as a disturbance or not one according to the elements that have been acquired by the structure in formation" (1975/1977:39).

In his newly revised equilibration model, Piaget (1975/1977) explains cognitive growth in terms of affirmations and negations. Affirmations are the observable facts, as understood within the limits of the child's cognitive structural framework, whereas negation is the compensatory construction of what is not present. In a constructivist psychology the "observable facts" have a subjective character. Piaget clearly states, "The observables must . . . be defined by what the subject believes he perceives and not simply by what is perceivable" (1975/1977:44). Negation is a construction which goes beyond the perception of positive attributes and which utilizes the cognitive activity of inference. An initial state of nonbalance exists as the subject affirms the observables of an object, but does not cognize the negative component. The nonbalance becomes the impetus to further cognitive development. The construction of the negative constitutes a correcting or compensating force which brings the subject-object relation into a new balance or equilibrium characterized by more adaptive understanding. A state of equilibrium is not to be conceived of as permanent, for it is always vulnerable to new circumstances which will induce further disequilibrium and, hence, a renewal of the equilibrating process. In Piaget's theory, equilibration is the backbone of development, and it is not confined to any one stage but instead is found occurring throughout development from the sensorimotor period onward.

Applying this model to the conservation of substance discussed above, the nonconserving preoperational child affirms what he sees, namely that as the ball of clay is drawn into a sausage shape there is an addition of length. Since he is not yet capable of constructing the negation, he fails to take into account the subtraction of matter from the object's width, hence concluding that there is now a greater amount in the sausage-shaped clay. The preoperational child disregards the simultaneity of addition (length) and subtraction (width) in the single act of transforming the ball of clay into a sausage shape. That material is simply being displaced from one part of the object to another, without any change in the overall amount, is not recognized by the child. However, through a series of regulations every child advances to the stage of quantitative conservation, comprehending that each affirmation or addition is compensated for by a corresponding negation or subtraction. Once the child is able to coordinate both affirmation and negation, quantitative conservation has been achieved.

A CONSTRUCTIVIST VIEW OF MEMORY

Piaget and Inhelder (1968/1973) have formulated a novel and stimulating position on memory; one which is consistent with a constructivist psychology and based upon empirical investigations. The essential methodology has been to show the subject a stimulus which he is then asked to describe or draw immediately upon its removal. Without benefit of intervening exposure to the stimulus, the subject is asked once again to describe or draw it several months after the initial presentation. The stimuli utilized in the experiments were those of the familiar Piagetian tasks such as the seriation of varying-sized sticks. The results demonstrated qualitative improvements in recall after many months' duration rather than a fading of memory which would be predicted from a traditional storage-retrieval model. Piaget explains that in each case the child draws not what he had seen but what he knows. In other words, what had been observed is assimilated to the child's level of operative schemes. A preoperational child may observe a series of sticks arranged systematically in ascending order. However, once the sticks are removed and he is asked to draw what he had seen only minutes previously, he will not be able to accurately reproduce the sticks in proper order. What he draws will be commensurate with his stage of developing seriation competence. If over the next several months he progresses to the concrete operational period, hence attaining the completed seriation structure, then the child will accurately draw the sticks in ascending order. There occurs a reorganization and transformation of what has been recalled, resulting in a qualitative improvement of memory due to cognitive-structural development. Piaget does not contend that all memory is enhanced with time, but only that which derives from structural knowledge. Rote learning such as committing to memory a telephone number is subject to fading over time in the absence of repeated exposure or use.

A well-balanced review of the literature on memory from a cognitive-developmental perspective can be found in Liben (1977). The clinically oriented reader who would find a comparative analysis of Piaget's and Freud's views on memory to be of interest may turn to Casey (1980).

PHYSICAL CAUSALITY

The theme of causality unfolds throughout Piaget's material. It is present in his early works as he discusses the child's worldview (Piaget 1926/1960a, 1927/1969b) and in his discussion of the infant's understanding of the immediate environment (Piaget 1936/1971a). More recently a summary of about 100 studies on causality was published (Piaget with Garcia 1971/1974) with the promise that the studies would be published separately in a set of small books at later dates. Thus far none have appeared in English.

In a general commentary on the acquisition of knowledge about physical causality, Voyat states:

At the concrete operational level, causality becomes detached from its egocentric quality to proceed towards the direction of a deduction applied to the real. The overall evolution of the concept of physical causality during the individual development is directed through this dual process of decline of egocentrism and the replacement of the empirical appearance through the discovery of deeper abstractions not directly perceptible but logically deduced. (1982:132)

The early work of Piaget on causality studies the subject from the standpoint of the child's beliefs about natural phenomena (see Chapter 2, this book). The more recent studies focus upon causality in relation to physical objects in the child's environment "within a more defined context of action, forces, and reaction" (Voyat 1982:133).

Piaget's explanation for the psychogenesis of causality revolves around the interaction between objects and operations. Ultimately he maintains "the interpretation of causality as operational structures attributed to the object" (Piaget with Garcia 1971/1974:133). But then what is the source of an operation itself? Operations are constructed as a result of the child's own actions upon objects and an accompanying process of reflexive abstraction. It is not that they exist in an a priori fashion and are then superimposed as a causal explanation upon objects. For example, the preoperational child does not possess the transitivity operation. Competence at transitivity is achieved by the concrete operational period through a series of activities that the child has initiated with the objects in his environment. This in turn enables him to attribute the operation of transitivity to objects as a causal explanation when appropriate. Piaget illustrates this through a discussion of tasks involving what he calls immediate and mediate transmissions. The child grasps the first of these quite early in development, observing that moving object A can have the effect of dislocating object B upon coming in contact with it. However, force traveling through mediate transmission is not directly observable, and it involves an inference going beyond the data presented to the senses. Imagine a set of four marbles A, B, C, and D. Marbles B, C, and D are adjacent to one another. Marble A is set in motion so that it bumps into B. The observable effect is that while B and C remain stationary, D is jolted forward. The transitivity operations allows the child to consider the possibility that a vibrating force is passing through the stationary marbles from A to D even though the passage is unobservable and despite the fact that A never comes into direct contact with D (Forman and Sigel 1979).

Piaget's later work on causality is quite intricate and the present formulation is a simplified version, to be sure. The work is of major importance, however, and it has served as a springboard for contemporary research by Piaget and the Geneva School. Brief but excellent accounts of this material can be found in Piaget (1972b) and Vuyk (1981).

CONCLUSION

Knowledge, in the Piagetian view, inheres in neither the knowing subject nor the known object. Rather, it is by its very nature a relation between subject and object. The relation changes with development as the knower's self-regulative activity constructs new cognitive structures through which the external world becomes known with increasingly greater objectivity. De Lisi (1979) points out that each stage of intellectual development constitutes a subject-object relation that is qualitatively different from that of other stages. Recently, Kegan (1982) has constructed from this cardinal theme of Piaget's paradigm a new and comprehensive developmental theory of personality, attempting to account for both affect and cognition.

In contemplating Piaget's theory, it is important not to conceive of it merely as the study of logic. It is more accurately to be understood as a study of the evolution of natural thought in the individual, which moves in the direction of increasingly more effective reasoning strategies and, hence, adaptation. Natural thought evolving is thoroughly rooted in the same general biological processess of organization and adaptation that govern all living organisms.

The full scope of Piaget's work is staggering. Beyond what has been presented in this overview, he has authored books on space (Piaget and Inhelder 1948/1967), geometry (Piaget, Inhelder, and Szeminska 1948/1960), time (Piaget 1927/1971b), movement and speed (Piaget 1946/1971c), imagery (Piaget and Inhelder 1966/1971), chance (Piaget and Inhelder 1951/1975), and perception (Piaget 1961/1969c).

It is perhaps a matter of historical interest that the book on time and its sequel, the one on movement and speed, were the eventual outcome of several questions advanced by Albert Einstein, who had some familiarity with Piaget's work.

The reader may well be expected to wonder what Piaget has had to say about affect throughout his career. It should be kept in mind that affect was not the subject of Piaget's work, and he did not pretend to have offered a comprehensive theory of personality. Nevertheless, he did take the position that cognition and affect were not separable. Cognitive activity is always accompanied by some affect, even if it is only the interest necessary to perform the activity. Of course, one could further suggest that there is the satisfaction of joy that may accompany successfully working on a difficult intellectual problem, as well as the frustration that comes from being stymied in the pursuit of intellectual activity. On the other hand, affect never appears in a vacuum, but is always channeled by the cognitive structures present at any particular stage of development. One cannot have any feeling about that which one cannot conceive, for example. Although inseparable, cognition and affect are different by their very nature, in Piaget' view. He addressed the topic of affect only minimally in all of his works. Nevertheless, in a recently published monograph, long unavailable in English, Piaget (1954/1981) has set forth his views on affect and its relationship to intelligence. A shorter version of these views may be found in Piaget (1962b). While not elaborated upon at length, there is a recurrent theme in Piaget's work with respect to the role of affect in cognitive development which bears special attention. Tenzer formulates it succinctly and well: "Piaget states that emotional and other factors may affect *when* something is learned or *whether* it is learned but *how* it is learned remains the same" (1983:326).

Piaget's supreme influence and contribution within the field of cognitive-developmental psychology is indisputable. Nevertheless, the last few years have witnessed the emergence of neo-Piagetian models, as found in the works of Case (1978) and Fischer (1980). Alternative approaches offering vigorous challenges to Piaget's theories have also been surfacing (Bryant 1974; Siegel and Brainerd 1978; Gelman and Gallistel 1978). A full-length critique of Piaget's work is presented by Brown and Desforges (1979).

Exciting new developments have extended the Piagetian paradigm into studies of the child's social world (Damon 1977), children's conceptions of society (Furth 1980), the acquisition of social and moral knowledge (Turiel 1983; Rosen 1980), children's relationships to peers and parents (Youniss 1980), and the evolution of the child's interpersonal understanding (Selman 1980).

The impact of Piaget's work has been felt in such fields as philosophy, education, psychotherapy, psychopathology, and developmental psychology. Despite earlier and still occasional references to psychoanalysis, Piaget's work has been pursued independently of Freud's and of recent psychoanalytic refinements. There are certainly differences between Freud and Piaget, but these are open to reconciliation, as their respective emphases upon affect and cognition are more complementary than antagonistic. In a lecture given to the American Society of Psychoanalysis and later published, Piaget (1973) suggested that thought be given to developing a general psychology which would integrate the findings of both psychoanalysis and genetic epistemology.[3] He acknowledged that there are many problems yet to be solved.

3. See Anthony (1976), Basch (1977), Haan (1977), Greenspan (1979), Malerstein and Ahern (1979, 1982), Feffer (1982), and Levick (1983) for various attempts at comparing, contrasting, and integrating genetic epistemology and psycholanalysis.

Perhaps it was his purpose to incite our curiosity, initiate a new cognitive conflict, and to serve as an impetus toward reequilibration. This in turn would lead to coordinating psychoanalysis and genetic epistemology, structures in the history of ideas, and ultimately to the emergence of a new construction that would enable us to better understand ourselves and fellow human beings.

CHAPTER 2

Emerging and
Declining Egocentrism

Human development in the Piagetian system may be construed as a series of progressions toward objective relativism. Objective relativism, which allows for maximum adaptation to the environment, is achieved through the decline and conquest of egocentrism. The concept of egocentrism pervades Piaget's cognitive-developmental psychology, and a sound grasp of it is essential to comprehending his work. Although Piaget's emphasis has been upon cognitive development in relation to the physical world, it has been proposed that egocentrism may prove to be a significant link between cognition and personality dynamics (Feffer 1967; Elkind 1974). Furthermore, since egocentrism is a negative and limiting feature of development, it provides fertile grounds for exploring psychopathological phenomena in both the intrapsychic and interpersonal realms.

Despite his emphasis upon the physical world, Piaget was quite mindful of the contribution of social interaction to cognitive development and, indeed, of the contribution of cognitive structures to interpersonal relationships in both the moral and social spheres (Piaget 1932/1965b, 1947/1966). Because of the potential relevance of egocentrism to clinicians in the helping professions, this chapter will examine its nature and decline in depth.

Piaget's cognitive-developmental psychology is comprised of an unvarying sequence of major periods, stages, and substages. As the child interacts with his environment, he constructs new cognitive structures over time which afford him increasingly more adaptive prowess within his physical and social worlds. Each period is characterized by a superior set of newly developed structures which move in the direction of greater complexity and coordination. Although development at each advanced level introduces qualitatively different and better-organized structures, there is a common reemerging negative characteristic that stands as a limitation at the threshold of every new period. This reappearing phenomenon is egocentrism. In the most general sense it refers to a lack of differentiation between subject and object, between knower and known. Despite this basic definition, egocentrism will be seen to take diverse forms determined by the particular developmental period under examination.

There are fundamentally two types of egocentrism, one existing on the ontological plane and the other on the logical plane (Piaget 1926/1960a). The former illuminates for us the child's worldview of reality and causality, whereas the latter reveals a great deal about his judgment and reasoning. In ontological egocentrism the child does not experience the resistance of matter. Piaget states, "Reality is impregnated with self and thought is conceived as belonging to the category of physical matter. From the point of view of causality, all the universe is felt to be in communion with and obedient to the self" (1926/1960a: 167). The child's own desires and commands are felt to reign supreme because for him there exists no other point of view. In logical egocentrism, the child is unaware of the fact that others may have viewpoints which differ from his. He feels as if his own perspective is the only one possible, and, therefore, he does not recognize a need to offer proofs or verify his assumptions and assertions. It can be readily appreciated that his deficiency is likely to precipitate serious social difficulties, especially if carried over into adulthood. Underlying both types of egocentrism is a confusion between the subject's own convictions and those of others and between himself and the outside world. Although Piaget does use the word "confusion" in this context, it might be even more apt to speak of a "fusion" between inner and outer, between subject and object.

RADICAL EGOCENTRISM

During infancy there exists the most radical type of egocentrism, in which self and external world are totally undifferentiated. In fact, initially there is no self at all, and it is only through a gradual process of interaction with the environment that the infant simultaneously builds a self and differentiates from the objects in the milieu. Piaget writes, "Intelligence thus begins neither with knowledge of the self nor of things as such but with knowledge of their interaction, and it is by orienting itself simultaneously toward the two poles of that interaction that intelligence organizes the world by organizing itself" (1936/1971a: 400). The early infant does not differentiate between his own actions upon things and the independent existence of objects upon which he acts. Similarly, the sensations and perceptions he experiences are fused with the objects which are not accorded any separate permanence outside of the infant's sensating and perceiving activities. The infant takes his own activities to be the cause of effects in the environment, even though there may be no spatial contact. For example, an infant who produced the sound of a rattle by accidentally kicking it may be observed at a later time attempting to produce the same sound by kicking his feet in the air without any striving for proximity or contact with the rattle. Although this problem is resolved on a practical level by the end of the sensorimotor period (eighteen to twenty-four months), it is the precursor of the problem of psychological causality in the following period of preoperational thought.

By surmounting the problem of object permanence in particular, the infant contributes greatly toward the decline of radical egocentrism. At the start of life, he gives evidence of having no appreciation whatsoever, even on a purely practical level, that an object removed from his vision continues to exist. Through a series of six successive stages, however, he does obtain a cognitive structure or schema, as Piaget calls it, to deal with object permanence. Prior to the fourth stage, a child who has been playing with a ball which is then taken from him and hidden under a cushion will make no effort to retrieve it. At the fourth stage (eight to twelve months), the child will retrieve the ball under the condition described. However, at the time when he is just able to engage in this strategy, if he observes the ball being removed from cushion A and placed under cushion B, he will continue to seek the ball under cushion A, the place where he first found it. It is not until the fifth stage (twelve to eighteen months) that he develops the ability to cope with visible displacements, which means that he will go directly to cushion B to retrieve the ball, even though he had previously discovered it under cushion A. However, his capacity for doing this at stage 5 is contingent upon observing the ball as it is being moved from A to B. If in the process of the movement the ball were to be concealed in the hand of the experimenter, the child would revert to looking under cushion A and would make no attempt, upon not finding it, to look under cushion B. According to Piaget, the strategy for handling invisible displacements does not appear until the sixth stage (one and a half to two years).

There are many subtleties and subtstages to the development of object permanence which have not been covered in this highly schematic presentation. Nevertheless, it is hoped that the reader will derive a sense of the gradualness with which cognitive structures are constructed through stages. By the end of the sensorimotor period the child has undergone a profound evolution from primitive reflex activity, such a grasping and sucking, to the attainment of the symbolic function which permits representational thought. Developments in space, time, causality, object permanence, and means-end behavior have led to a differentiation between self and external world on a practical sensorimotor plane. The most primitive experience of egocentrism has been conquered. In the words of Piaget, "The elaboration of the universe by sensorimotor intelligence constitutes the transition from a state in which objects are centered about a self which believes it directs them, although completely unaware of itself as subject, to a state in which the self is placed, at least practically, in a stable world conceived as independent of personal activity" (1936/1971a:395).

ONTOLOGICAL EGOCENTRISM

In the study of the child beyond infancy, we encounter another array of fascinating developments bearing on egocentrism. These are to be found mainly in Piaget's first five books (1923/1955, 1924/1969a, 1926/1960a, 1927/1969b, 1932/1965b).

The child before the age of seven or eight does not recognize chance in the course of events. All that occurs in nature is seen as willed. There is a constant search for justification and motivation of events which, in fact, do not permit such explanation, because, as the child only later comes to recognize, they are due to chance or determined by physical laws. More positive and accurate explanations of causality emerge at seven to eight years of age, and by eleven to twelve years there has developed a genuine understanding of physical causality.

The child has progressively undergone a separation between self and universe. Causal sequences, which had been conceived of as occurring without intermediary links, are eventually objectified, and the need for such links, rather than one's own desires or existence, is recognized as a causal factor. There are as many as seventeen different types of causality in child thought as observed by Piaget. Only a few will be cited here to illustrate the manner in which the child's own subjectivity interpenetrates with his universe.

First, there is psychological causality or motivation. As an example, Piaget (1927/1969b) cites the fact that children often believe God has sent them a dream because they have done something wrong. As another example, Piaget tells of a child who explained a large mountain and a small mountain by saying that the former existed for adults and the latter for children. There is also phenomenalistic causality in which two facts observed contiguously in time and space are taken to be causally related, even though there may be no actual causal relation. For example, a pebble which has sunk to the bottom of the water has done so because of its color, or the moon is suspended in the sky because it is yellow. Piaget puts it succinctly: "Anything may produce anything" (1927/1969b:259). Relationships are readily seen between things in the universe when, in fact, none exist. Until age four or five, children tend to believe not only that the moon follows them, but that it is their own movements which force the moon to move along with them. Piaget refers to this as magical thinking. At age four or five, the child shifts from magical to animistic thinking and believes that the moon is following him because it is alive and willfully attempting to do so. Artificialist causality is the belief that things are made by humans through their own activity. Therefore, such things as bodies of water, mountains, and the stars are viewed as products of man's own activity. Finalistic causality is founded on the belief that all things are created for a purpose. Relevant to the preceding comments, Piaget has written, "In fact the child always begins by regarding his own point of view as absolute. . . . In so far as he ignores that his own point of view is subjective he believes himself the centre of the world, whence follow a whole group of finalistic, animistic, and quasi-magical conceptions" (1926/1960a: 126–127).

Animism is an intriguing aspect of child development. The young child generally conceives of everything in the universe as being alive or at least potentially alive. He virtually endows inanimate objects with such living properties as will, consciousness, and purposiveness. Initially all objects may be the locus of conscious activity. Although not said to be conscious at all times, a rock, for example, may feel nothing, but if moved may feel something. One child queried at age eight and a half and again a year later replied that the sun could see, a button could feel pain if torn off material, and a twisted piece of string that was unwinding was aware of its condition and wanted to get untwisted. As in so many of the areas uncovered by Piaget, progress is made through an unvarying sequence of stages. In the second stage of animistic thinking, consciousness is ascribed only to things which move spontaneously or whose special function it is to move, such as clouds, rivers, and bicycles. Upon arriving at the realization that such things as bicycles do not possess an intrinsic capacity for motion, the child no longer ascribes consciousness to them and reserves that attribute to things he continues to believe are capable of spontaneous motion. A child of eight years four months, in the third stage, told Piaget that a bicycle wasn't alive "because it has to be made to go" (1926/1960a:185), while at the same time he exclaimed that water can feel because it flows, fire because it is alive can move, and grass can feel because it is alive and it is alive because it grows.

Finally, in the fourth stage, which is not reached on the average until eleven to twelve years of age, the child restricts consciousness only to animals. One can readily discern in this progression a diminishing anthropomorphic extension of the child's own attributes to the external world. Gradually he forges a proper separation between himself and the objects populating his world. Although ages have occasionally been quoted to provide the reader with some guideposts, it is important to remember that they reflect only averages and that wide variations will be found on an interindividual, as well as intercultural, basis. It is the sequences of the developmental stages in each area which are not likely to vary. Additionally, the various phenomena which have been under examination here are not found in the child in the form of an aware, carefully thought out in advance, system of thought. Piaget is clear in stating, "In the child, animism is much more a general trend, a framework into which explanations are fitted than a consciously systematic belief" (1926/1960a:188).

The final concept to be examined in this section is intellectual realism, which is grounded in the child's confusion between the physical and the psychical. The young child takes an essentially psychic event and ascribes to it an external reality. Names are conceived of as being an attribute of the object named, and, during an intermediary stage of development, they are believed to be dissociable from the object, but not yet accorded the status of a purely mental activity. Hence, one youngster was able to say that her cousin's name remained at the airport when the cousin boarded a plane and flew off for a trip. However, in the first stage of nominal realism, the object is virtually believed to contain the name, so that the white object which is the moon actually contains within it the name "moon." Eventually, of course, this confusion between the signs and the things signified disappears and the two are separated.

The child's early attitudes about dreams serve as still another and quite excellent example of realism. In the first stage (approximately five to six years), the child thinks the dream has originated outside of himself, and even after awakening he views it as true in the same sense that other memories of his previous activities are a record of actual events. During the intermediary stage, the child (average age seven to eight years) recognizes that the dream has originated within himself, but continues to ascribe external existence to it. Finally, in the third stage (about nine to ten years), he appreciates that the dream is purely a mental event and he no longer believes that it has any objective status.

In summing up this portion of our exposition on ontological egocentrism, Piaget's own words are most pertinent:

These diverse manifestations of this early thinking are consistent in their prelogical character. They all manifest a deforming assimilation of reality to the child's own activity. Physical movements are directed toward a goal because the child's own movements are goal-oriented. Force is active and substantial because it is conceived on the model of muscular strength. Physical reality is animated and alive, while natural laws must be obeyed. In short, all of reality is construed with the self as the model. (1964/1968: 28–29)

THE LOGICAL FORM OF EGOCENTRISM

A classic example of the young child's inability to take the perspective of another is clearly illustrated in the three-mountain problem cited in Piaget and Inhalder's book on space (1948/1967). Although the ultimate achievement involves a series of subtle advances, only a brief, but essential, exposition will be presented here. Placed before the child is a simulated model of three mountains, each containing such items as trees and log cabins variously situated. The task of the child is to tell what the view of the experimenter seated across from him is. In a variation of this, the experimenter places a doll at different spots around the model, with the expectation that the child will report what he thinks the doll's perspective is. The basic finding in this experimental task is that the child's capacity for accurate reporting shows a definite progression through stages as he grows older.

More striking, however, is the fact that the child in the experiment persists in describing only his own point of view even when asked to describe a variety of viewpoints as the doll is moved around the model. The opportunity to view photographs of several views from varying positions or to actually walk around the model to observe the viewpoints has no effect on the resilient egocentrism of the child. Invariably, despite being exposed to these opportunities, the child reports his own viewpoint upon resuming the task. The problem is solved as the child develops from egocentric realism in which his own viewpoint is taken as an objective absolute to a capacity to entertain multiple perspectives simultaneously and, hence, engage in relational coordination. The egocentric child tends to center on one aspect of a reality at a time and is easily milsed by perceptual cues. The decline of egocentrism is related to the increasing capacity to decenter or take into account multiple perspectives simultaneously. The egocentric child lacks awareness that he holds a viewpoint which is differentiated from those of others, and he ascribes a false absolute to his personal centration. In time he constructs the cognitive structures which enable him to differentiate his own distinct viewpoint from those of others and to coordinate it with the various other perspectives. Thus, he eventually achieves objective relativity.

The inability to take the perspective of another was discussed at length in Piaget's first book (1923/1955), which was devoted to language and thought. Piaget's observations have led him to distinguish between egocentric logic and communicable logic. In the former, thinking is more intuitive than deductive and little effort is made to be explicit about the line of reasoning pursued. The child jumps in his reasoning from premise to conclusion without appropriate intermediary logical links. He does not feel constrained to verify his propositions or to offer proof of his assertions to those whom he addresses. Pronouns are freely utilized without clarity regarding the objects or people to whom they refer. In addition, causal connections such as "because" and "altogether" are rarely used properly. It is not until age seven or eight that communicable logic emerges, leading to socialized speech in which a desire to be truly heard and understood becomes evident. When the child is still predominantly egocentric he lacks the desire to effectively communicate and to genuinely understand what others are attempting to communicate. The reader is cautioned to bear in mind that shades of socialized speech will gradually appear prior to the suggested average ages of seven or eight, just as egocentric speech will persist to some degree beyond those ages. The young listener also poses problems in achieving genuinely socialized communication. He frequently believes he has understood what has been conveyed to him when, in fact, he very often has not. Piaget addressed this problem directly:

When the child hears people talk, he makes an effort, not so much to adapt himself and share the point of view of the other person as to assimilate everything he hears to his own point of view and to his own stock of information. An unknown word therefore seems to him less unknown than it would if he really tried to adapt himself to the other person. (1923/1955:64)

Egocentrism is, of course, characterized by being locked into one's own perspective and an accompanying inability to take the point of view of another. Consequently, it would follow that an egocentric speaker would not be able to discern the informational needs of the listener and that this would be reflected in the paucity of his syntax. Similarly, the young listener does not realize that an alternate viewpoint is being conveyed and that he must make an effort to understand on the speaker's terms if genuine communication is to transpire. Yet speaker and listener both labor under the impression that they have been understood and do understand respectively.

Additionally Piagetian contributions involving perspective taking, sometimes called role taking, can be observed in his comments on relationship. One type of common error is made when the child centers only upon himself and, hence, can recognize that he may have two brothers, but fails to see that he is also a brother to them and that, therefore, there are three brothers in the family. The young child has not yet developed a reciprocal schema (cognitive structure), which would enable him to deal with the reciprocity implied in the term "brother." In other words, if I have a brother, then I must also be a brother. He does not distinguish between the sibling and parental type of relation, in which he could have a father without, himself, being one. Younger children do not even conceive of a brother in relational terms. For example, a brother is seen in absolute terms simply as a boy who perhaps "is a little person who lives with us," or "A brother is a boy who is in the same flat" (Piaget 1924/1969a).

The notion of relativity is also seen to undergo development in the area of right and left. Progress moves through three stages toward socialization as subjectification diminishes. During the first stage (five to eight years), questions regarding right and left are answered from the child's point of view. Consequently, when asked to identify the left hand of a person facing him, the child will point to the right hand of the person opposite him. In the second stage (eight to eleven years), the child is able to identify right and left in relation to a person facing him. For example, the child will answer correctly when the person opposite openly holds a coin in his hand and asks whether it is in the right or left hand. However, at this time the child still does not understand the relative nature of left and right, but conceives of them as absolute positions. It is not until the third stage (eleven to twelve years) that he grasps the actual relativity of left and right regarding objects. It is at this time that the expression "to the left of" takes a genuine meaning as opposed to merely signifying left or right as absolutes. Previously, given an array of objects, A, B, and C, the child would simply state that B was in the middle. In the third stage, he recognizes that B is neither to the left nor to the right in any absolute sense. What he grasps is that B is simultaneously to the right of A and to the left of C, from his position. In summary Piaget states the following:

During the first [stage] the child places himself at his point of view, during the second at the point of view of others, and during the third at a completely relational point of view in which account is taken of objects in themselves. The process is therefore precisely that of the gradual socialization of thought-egocentrism, socialization, and finally complete objectivity. The curious thing is that the three stages are determined by ages which happen to correspond to the ages of important changes in the child's social life viz. 7–8, diminution of egocentrism, and 11–12, the stages of rules and of thought which has become sufficiently formal to reason from all given points of view. (1924/1969a:112–113)

The ability to deal properly with relations is made possible when the reciprocity involved in different perspectives is realized.

EGOCENTRISM IN OPERATIONAL THOUGHT

Concrete operational thinking generally appears at around six or seven years of age. The preceding preoperational period is really a preparatory phase for the eventual emergence of concrete operations. Thinking in this period is no longer misled by perceptual cues, but instead is capable of dealing with transformations. Hence, it is decentered, nonstatic, and reversible. By this time the cognitive structures of the mind have organized into a systematic network which provides the foundation for genuinely logical thinking. The child can now deal competently with tasks involved in conservation, classification, seriation, number, and transitivity. His logical prowess, however, is confined to real objects known to him through experience. Although the preoperational period is the one generally considered the most egocentric, it will be remembered that the onset of each new period, despite its advances, is marked by a new level of egocentrism which is itself inherent in the nature of the progress made.

The concrete operational child cannot as yet apply his newfound logical abilities to hypothetical situations. It is difficult for him to accept a premise for which he has no immediate verification and to reason on a deductive plane from it. To do this he would be required to psychologically take the point of view of the speaker presenting the hypothesis. The extent to which the concrete operational child can reason deductively is limited to the beliefs which he, himself, already has conviction about. It is his own worldview from which he can accept premises as a point of departure for his reasoning. If, however, the child is asked to deal with a problem that assumes that dogs have six heads, he will refuse to attempt a resolution because he rejects the hypothesis.

It is only in the formal operational period that an absurd hypothesis will not be a barrier to purely deductive thought. The formal operational thinker is not rooted to empirical necessity (dogs cannot have six heads), and he, therefore, is free to make deductions from any premise. The egocentrism of the concrete operational child consists of his inability to forego his own point of view or the one salient at the moment and to place himself in the role of the other in order to accept a nonevident premise from which he may deduce logical, although perhaps nonverifiable, conclusions. Piaget observes:

> It is only from the day that the child has said "I understand. Let us admit your point of view. Then if it were true . . . this is what would happen . . . because . . .," that a genuine hypothesis or a genuine assumption (i.e., one which is not believed in at all, but nevertheless analyzed for its own sake) has really dawned in his mind. Here again it is social intercourse, but of a far more delicate order than that which we have spoken of previously, that modifies the structure of thought. (1924/1969a:72)

Elkind (1974) has taken a position on egocentrism in the concrete operational period which is a modified, although still congenial, version of Piaget's work. In Elkind's view, the essence of the egocentrism is the child's confusion between empirical reality and his own assumption. The child will frequently interchange hypothesis and fact, dealing with one as though it were the other. Elkind's point is that the concrete operational child is more likely to take new evidence that runs counter to personal assumption and to attempt to make it conform to the assumption rather than to alter the assumption to match the facts. As a result, youngsters during this period hold many beliefs about people and social relations which are based only on partial information and which do no yield even when the child is presented with contradictory facts. Elkind calls these beliefs assumptive realities. The resemblance to delusions is superficial, for the assumptive realities are not characterized by either the narcissism or systematic character of delusions.

In the formal operational period (eleven to twelve years), the adolescent has at his command cognitive structures (operations) which enable him to test hypotheses in an experimental fashion and to revise his assumptive realities so they are in keeping with any contrary evidence which is discovered. He is now capable of hypothetico-deductive reasoning and of conducting a strict scientific experiment, involving holding all variables constant except one which is tested for its effect. He is capable of combinatorial thinking which enables him to systematically and exhaustively try out all possible combinations of a set of elements. He has also become capable of thinking about his own thinking, as well as reflecting upon the thoughts of other people. In the most general sense, the highest achievement of the formal operational period is that reality has become a subset of the possible for the young adolescent. Where, then, is the deficiency of egocentrism amid such a powerful spectrum of intellectual tools?

The adolescent begins to think of his present and future roles in society and, in so doing, contemplates a change in a limited, or perhaps even unlimited, sector of that society. The capacity to have thought about thought leads him to construct "systems" or "theories" which to his mind can possibly be superimposed over society. The theories generated may be of a political, philosophical, aesthetic, or scientific nature and often serve to breathe life into burgeoning reformist spirit of the adolescent. Inhelder and Piaget suggest that the preceding description reflects most accurately the intellectual and student classes, whereas this development will most likely assume other forms among the adolescent working and peasant classes. The basic process will remain the same, however; it is one in which the adolescent "is motivated also to take his place in the adult social framework, and with this aim he tends to participate in the ideas, ideals, and ideologies of a wider group through the medium of a number of verbal symbols to which he was indifferent as a child" (Inhelder and Piaget 1955/1958:34). The formal operational adolescent undergoing this process does not fully distinguish between his own perspective as he organizes a life plan and the viewpoint of the group he anticipates reforming. The reveries and plans he forges are grandiose and usually are later abandoned. Inhelder and Piaget are quite specific in explaining how their description of cognitive development in the formal operational period produces a type of egocentrism:

The indefinite extension of powers of thought made possible by the new instruments of propositional logic at first is conducive to a failure to distinguish between the ego's new and unpredicted capacities and the social or cosmic universe to which they are applied. In other words, the adolescent goes through a phase in which he attributes an unlimited power to his own thoughts so that the dream of a glorious future or of transforming the world through Ideas (even if this idealism takes a materialistic form) seems to be not only fantasy but also an effective action which in itself modifies the empirical world. This is obviously a form of cognitive egocentrism. (1955/ 1958:345-346)

Elkind (1974) has once again contributed to our understanding of egocentrism by offering the following observations about the adolescent's cognitive development. The youngster is now able to consider the thoughts of others, but he makes no distinction between his object of preoccupation and what may be of primary concern to others. Therefore, he believes that others are just as taken with the thought of him as he is himself. Put simply, while he is now taking into consideration what concerns others, he believes that it is his appearance and behavior they are concerned with. The adolescent anticipates the reactions of others to him and he expects these to be the same as the reaction he has to himself, whether positive or negative. Elkind coins the phrase *imaginary audience* to signify this phenomenon. Akin to this is what Elkind calls a *personal fable*—an untrue story which the adolescent accepts about himself. The young person believes there is a special uniqueness to his own experiences, and he conveys the impression that only he can feel so deeply in love and sorrow. The strong male may believe that he will never fall ill or die and the young female may believe that she will never become pregnant, even though she engages in sexual encounters without benefit of contraceptive devices. Both have the fantasy, the personal fable, that somehow they are special enough to be exempt from these common human experiences.

THE DECLINE OF EGOCENTRISM

It is apparent from the preceding that egocentrism is a state in which the knower is centered upon one point of view only—his own. Furthermore, he lacks awareness of other perspectives as well as the fact that he is confined exclusively to his own perspective (Flavell 1963). As self and object are differentiated, the knower simultaneously becomes increasingly more aware of his own self and point of view and of the point of view of others. The process involved in no longer focusing solely upon one centration, to the exclusion of other aspects of reality, is called decentration. In decentering, the cognizer also coordinates these various viewpoints as they become known to him, and he thus demonstrates a capability of entertaining multiple perspectives simultaneously. This progressive decentration at each developmental period leads to the disappearance of the egocentrism specific to the period.

Piaget sees the repetitive decentrations of the child's development as analogous to the decentrations occurring in the history of ideas, which brings to mind the often-cited phrase "ontogenesis recapitulates phylogenesis." A particularly apt example is the decline of radical egocentrism in which the child no longer experiences himself on a practical level as the center of the universe around which all else revolves, but comes to recognize that he is one of many objects in the milieu, each having positions in space relative to one another. The similarity of this achievement to the shift from the Ptolemaic system to the Copernican revolution is difficult to miss. In a stimulating comparison, Piaget further elaborates the recapitulation theory by stating, "The completion of the objective practical universe (end of sensorimotor period) resembles Newton's achievements as compared to the egocentrism of Aristotelian physics, but the absolute Newtonian time and space themselves remain egocentric from the point of view of Einstein's relativity because they envision only one perspective on the universe among many other perspectives which are equally possible and real" (1936/1971a:413).

To fully understand the mechanism leading to the decline of egocentrism, it is necessary to begin with the concepts of adaptation and organization which comprise the biological substratum of the Piagetian system and are referred to as functional invariants. They are so-called because they continue to perform throughout the developmental periods despite qualitative changes in the emerging cognitive structures. As noted in chapter 1, adaptation is comprised of two processes, assimilation and accommodation. Assimilation is the incorporation of external information into the preexisting cognitive structure (schema). Functioning in its present form, it does not involve any change in the structure and, hence, represents a conservative element in the meaning system or way in which the infant or child construes things. Accommodation is the effort made by the cognitive structure to conform to the external reality which is being assimilated.

Therefore, it promotes change in the structure and is considered a progressive element. Both processes are necessary for intelligent or adaptive functioning.

Initially, at the outset of infancy, the functional invariants are undifferentiated. The only existing schemas or structures are inherited or early acquired, such as sucking, grasping, and looking. Take grasping as an example. In the act of assimilating an object to his grasping schema, which is the infant's way of making sense out of his environment on a practical level, he must automatically accommodate his fingers to the shape of the object. Hence, the undifferentiated character of the infant's activity and the object. Flavell comments, "In short, agent and object, ego and outside world are inextricably linked together in even infantile action, and the distinction between assimilation of objects to the self and the accommodation of the self to objects simply does not exist" (1963:59). As a result, the infant at this point has no sense of spatial relations, independent existence of permanent objects, or causality. However, as the conservative assimilatory process attempts to reduce all of the external world to the present level of structural development, the progressive accommodatory process attempts to modify the existing structures in order to deal with novel features of the environment. For example, in exploring the physical world around him, the infant will begin to grasp objects with shapes that are new to him and that will require special accommodations to meet the demands of those contours. An opposition or antagonism, therefore, arises between assimilation and accommodation, although eventually these twin processes are fated to perform in a complementary fashion in which an equilibrium is established. In any event, the initial antagonism breaks up the undifferentiated state between assimilation and accommodation. Increasingly throughout the sensorimotor period, the infant will acquire the ability to differentiate between his own activity and the objects upon which he acts. Schemas themselves will become more and more differentiated as accommodation takes place, which in turn permits a much wider range of the child's universe to be assimilated to the newly constructed structures. The entire process is further promoted by the other functional invariant, organization.

Throughout development, structures are organized into complex systems. A simple prototype, however, is the young infant's attainment of coordination of the grasping and looking schemas. Whereas they both took place separately during the very early phase of life, within only a few months the infant can be observed to grasp what he looks attentively at and to look attentively at that which he grasps. This organized property of schemas further facilitates the differentiation between subject and object on a practical or action level. Further accommodations to the environment in the area of intentional behavior also greatly promote the decline of egocentrism. In an early stage there is little differentiation between ends and means. For example, having accidentally pulled a string attached to a rattle, the infant will again pull the string to reproduce the sound of the rattle. Note, however, that the pulling of the string and the reproduction of the desired effect are performed in virtually a single act. At a later stage the infant will, when desired to grasp an object, strike aside an obstruction, such as an experimenter's hand, in order to achieve it. In both illustrations we find a form of intentional behavior, but in the second example, which comes later in the infant's development, there is to be found a greater differentiation between the child's own actions and the object sought.

In the area of causal development, the infant initially assimilates all cause and effect relationships to the center of his own being. He behaves as if believing that only he can create effects in his universe. Gradually as he accommodates further to the external world, he exhibits an awareness on a practical or behavioral plane that the locus of causation may reside not only in himself, but also in other people and objects. In brief, through adaptation and organization the radical egocentrism of the sensorimotor period disappears. The infant emerges onto a representational plane of development in a world that has become spatialized and objectified. As with every cognitive advance, a new form of egocentrism appears, which in turn must be conquered.

The major factor contributing to the decline of egocentrism beyond the sensorimotor period is social interaction, particularly with one's peers. The child who wishes to communicate and be understood must adapt to the informational needs of his listener. He cannot continue to assimilate reality to his own private schemas, but must also accommodate to the point of view of the other. The desire to effectively persuade and to have others accept his ideas will require this accommodation. He must, if he is to be understood, begin to identify the referents of pronouns in his speech and to link events in proper causal fashion reflected in his syntax. He can no longer juxtapose unrelated events as if these were meaningful to the listener. He can no longer make contradictory statements, as he does in the preoperational period, and yet continue to remain unaware of their contradictory nature. He will come in contact with others who will challenge, offer rebuttal, and demand clarification. Logical proof and verification will be sought in social exchange. The personal point of view of the child, adopted as universal and absolute, will not be at all evident to his peers. The desire and movement toward socialized thought not only facilitate the development of logic, but also serve to prevent the child, or even the adult, from a pathological subjectification. Piaget comments as follows:

What then gives rise for the need for verification? Surely it must be the shock of our thought coming into contact with that of others, which produces doubt and the desire to prove. If there were not other people, the disappointments of experience would lead to overcompensation and dementis. We are constantly hatching an enormous number of false ideas, conceits, utopias, mystical explanations, suspicions and megalomaniacal fantasies, which disappear when brought into contact with other people. The social need to share the thought of others and to communicate our own with success is at the root of our need for verification. Proof is the outcome of argument. (1924/1969a:204)

The central role of social interaction in the decline of egocentrism persists throughout the developmental periods including adolescence, when it is well known that youngsters in their teens seek out peer reference groups and confidants to test with one another in endless discussion their newly generated ideas, theories, and utopias. In doing this the youngster accelerates the intellectual decentering process, for feedback from his peers will often pointedly underscore the weaknesses and limitations of his newfound ideas and ideologies. Piaget identifies an even more specific source of decentration for the formal operational youngster, which is his entry into a vocation or commencement of professional training (Inhelder and Piaget 1955/1958). It is ultimately in assuming a real job that the adolescent is ushered into adulthood, and the tendency to engage in undue formal theorizing is diluted as he is brought back into the world of reality. However, although the final egocentric flight of adolescence disappears, the youngster will retain into adulthood formal operational structures which permit the creative and scientific reasoning that set him apart from all other creatures and objects in the universe.

Elkind (1974) suggests that by the time formal operations are firmly established (fourteen to fifteen years), the adolescent has used his scientific schemas to test out the concept of the imaginary audience, which is regarded as a hypothesis, and he revises it to conform with the real audience which he discovers. Henceforth, the adolescent can differentiate between his own preoccupation with self and the concerns of others. The personal fable, which may never be entirely overcome, yields to some extent to relationships of intimacy. It is through the sharing of mutual feelings, fantasies, and goals which characterizes such relationships that each participant comes to realize the illusion of his being unique in experiencing life's emotions so intensely.

CONCLUSION

It may not be apparent thus far, and, therefore, will be emphasized here, that not all individuals attain the cognitive structures of the formal operational period. Further, even for those who do, there will surely be remnants of previous periods adhering to their present functioning. It is not likely that even a formal operational adult will function at that level in every area of his life at all times. It is even questionable whether this would be desirable. The various types of egocentrism which have been examined in this chapter are certainly not completely abandoned, and traces of them will be found in everyone at different times. The presence of exceptionally large measures of egocentrism may well explain serious interpersonal difficulties and pyschopathologies. The reader who is interested in the application to psychopathology of the Piagetian concept of egocentrism may wish to consult the following: Odier (1956), Anthony (1956, 1957), Freeman and McGhie (1957), Neale (1966), Feffer (1967), Clarke (1969), Schmid-Kitsikis (1973), Lidz (1973), Chandler, Greenspan, and Barenboim (1974), Pimm (1975), and Steinfeld (1975). Although it does not deal primarily with psychopathology, an excellent review of egocentrism and extension of the concept across the lifespan is to be found in Looft (1972).

By now, the term egocentrism has become too deeply embedded in the Piagetian literature to be extracted successfully. Nevertheless, Piaget has voiced regrets over having adopted it because of the unfelicitous connotation of a selfish or egotistic personality which the word carries. He has, therefore, sought to disavow use of the word in that sense and to highlight his own cognitive meaning, which is that of the ego centering on itself and, consequently, lacking the ability to deal with multiple perspectives simultaneously. In fact, the child is unaware of his egocentrism and, therefore, cannot recognize his own cognitive deficit.

It was stated in the opening paragraph of this chapter that Piaget conceives of human cognitive development as moving in the direction of increasingly attaining objective relativism. The concept of object relativism and how it is acquired serves as a touchstone to understanding the basis of Piaget's system. The child's viewpoint becomes objective as he differentiates between self and external world, between psychic phenomena and the material universe, between internal, private events and the objects populating his environment. The term "relativism" refers to both relational or relative notions of reality and to the notion of reciprocity. The elimination of realism leads to the disappearance of the tendency to materialize and reify psychic events. As children grow older, they no longer think of such expressions as "in front of" or "behind" in terms of absolutes, which would indicate attributes of objects. Instead, they begin to grasp the relational nature of subjects in the world. A term such as "foreigner" is seen not to signify an absolute property of the person, but rather a relation which is reciprocal, so that if A is a foreigner to B, then B is also a foreigner to A. In a reciprocal relationship the individual is able to see things from the other person's point of view and not only from his own. Piaget points out that "it is because he fails to grasp the reciprocity existing between different points of view that the child is unable to handle relations properly" (1924/1969a:134). As the child decenters he achieves multiperspectives which he then coordinates simultaneously. It is this process of decentration and coordination which leads to the decline of egocentrism and toward the achievement of objective relativism.

CHAPTER 3

The Priority of Cognitive
Structures Over Language

A sound comprehension of Piaget's position on the relationship between language and cognition will contribute greatly to a complete appreciation of his epistemology. The traditional approach has maintained that, as the child gains linguistic ability, he uses his language to order and understand the world in which he lives. The radical constructivist psychology of Piaget has inverted this sequence. The construction and existence of cognitive structures will determine language acquisition and what can be known about reality. A child who does not have the appropriate structures may use certain words, but it can be demonstrated that he does not truly understand what he is talking about. It can be further demonstrated that certain language characteristics invariably emerge only after the corresponding cogni-, tive structures have developed. Piaget's contention essentially is that language is not necessary or sufficient for intellectual development to occur. Studies in language acquisition (Bloom 1970, 1973) strongly support Piaget on this important point, as does work by Furth (1966, 1973) on deaf children. Training studies by Sinclair-de-Zwart (1969) lend even further weight to his position. In brief, Piaget challenges the orthodox position in psychology which has held that thought is dependent upon language. An understanding of the rationale underlying Piaget's challenge will illuminate the nature of thought in his system.

INTENTIONAL BEHAVIOR PRECEDES LANGUAGE

The first major argument of the Geneva School for its position on language and thought is predicated upon infant studies revealing that cognitive development precedes the acquisition of any language. To support this contention, an exposition on the early progression of intentional behavior as observed during the sensorimotor period will be presented. The reader should bear in mind that this is one aspect of total development during this period, which also includes major isomorphic gains in areas of space, time, causality, object permanence, imitation, and play. As intentional or means-end behavior is often cited as a primary characteristic of intelligence, it has been selected for special consideration in this section.

Upon entering life the infant has no innate cognitive structures other than such basic reflexes as sucking, grasping, and looking. He has no sense of a self and, hence, cannot differentiate between self and external world. It further follows that objects beyond the boundaries of his own body are not recognized as such and have no existence for him beyond his own perception and activity with them. In interaction, objects are experienced only as an extension of his own body and as intrinsically a part of the activity he performs upon them. The reflexes, as with more complex structures to follow, provide the meaning system through which the infant comes to know the world. For example, the rattle comes to be known as something to suck, see, or be grasped. Assimilation is cited by Piaget (1936/1963) as the basic fact of psychic life, by which he means that, from the outset, the infant construes or takes in the world in terms of the reflex structures and that assimilation continues to occur throughout life regardless of how complex cognitive structures become. The cognitive structure or scheme, as it is called during the sensorimotor period, has an intrinsic motivation to function. Objects in the environment and even parts of the infant's own body serve as aliment or nourishment for the scheme which seeks to function, "the principal motive power of intellectual activity thus becoming the need to incorporate things into the subjects' schemata" Piaget 1936/1963:46). The scheme, needing to function, engages in continuous attempts to repeat its own activity. The repetitive acts, however, are not confined to complete rigidity, but instead generalize to varying objects in the environment. This varying of the objects acted upon forces the schema to differentiate according to the characteristic properties of the object. Hence, there comes into being a motor recognition, or recognitory assimilation. In more tangible terms, as the infant generalizes from sucking the nipple, to his fingers, to the rattle, the sucking schema itself must become less simple in its structure and more highly differentiated in order that the infant may adapt to the varying and specific demands of the objects he sucks. As each encounter with novelty in the environment occurs, this assimilating schema itself is slightly modified to accommodate the new. It is this ongoing process of assimilation and accommodation which constitutes adaptation and leads to intellectual development. There is also contained in this activity the nucleus for the infant's eventual ability to recognize external objects as existing apart from his own body and simultaneously in the process to develop a separate sense of self.

While the first stage of intentional development is characterized by the pure functioning of the reflex when triggered off by chance, the second stage ushers in deliberate attempts to coordinate activities so that the reflex may function. For example, in the second stage the child will not only suck when his thumb encounters the mouth by chance, but will make concentrated efforts to bring thumb and mouth together. As Piaget points out, while sucking is one of the few hereditary structures, coordination of hand and mouth is not hereditary. Instead, it is an example of the first acquired adaptation. The essential defining aspect of the second stage is the primary circular reaction. A circular reaction begins with a chance event, which the infant then seeks to repetitively reinstate. Since the series of actions is triggered by a chance occurrence, it is not considered essentially intentional, although it is an advance over pure reflex activity. There are three types of circular reactions—primary, secondary, and tertiary—which appear in the second, third, and fifth stages respectively. The primary circular reaction of the second stage centers upon activities involving the infant's own body. To illustrate how the present discussion pertains to the second stage of the sensorimotor period, the following is an observation made by Piaget of one of his own children.

The chance contact of hand and mouth set in motion the directing of the latter toward the former and . . . then (but only then), the hand tries to return to the mouth. (1936/1963:52)

Later in the same day Piaget brings the infant's hand to his mouth and observes:

After a moment, the hand lost the contact but rediscovered it. It is no longer the mouth that seeks the hand, but the hand which reaches for the mouth. Thirteen times in succession I have been able to observe the hand go back into the mouth. There is no longer any doubt that coordination exists. The mouth may be seen opening and the hand directing itself toward it simultaneously. (p. 52)

With meticulous detail, Piaget reports the increasing coordination of various schemas such as looking and grasping or hearing and seeing. The coordinated activity is designated reciprocal assimilation. In one intriguing example, Piaget comments upon the child turning to the face of a person who has just spoken. The child does not yet have a concept of the face as a separate object possessing the capacity to speak. Instead, the child is merely stimulated visually by the auditory stimulus. In turning to look, it is as if he seeks to assimilate the sound to the visual schema and the face to the hearing schema. The visual schema is especially fertile in its capacity to extend the infant's applicability of reciprocal assimilations across a wide range of interactions with the environment. No longer looking only to provide exercise for the visual schema, the infant will now look at an object as a thing to be swung or grasped, hence coordinating it with the appropriate schemas. Reciprocally, the infant may initiate the grasping schema not simply to give expression to the intrinsic motivation for grasping, but to coordinate that schema with the visual schema. As the reader may well have guessed, these coordinated activities do not occur fully developed, and we find that there are many substages leading to their full fruition, although these will not be documented here. There exist varying gradations of intentionality in the course of sensorimotor development. However, Piaget makes clear that the acquired adaptations of the second stage, even when an infant may grasp an object to look at it, do not qualify as intentional behavior. The criteria for such behavior will be introduced at a later point in this section.

The focal point of the primary circular reaction has been the infant's own body during the second stage. In the third stage there is an extension toward the external world in the rhythmic activity of secondary circular reactions. The infant now attempts to repeat chance events involving objects in the environment. There still does not exist a goal at the outset of behavior. For example, the child may accidentally pull a string attached to a rattle, which in turn will produce a pleasant sound. The child will repeat the action which, in turn, produces a pleasant sound, which leads to a repetition of pulling the string and, thus, a continuation of the circular reaction. Although the action of the secondary circular reaction is externally oriented, it should be noted that the pulling of the string and the hearing of the sound constitute a primitive differentiation between means and end behavior. The string, after the first chance contact, is pulled to reproduce and maintain the sound or effect. Nevertheless, the initial action of pulling in itself implies the end or effect. True, it is an advance over previous behavior, but the means-end arrangement is not a very differentiated or complex one.

The means-end behavior of the secondary circular reaction constitutes a single act or "self-enclosed totality," as Piaget calls it, rather than a progression through time of a serial arrangement of means-end behavior. Piaget asserts that while pulling a string to hear the sound of the shaking rattle to which it is attached is an advance over simply grasping an object when it is seen, the secondary circular reaction is still not yet truly intelligent behavior. Another feature of the third stage is the tendency of the infant to assimilate even relatively new objects into preexisting schemas. He may pause to observe the novelty, but will then proceed to initiate activities that entail assimilation over accommodation. Younger infants tend to disregard novelty in objects they encounter, while older ones demonstrate a greater effort at accommodation to that which is novel, even eventually inventing new structures for dealing with the novelty. At this third stage the infant can even be observed attempting to act upon objects at a distance in order to preserve an interesting spectacle. Wishing to reinstate the shaking of an object he cannot come in spatial contact with, the infant may initiate the procedure of swinging his hand or leg, ignoring the role of the string, which he normally pulls to produce the spectacle.

The fourth stage emerges at about eight to nine months and is defined as the first appearance of decisively intentional behavior. There is no longer a limitation of merely seeking to reproduce interesting effects. The infant at the fourth stage can actually coordinate two separate schemas in a serial fashion through time, utilizing one as a means and the other as an end. There takes place a major breakthrough in the decline of radical egocentrism in this manner; as Piaget states, "in proportion as the action becomes complicated through coordination of schemata, the universe becomes objectified and is detached from the self" (1936/1963:211). The infant is capable of constructing a new schema, the means-end schema, based upon the coordination of two preexisting schemas. An essential difference from the secondary circular reaction is that the end to be achieved is obstructed by intermediary obstacles. The end cannot be immediately achieved in the way that pulling a string which is attached to a rattle will immediately produce a sound. As an example, an experimenter may place his hand between the child and an object the child wishes to grasp. The child gropes with his environment to rediscover the familiar means of "striking aside," which he applies to the experimenter's hand and subsequently grasps the desired object. Hence, two familiar schemas, striking and grasping, are coordinated serially to obtain the goal. The means is subordinated to the end. Piaget has gone so far as to suggest that this attainment marks the prototype of logical reasoning in which premise is subordinate as a means to reaching the conclusion or end of an argument. In the circular reactions examined so far, there is simply an attempt to reproduce an effect encoutered by chance. Now we find the infant intentionally setting out to achieve an end which he had not just experienced. The goal is in mind from the outset even though groping with the environment to hit upon the means may take place. In Piaget's own words:

In the secondary circular reaction, the means utilized were discovered fortuitously and were applied just beforehand; hence it is only a question of rediscovering them. In the behavior patterns now under study, on the other hand, it is necessary to improvise means and remove obstacles which separate the intention from its final result. (1936/1963:228)

Piaget points out that inhering in the means-end schema is the beginning of a significant sense of a system of relationships. For example, to remove an obstacle in attaining a goal the infant is demonstrating a behavioral recognition of spatial and time relations. He now understands on the level of practical intelligence that the obstacle is "in front of" the goal and that its removal is necessary "before" the desired object can be picked up. Piaget is insistent, of course, that in referring to practical intelligence we are not speaking of the conceptual level to appear later, but of a demonstrated pattern of intelligent behavioral actions. In fact, it is precisely this point that Piaget has in mind when he contends that the origins of intelligence are in action and that later intelligence is internalized action. According to Piaget, at the sensorimotor period *success* and not *truth* must serve as the criterion for verification.

The fifth stage marks the appearance of the tertiary circular reaction and the discovery of new means through the growing infant's own active explorations within his environment. The reader will recall, having left the secondary circular reactions at the third stage, that circular reactions are triggered by chance, which the infant repetitively seeks to reproduce. However, in the tertiary circular reaction, the child no longer seeks to rigidly reproduce previous effects, but he modifies his behavior as he experiments to innovate new effects. He is now seeking to introduce novelty into his own environment. The child has become genuinely interested in the nature of external reality. He is intent upon exploring objects from the standpoint of their own properties and capabilities. Piaget tells of the child who engages in "the experiment to see" as he drops objects, being sure to vary their position, to watch how they fall, and even to observe their final resting place. There is a transition from the day before when the focal point was upon the act of letting go rather than the more externalized and independent character of the objects. It is the deliberate variation of the manner in which he drops the objects with the aim of altering the effects for study which is expressive of one of the major features of the fifth stage. The child searches for novelty and does so to acquire understanding.

A direct outgrowth of the experiment to see in the fifth stage is the distinctive activity of "the discovery of new means by experimentation." Recall that in the fourth stage there did not occur the construction of new means in problem solving, but rather an application of old means to new situations. The striking schema had already existed; it had simply not been employed previously to strike aside an obstacle in order to grasp an object. However, in the fifth stage there occurs the virtual invention or construction of a new schema or means for achieving an end. Piaget elaborates upon a particularly interesting example known as the behavior of the support. It involves bringing an object which is out of reach closer by pulling the support upon which it rests. In the fourth stage the infant has no schema offering him an understanding of the relation Piaget calls "placed upon." He is referring here, of course, to the fact that when an object is placed upon a support, such as a cushion, it can be attained by first drawing the cushion to oneself. The infant virtually invents a schema of "placed upon" that enables him to understand the appropriate relation by engaging in a process similar to the experiment to see, when he enters the fifth stage. The infant may possibly draw a support with a desired object upon it toward himself during the fourth stage, but this is not in itself proof that he has constructed the schema of "placed upon" as yet. The test is that at this time the same child can also be observed pulling a support toward himself even when the clearly desired object is behind, beside, or being held above the support. In other words, the behavioral criterion of success will not be met, even though in drawing the support to him the child expects it to be. He does not yet recognize that the object must be placed upon the support and not simply in proximity to it, for success to occur. Disconfirmation leads to a series of concentrated efforts in which the child intently studies the connections between support and object, eventuating in the fifth stage with the invention of the schema "placed upon."

Another significant advance in the same vein, discovering new means through actively experimenting, involves a pattern of behavior using a stick. There is a very gradual build up of a behavioral recognition that the stick can be utilized to bring to the child an object he desires, but which is out of his reach. Even after the child knows that he can displace an object by hitting it with a stick, he must still experiment with a series of cumulative accommodations to effectively bring the particular object sought to him. Therefore, he undergoes a series of random or groping acts as he hits the object repeatedly with the stick. In accord with the fifth stage search for novelty, he varies the way he hits the object to see what will happen. However, unlike the tertiary circular reaction or search for novelty, his movements are much less random as they are guided by a specific goal rather than simply a desire to see what happens in general. In connection with this development, Piaget makes an especially interesting observation about the role of chance. What if the infant hits an object purely by chance and in so doing displaces it? The event is of very little value without the intelligence to undergo a series of coordinated assimilatory and accommodatory actions moving the child progressively toward achievement of the goal. In a bold comparison, Piaget states:

Chance, therefore, in the accommodation peculiar to sensorimotor intelligence, plays the same role as in scientific discovery. It is only useful to the genius and its revelations remain meaningless to the unskilled. In other words, it presupposes a directed search and is incapable of orienting it by itself. (1936/1963:303)

What now remains to be accomplished in the sixth stage? It is at this stage that the shift to representation in thought is made. The child need not rely any longer upon behavioral trial and error or guided groping in the environment to achieve his goal. He continues to invent new means, but the action is now literally interiorized. Piaget refers to this new activity as "invention through deduction or mental activity," cautioning that the old behavioral repertoire is not discontinued, but that this new ability becomes the highest level of intellectual achievement to appear so far. In one such instance, Piaget tells of his daughter attempting to kneel down, beginning to do so by leaning against a stool on the floor. As she leans upon the stool, she pushes it away from her. She then stands up, places the stool against a firmly resting sofa, and proceeds once again to kneel by leaning against it. There is no intermediary phase of directed empirical groping necessary. Instead, the child is able to internally deduce a solution to the problem, which she executes flawlessly without hesitation. Piaget introduces several examples of this type, some manifesting transitional substages, but all basically predicated upon the principle of internal invention of a new means.

In another particularly illuminating example, the child seeks to obtain a chain which is contained in a matchbox that is left slightly open. The slit is not sufficient for the child's fingers to directly enter the matchbox. She attempts this, but does not succeed. She has had no previous experience with the opening and closing nature of a matchbox. Yet now she is observed pausing, while successively opening and closing her mouth. Piaget believes that she has thought out the situation. The opening and closing of her mouth is a transitional phase in which the symbolic behavior is in the process of being interiorized. Transitionally there occurs an overt imitation of the solution which is once removed from empirical groping. Following the pause and expressed imitative behavior, the child goes to the match-box, opens it wider, and retrieves the chain. In so doing, she does not perform any unnecessary actions. Later, the thinking activity is en-tirely interiorized without benefit of the observed imitation. The child has invented a new means through mental representation. Piaget emphasizes that the problem is clarified for the child when her first attempt at securing the chain fails. Her initial hypothesis is discon-firmed. She assimilates the situation to previous schemas of experience in which she has opened and closed boxes. Piaget comments, "Those are the schemata which confer a meaning on the present situation and which at the same time direct the search" (1936/1963:374). Invention is the accommodation of those schemas to the particularized features of the matchbox with its narrow slit, and it is unmistakably a *creative* act in Piaget's view.

The above account of intentional behavior is a highly abstracted version of Piaget's original work. Nevertheless, some of the most salient aspects are contained in it, and it is hoped that they will convey a sense of the majestic achievements which envolve during the intel-lectual development of the sensorimotor period. All this occurs with-out benefit of language. In a very real and significant way, Piaget justifiably asserts that ontogenetically, intelligence precedes language.

THE SYMBOLIC FUNCTION

Central to understanding the role of language in the Piagetian system is a recognition of its relationship to the generic concept of the symbolic function (Piaget 1946/1962a). Prior to the sixth stage of the sensori-motor period, which virtually ushers in the first phase of the preo-perational period, the child cannot mentally represent objects to himself. There are, of course, early precursors to representation. Primary among these are the signal and the index, which are in some way part of the object. For example, the footsteps of the mother coming from another room signal her approach. The tracks of a bird walking on the sand or the exposed tip of an object otherwise concealed by something over it are indices of their presence. The child is also capable of perception prior to the sixth stage, but a percept by its very nature requires the presence of the object perceived. Representation, appearing as it does at the sixth stage, frees the child from the constraints of the immediate presence of objects. He can now represent to himself objects which are no longer present. He does this through the use of either symbol or sign. These are distinct from an index or percept in that they are differentiated from that which they stand for. The symbol differs from the sign in that the former is personal and resembles that which it represents, whereas the latter is social and bears no necessary resemblance to that which it represents. That which is represented may be referred to as the signified, and the representation itself is called the signifier. The significate is the actual meaning ascribed to the representation, and this is determined by the level of schematic development to which the representation is assimilated.

Ths symbolic function, more recently called semiotic function, is comprised of symbols and signs, and is distinguished by the capacity to evoke, on a symbolic plane, objects that are absent from the immediate environment. Signs specifically refer to language, which eventually becomes public and is socially shared. However, with the advent of the symbolic function, it is not language which the child as yet has the most mastery over. The beginning use of language has private meaning attached to it, is limited by the child's structural development, and retains facets of the action-laden sensorimotor period. It is the symbol, as opposed to the sign or language, which the child demonstrates the most facility with at first. The major symbols are play, imitation, and image. Progressively more complex playful behavior can be observed in the infant during the sensorimotor period. But it is not until the symbolic function develops that the child begins to play with objects that represent absent objects. The child may play symbolically with a stick that represents a rifle or use a crumpled piece of cloth to represent a pillow as he pretends to sleep. The real nature of the objects used are distorted or assimilated by the child to take on the symbolic meaning he ascribes to it.

Another example of the ludic symbol given by Piaget (1946/1962a) is a cardboard box and a shell manipulated by a child such that they symbolize a cat walking along a wall. Imitation becomes symbolic when, in the sixth stage, the child can be observed for the first time engaging in deferred imitation. As with play, imitative behavior becomes increasingly more complex throughout the sensorimotor period, but it is not until the symbolic function emerges that the child is able to imitate behavior which he has previously observed, but which is not being observed at the time of the imitative behavior. Piaget (1946/1962a) offers the example of his daughter, who one day observed a child having a temper tantrum. Twelve hours later she had her own first temper tantrum in which she distinctly emulated the sounds and movements of the other child. She was sixteen months old at the time. Just as assimilation predominates in play, it is accommodation that predominates in imitation.

The image, a third type of symbol, is actually the interiorization of imitation. It is not, as some have maintained, a faint memory trace of a previous perception, but an active reconstruction. Through an attempt at internalized imitation, the child now tries to accommodate the contours of the signified. Hence, an image is personal or specific to the individual constructing it and is based on material or sensorial properties of the object, even though the object is no longer present. The reader may recall the child who opened and closed her mouth in a fashion analogous to the matchbox. Piaget suggests that this transitional act witnesses the gradual interiorization of imitation, which leads to the image. It can be seen that through the use of play, imitation, and image the child may disengage from the immediate context to which the sensorimotor child is limited and thereby vastly enlarge upon the scope of his universe. But where does language fit into this scheme of things? Piaget states:

As language is only a particular form of the symbolic function and as the individual symbol is certainly simpler than the collective sign, it is permissible to conclude that thought precedes language and that language confines itself to profoundly transforming thought by helping it to attain its forms of equilibrium by means of a more advanced schematization and a more mobile abstraction. 1964/1968:91–92)

It should be apparent from the above comment that, while Piaget subordinates language to thought in development, he does not slight its highly facilitative role.

FIGURATIVE AND OPERATIVE KNOWING

Piaget posits two aspects to cognition—the figurative[1] and the operative. Furth (1970) has elaborated upon these in an effort to deepen the understanding of the role of language in thought. Figurative knowing is the static configuration of things and stresses the sensorial component. Operative knowing is an act of transformation through which incoming data are understood. Figurative and operative knowing are not two totally separate ways of knowing, but are two aspects under which things are known. There is a potential for confusing operative and operational which should be avoided at the outset. Operational thought refers specifically to the last two periods of development, starting with the concrete operations of age six or seven and extending to the formal operations beginning at approximately age eleven or twelve. Operative knowing, however, is a broader concept which encompasses all of cognitive-structural development from birth onward. The meaning imposed upon the figurative element is derived from the particular level of operative development. Furth uses an example involving the White House to demonstrate these concepts. Figurative knowing refers to the perception or image which provides a static configuration. This sensory input is then subject to a transformation determined by the operative or structural level of the knower. It may come to be known as simply a house where people live, a place where politicians work, or possibly the building where representatives of the people make laws that govern the country. The last of these can itself be understood in terms of varying levels of maturity, depending upon such structures as classification, justice, and ratio, to cite only a few. The point is that the knowing derived from the figurative component cannot go beyond the operative level of development. Therefore, as Furth has pointed out elsewhere:

It is the operative component, present in any perceptual or symbolic behavior, which primarily determines the level of understanding reality. Thus neither symbolic nor figurative functioning can explain intelligence since these cog-

1. Piaget utilizes the term "schema" to denote figurative knowing. In contradistinction, the term "scheme" is reserved for operative knowing. However, in his earlier writings this distinction had not yet been made, and this has been a source of confusion at times.

nitive aspects are fully tied to and dependent on the level of operative thinking. (1969:104)

Furth (1969, 1970) stresses that a symbol does not possess an intrinsic meaning, as the meaning is derived from the operative level, which itself changes as it is restructured in development. He points out that the figurative aspect of the symbol is an internalization of that which is external to the child. In other words, the static configuration of an image is based upon an internal accommodation of an object which, although not present, resides in the real environment, or at least did so at some time. However, the object as it exists outside the knower does not provide the *meaning* to him, for this is derived from an assimilation to the operative structure of the image. To elucidate this, Furth states, "An operative structure in itself has no figurative component and does not represent the known event but *is* the known event and the prerequisite for its symbolic representation" (1970:249).

In further interpreting Piaget's theory, Furth (1970) distinguishes between operative activity as the *form* which is abstracted from the specific situation or content and the figurative aspect as derived from the *matter* of the specific situation. A child playing with six cubes may by his actions with them invent an operative structure which provides knowledge that the sum total of the cubes remains the same regardless of how they are combined. That is, $4+2=6$ just as $2+4=6$ and $5+1=6$. The order or clustering has no bearing on the outcome. The knowledge gained is not based upon any properties of the objects, but is derived from an abstraction of one's actions upon the objects, from which an operative structure is constructed. This is logico-mathematical knowledge as opposed to physical knowledge, which deals directly with the particular properties of objects.

Furth (1970) insists that in comprehending Piaget's position on language and thought, it is vital to distinguish between the child's repertoire of language symbols and how he is able to employ them in areas involving logical thought. A preoperational child may have a fairly wide range of linguistic symbols available to him, but is delimited in his use of them by the operative structures of that period. Thus, the lack of reversible thought structures will lead to inaccurate verbal responses in such tasks as classification and conservation. The child who says that there are more yellow primulas than there are flowers in a bunch of ten yellow primulas and two red roses does so not because he does not have the vocabulary to give the proper response, but because he lacks the operative structures to promote his understanding of the logical requirements of the task. His use of the language cannot go beyond his preoperational understanding of classification. Similarly, a child who can count a row of ten pennies and a second row of ten buttons situated below in a one-to-one correspondence will say that there is the same amount of objects in each row. Judging from his verbal response, it would appear that he understands something about counting and number. Yet if one of the two rows is condensed, he will say that there are more in the unchanged or longer row. He will persist in this even after he has recounted the two rows. The child has not yet developed conservation structures, and, thus, his use of language cannot go beyond his level of operative development. Both Furth (1970) and Piaget (1964/1968) have pointed out that, even when in the concrete operational period, the child must apply his logical structures on actual objects or their representations. While he is now capable of dealing with classification, seriation, and transitivity on a concrete level, hypothetical questions in these areas which would require a purely verbal response will prove beyond his ken until the formal operational period, at which time language takes on the greatest relevancy as an instrumentality in thought.

There is a fine question that should be examined in this context—does language have a figurative aspect as do perception, imitation, and image? Furth (1969) indicates that Piaget deemphasizes the figural aspect of language and likens it more to general schemas. Furth would prefer to emphasize the figural aspect of language in the developing child. He points out that although they do not resemble the signified in the way that perception, imitation, and images do, the auditory and vocal features of language are figural. Furthermore, the young child's language is highly egocentric and embedded in specific, private meanings. The early use of linguistic symbols bears the mark of their sensorimotor heritage. A single word such as "momma" may not simply stand for the mother as such, but may convey an entire range of actions. It may be a request for the mother to bring food or engage in comforting or helpful activities of various kinds. Furth (1970) compares a young child gesturing as if throwing a ball to his exclaiming "ball" to convey knowledge of a ball as something to be thrown. In both instances, the motoric activity and its vocalized alternative, there are figurative aspects to the representation which attempt to accommodate to the action of a ball as a thing for throwing. Furth is clear on his position regarding this question. He comments, "It would seem to me more appropriate to include the language of the growing child in the category of figurative instruments to the same extent as mental images" (1969:141)

PRELINGUISTIC ROOTS OF CONCRETE OPERATIONS

Piaget maintains that intelligence is action. Through his own actions upon objects, the child comes to abstract and construct knowledge of the world. He combines and dissociates objects, he orders and reorders them, he engages in a multitude of motor activities as he acts upon and interacts with the things in his world. Conceptual knowledge is internalized action, and as he masters it, sooner or later, the child begins to show an ability to put it into language. At about six or seven years of age the child begins to give correct verbal responses to tasks involving classification, seriation, conservation, and transitivity, when the objects in the task are present and can be directly manipulated by him or the experimenter. However, Piaget (1964/1968) has underscored the fact that conceptual mastery of these tasks has its roots in the sensorimotor period on the behavioral plane. In other words, the genesis of concrete operations is prelinguistic.

We have already seen how intentional behavior progresses without benefit of language, although it is certainly the case that later the child will engage in much self-aware problem-solving activity that will be formulated in words. One does not have to stretch the imagination to recognize the development of object permanence as the prototype of conservation. Recognitory assimilation during the sensorimotor period is, indeed, an early prelinguistic form of classification. The infant who, when hungry, rejects non-nutriment-providing objects and chooses to suck only on the nipple of a breast or bottle has engaged in an act of primitive classification on a purely behavioral level. Piaget (1936/1963) observes his infant daughter seriously, effortlessly, and briefly shake her leg upon spying a toy doll which she has often swung. He interprets this as a prelinguistic act of classification. Through recognitory assimilation the child ascribes the meaning of the doll as being a thing to be swung. She has no recourse to language, as yet, and so relies on a behavioral mode of expression. Prototypical examples of relations or seriation can also be found in infancy. Observing his son at four months and twenty-one days of age, Piaget states, "When he strikes with his hand the toys hanging from his bassinet . . . he visibly gradates his movements as function of the result: at first he strikes gently and then continues more and more strongly, etc" (1936/1963:185). Here we see an illustration of a prelinguistic sense of quantity and of ordering things in relation to one another.

Piaget (1964/1968) has also pointed out that, although the child can handle concrete operational tasks from about six or seven years on, he cannot handle the tasks on a purely verbal level if the objects involved are not within his perceptual range until he enters the period of formal operations. He has the structures which enable him to properly combine and dissociate concrete objects which he can personally manipulate, but if asked questions in the abstract about universal classes, he will not succeed until early adolescence. Piaget's emphasis is that, even though the concrete operational child can coordinate actions in a logical and systematic way in the real world, he still has not yet mastered these operations on a purely linguistic level, where he would have to operate with abstractions and universals. Therefore, it follows that language cannot account for the development of logical structures of the concrete operational period.

A final prelinguistic example, with sensorimotor roots, which Piaget offers deals with transitivity. Transitivity involves drawing a conclusion between two elements by comparing them with an intermediary element, but not directly with each other. If A is greater than B and B is greater than C, it must follow that A is greater than C. The concrete operational child can perform this task on a concrete level by first comparing sticks A and B and then sticks B and C. Having done so, he can conclude that stick A is greater than stick C. However, if asked to solve the following problem on a purely verbal level, he cannot do so until he arrives at the formal operational period. "Edith is fairer than Susan and darker than Lily; who is the darkest of the three?" Here, of course, we have another example of the preceding argument in which a concept can be handled structurally at the concrete level by manually handling the objects, but is not yet mastered linguistically. However, let us also trace this back to the level of practical intelligence. Piaget has set up a task in which a child toward the end of the sensorimotor period can observe an object being placed under a blanket. What he does not see is that under the blanket is a hat under which the experimenter actually places the object. In seeking to retrieve the object, the older infant will lift the blanket, and when he finds the hat he will then remove it, fully expecting to find the object. Piaget suggests that this is a seminal illustration on the behavioral plane of transitivity relations. In effect, the child grasps on a behavioral level that, if the object is under the hat and the hat is under the blanket, the object is under the blanket. He contends that this is the functional equivalent of not only transitivity on a representational plane, but also of class inclusion, both of which are first mastered at the concrete operational period.

The role of language in formal operational thought will not be elaborated upon at length. Because of the hypothetical and propositional nature of such thinking, it would appear that language is a necessary element in formal reasoning. However, it should be obvious that the mere presence of language does not assure a formal operational capacity. If it did, all people who normally speak a language, the vast majority by far, would be at the formal operational period. Research and common observation, however, tend to disprove any such conclusion. In fact, Cromer (1974) suggests that there appears to be little difference between the language of the formal reasoning person and the nonformal reasoning person, except in the sphere of linguistic structures. As at all previous levels, this is determined by operative level of development.

LANGUAGE AND COGNITION IN THE DEAF

Furth (1964, 1966, 1971, 1973) is a foremost contributor to our knowledge about the cognitive development of deaf people. A study of the deaf provides a natural opportunity to explore intellectual development in the absence of language. Furth maintains that, while a deaf child is not without symbols, he does not possess a conventional linguistic system. Furth discards as insignificant the relatively few words acquired by the deaf child by the time he is five years old, because, in contrast to the hearing child, his vocabulary is not informed by the rules of linguistics. Furth regards the gestures of deaf people which are used in communication as a human language; however, he points out that the vast majority of young children who grow up deaf are not exposed to American sign language. Further, he points out that, even until recently, the official educational position was not to teach or encourage deaf schoolchildren to learn the conventional sign language used by deaf adults. Generally it has not been until after ten years of age that deaf children have begun to learn American sign language. Gestures utilized in communication prior to that time tend to be spontaneous and are not grounded systematically in linguistic rules. American sign language, which is eventually learned, is predicated upon linguistic rules and is described by Furth as a human language without speech. However, the significant aspect for our discussion is the fact that almost all deaf children have been growing up during their first decade without a language, whereas their hearing counterparts have been learning a formal conventional language during comparable years. In other words, the young deaf child has been deprived not only of speech, but also of language—the former by an act of nature and the latter by neglect and official policy. Furth defines intelligence as an ability to successfully perform learning tasks of a complex nature, and he maintains that a distinction between language and intelligence is conceptually sound. To define intelligence in a manner that makes language intrinsic to it is to beg the question.

It should be obvious that by studying the ability of deaf children to handle complex learning tasks and by comparing them to hearing children, we may learn something of the relationship between language and cognition. Furth has been engaged in conducting and reviewing such research over the past several years. His general observations and results will be summarized here. The research covers memory, perception, and conceptual development. Many of the tasks utilized Piagetian problems, and all of Furth's theoretical observations are couched within the framework of Piaget's developmental psychology.

Based on his research, Furth has drawn a fundamental distinction between symbol discovery and symbol use. In experiments involving the discovery of a symbol, Furth found that deaf subjects, most notably the younger ones, performed in a manner inferior to the hearing subjects. However, once the deaf subjects understood the symbol, they were able to use it as well as those who could hear. Furth succinctly states, "On a task using a discovery principle the deaf lagged behind, but on a task requiring comprehension and use of a principle they were equal to the hearing" (1966:147). Furth adopts the position that where deaf children are found to be markedly deficient in a cognitive comparison to hearing children, it is not due directly to their language deficiency but to their social environment. Because of the way society has related to deaf children, Furth finds that they have not been encouraged to develop a spirit of curiosity or inquiry nor to actively reason about their world. He emphasizes that it is precisely in areas where initiative and challenge are called into play that deaf children prove inferior to hearing children. In comprehension and use of concepts they do not exhibit the same retardation. Hence, where intellectual motivation to explore and raise questions is called into play, the deaf children do not fare well, because of their impoverished social milieu. Nevertheless, this is to be distinguished from their basic intellectual capacity, involving the understanding and application of concepts, at which they perform well.

In further support of his position, Furth cites a study by Furth and Youniss (1965) in which a rural group of children were given tests on the symbolic discovery and symbolic use tasks. The rural children were drastically different from the deaf children in they that they possessed a basic linguistic competence and, hence, were similar in this aspect to the original control group used with the deaf children. At the same time they came from a culturally deprived environment which lacked much of the stimulating enrichment the control group enjoyed. In this respect, they bore a greater resemblance to the deaf children. Strikingly, they performed poorly on the symbol discovery tasks and were equal to the average on the symbol use tasks. In brief, they exhibited capacities comparable to the deaf group rather than the hearing group. Language, per se, did not seem to be the significant variable, but certain aspects of the intellectual environment did seem to be significant. In general, across the range of all the various cognitive tasks utilized, deaf children did as well as hearing children or at the most lagged one or two years behind, as in some conservation tasks. The one exception was in symbol discovery tasks. Tasks which relied heavily on verbal comprehension, of course, did not find the deaf children faring well. The deaf children did manifest a lack of basic information usually found to be in the repertoire of hearing children. Although the deaf children did not do well at unstructured situations (symbol discovery), exhibiting traits of rigidity or passivity, much of this limitation was no longer present by adulthood. In a conclusion to his classic book *Thinking Without Language,* Furth states:

Apart from these listed effects, the basic development and structure of the intelligence of the deaf in comparison with the hearing is remarkably unaffected by the absence of verbal language. One can reasonably assume that the major area in which the deaf appear to be different from the hearing is in variables related to personality, motivation, and values. If substantial differences are found, they will likely be due to experiential and social factors of home, school and the deaf community. (1966:227)

Furth does not view the impoverished learning climate of the deaf child as inevitable, and he urges formal systematic nonverbal communication instruction for the very young child. Recognizing that verbal language is not a necessary condition to thinking should accelerate the development of practices and policies in this endeavor.

A final comparison of some interest is that between deaf children and blind children (Sinclair-de-Zwart 1969). As Sinclair-de-Zwart points out, although deaf children lack linguistic competence, their normal interaction with the environment during infancy lays the foundation of sensorimotor structures. In the case of blind children, however, while they normally acquire linguistic facility, their restricted environmental exchanges delimit the development of significant sensorimotor schemes. Consequently, deaf children manifest at most only a slight lag in development compared with normal children on tasks involving concept comprehension and use, whereas blind children are observed to be an average of four years behind normals developmentally on the same tests. Sinclair-de-Zwart emphasizes that the language ability of the blind children is insufficient to counter the schematic retardation derived from their limited actions upon the environment during infancy and early childhood. It should be noted, however, that the gap in cognitive development is eliminated in time.

RESEARCH FROM THE GENEVA SCHOOL

Sinclair-de-Zwart (1969), Inhelder and Sinclair (1969), and Sinclair (1971) have conducted research on the relationship between language and cognition which offers compelling evidence of the ontogenetic priority of the latter over the former. Their primary aim was to discover whether the emergence of concrete operations is accompanied by a parallel change in language. In addition, they sought to determine whether verbal training of those lacking the operations in the linguistic devices utilized by those possessing them would, in fact, lead to the acquisition of the operations.

A vital distinction between vocabulary or content and syntax or form was made. Children could be divided according to this distinction into two groups. All of the children had the appropriate vocabulary at their command, but there were two distinct ways of utilizing it in evidence. In describing pencils placed before them, preoperational children would string adjectives together serially rather than cross multiply them. They would make such comments as "This pencil is long, this one is short; this one is thin, this one is fat." In contrast, children who had already shown an ability to conserve would say, "This one is longer and thinner [than the other one]." Inhelder and Sinclair (1969) draw attention to the fact that this phraseology demonstrates the conservers' linguistic capacity to coordinate the descriptive terms and to integrate the comparative judgement into one syntactical arrangement. The preoperational children, while they had the particular words needed within their repertoire, failed to employ such a grammatically economical approach. The linguistic method of the concrete operational children was determined by their operative development, which permitted them to employ compensation in conserving. For example, the conserver will often respond to a conservation task in which one of two equal balls of clay is elongated by saying that the amount remains the same because while it is longer it is also thinner. In other words, a structural advance in the concrete operations enables the child to simultaneously coordinate two dimensions. The structural change is reflected in a parallel linguistic modification.

An attempt was then made to train children who were preoperational to adopt the syntax utilized by the concrete operational children to see if this would lead to conservation. It proved quite difficult to inculcate the more advanced linguistic expressions, and when they were acquired, there was not any appreciable shift to conservation. The trained children began to convey the dimensions in their verbal responses and yet still continued to draw nonconservation conclusions. It is once again apparent that language facility can be misleading and that without cognitive structural development there is no genuine conceptual understanding.

Beilin, however, challenges the Geneva School's position on the unidirectional priority of cognitive structures over language. It is his contention that linguistic training utilizing "verbal rule-instructional methods" can lead to the attainment of operational knowledge. He states that "the theoretical relation between cognition and language is one of partial autonomy for each system. . . . Thus the most simple and plausible way to conceive of the relation between cognition and language is as each deriving from some common, more abstract structure" (1981:120). Further, Beilin believes that Piaget was moving in the direction of giving credence to this interpretation as evidenced in a commentary offered by him (Piaget 1971d).

CONCLUSION

Language has been introduced as one of several symbolic functions which comes into being as the capacity for representation develops at the threshold of the preoperational period. A distinction was made between figurative and operative knowing, in which the first of these is tied to sensorial content, while the second is freed of material aspects and is based on a mental act of transformation. Figurative and operative elements are not totally separate, but are two aspects of cognition. The genesis of advanced reasoning which can be rendered into sophisticated syntactical arrangements is found in the sensori-motor period in such domains as intentionality, object permanence, primitive classification, relations, and transitivity. At the concrete operational period, systematically logical structures are brought into play with materials that can be manipulated in the environment, but the linguistic ability to deal with these tasks on an abstract level is not present until the development of the formal operations. A comparative study of deaf children with a normal group indicated that with minimal lag, and in some cases none, there was comparable reasoning capacity. Reasoning on complex intellectual tasks without benefit of language was established. It was seen that operative development is paralleled by appropriate syntax, but that linguistic training when successful is not accompanied by operative understanding. The weight of evidence supporting Piaget's position on the language-cognition controversy is succinctly stated by Sinclair-de-Zwart when she asserts, "Language is not the source of logic, but is on the contrary structured by logic" (1969:325).

CHAPTER 4

Social-Cognitive Development

The focus of this chapter is upon the child's gradual construction of knowledge pertaining to social aspects of his world and his participation in social interaction processes. In particular, we shall examine the development of moral judgement, the distinction between moral and conventional domains, perspective-taking abilities, and adaptive communication. In the view of some theorists, all knowledge is social in origin and character. Others distinguish sharply between "cold" knowledge of the physical world and the "hot" knowledge of social concepts. The social world is more complex and unpredictable, more elusive and uncontrollable, than the physical world. The child must discover that others may view things differently from himself and how to coordinate diverse viewpoints. He must evolve many social concepts bearing on self, justice, fairness, sharing, authority, friendship, work, politics, and economics. Further, he must learn to speak effectively by adapting his messages to the listening needs of the other and to listen effectively by accommodating to the intended meaning of the speaker. All of the knowledge and skills that accompany social-cognitive development will equip the child for competent living in the real world.

MORAL REASONING

Toward Autonomy in Moral Judgment. Piaget's fifth book (1932/1965b) is a major treatise on moral development, albeit the only work he ever devoted exclusively to that subject. One method he used to elicit from children their moral concepts was to play the game of marbles with them, pretending not to know the rules, while probing the children to discover their conceptions about the nature of rules. The other major approach he utilized was that of posing a variety of stories to children dealing with stealing, lying, clumsiness, and sharing. Many of the stories revolved around issues of justice and punishment. The exposition that follows was devised by Piaget from these procedures.

There are two basic epochal developments in moral judgement—the morality of constraint and the morality of cooperation. The former involves the imposition by an outside authority of specific rules which must be followed by the individual. This is known as the period of heteronomy, which lasts until about age eight, as opposed to the autonomy to follow, and is characterized by duty and submission to authority. The command of recognized authority determines what is right, and this is the accepted criterion regardless of circumstances. Moral realism governs a morality of constraint. A general definition, as formulated by Piaget, is as follows: "We shall therefore call moral realism the tendency which the child has to regard duty and the value attaching to it as self-subsistent regardless of the circumstances in which the individual may find himself" (1932/1965b:111).

There are three main elements characterizing moral realism. First, heteronomy is the foundation of duty. The good is defined by obedience to the external rule or adult command. Second, only a literal application of the law is permitted. Any attempt to obey the spirit, rather than the letter, of the law would be a movement toward reason and intentionality or subjectivity. Third, intentionality is not considered in making moral judgements. Responsibility is assumed on a purely objective level in which acts are viewed from the standpoint of rigid compliance with predetermined rules. Objective responsibility and intentionality are not viewed by Piaget as two distinctly sequential stages. Among younger children there is a preponderance of responses to stories which exhibit their belief that others are culpable for those actions which have negative physical consequences regardless of their motives. Nevertheless, some of the same children's responses reveal intentionality considerations as well. What occurs with age progression is a gradual diminution of objective responsibility responses in children accompanied by a gradual increase in subjective responsibility responses. There are no clear instances of objective responsibility found after age ten.

The same trend is apparent in the areas of lying. Younger children consider more naughty the child who unwittingly conveys an untruth of large magnitude than another child who transmits a small untruth with intent to deceive. Older children, on the other hand, will increasingly take into account whether or not the child is intentionally lying. Piaget points out that truth holds no value to the younger egocentric mind, which is more likely to assimilate reality to the end of achieving its own satisfaction. The need to speak and pursue the truth is derived from one's participation as a social member in cooperation with others. It is, therefore, predicated upon mutual respect and reciprocity. The young child up to seven or eight years of age finds it difficult to observe the rule not to lie, because his attitude toward it is based on unilateral respect for the adult, who is the source of the rule. As the child develops he recognizes lying as intrinsically wrong and that it is not wrong merely because he will be punished for lying, as he held earlier. The rule becomes dissociated from its origin, the adult, and embellished by the child's own reasons, which elevates it to a universal status. Piaget maintains, however, that heteronomy still characterizes the rule because it continues to be construed as a command which has not yet been interiorized and made a part of the child's own mind. It is when children reach the ages of ten to twelve that reciprocity and mutual agreement are seen as prerequisites to social relations. It is the destruction of trust and affection brought about by lying which makes it intolerable.

Gradually the morality of constraint yields as a morality of cooperation develops. A bond of solidarity with others supplants external authority. Personal motives and subjective responsibility are taken into account when making moral judgments. The growing child moves in the direction of equality with adults, and unilateral respect declines. Mutual respect and autonomy of conscience undergird the morality of cooperation. In the period of autonomy, the good is founded upon a sum of relations between individuals and is not imposed from without. The good is no longer equated with the existing rule or command, but is dissociated from it, allowing the individual to pursue what ought to be rather than merely what is.

As congnitive development progresses, the child increasingly acquires a capacity for reciprocity of relations. The dissolution of preoperational egocentrism promotes his ability to take the point of view of another, and as he decenters, his judgment regarding the rights of others takes into account multiple perspectives. To acquire this role-taking ability, it is necessary to engage in social activity. An awareness of one's own self is forged from repeated comparisons between self and other people. The young child does not recognize the need in social life to verify his thoughts and to subject them to rational disputation. Similarly, his feelings are accepted as having universal validity, and it is not until he encounters the "judgements and evaluations of others that his intellectual and affective anomy will gradually yield to the pressure of collective logic and moral laws" (Piaget 1932/1965b:401).

Autonomy is a necessary prerequisite to justice, which cannot be based upon obedience to authority. In the exercise of adult authority, duty is supreme, whereas justice is derived from reciprocity and equality, which in turn require the consent of the actor. Little children mistake prescriptive law, held before them by adult authority, for justice. Piaget draws attention to the fact that many adults have themselves failed to achieve autonomy of conscience and, therefore, act solely upon social prejudices and encoded law rather than from a sense of justice. It is only through cooperation between children and eventually between child and adult, as adolescence nears, that a sense of justice develops.

Piaget rejects the notion that justice and love are incompatible. It is only when a stark equality or mathematical equivalence is meeted out as justice that this would seem to be the case. Indeed, children below eleven or twelve seem to evidence this "blow for a blow" mentality. Even then, reciprocity seems to be the critical component, not revenge, for many of the children. A lad who insists on rendering "a blow for a blow" is seeking to return an exact mathematical equivalent and is careful not to give more than he receives. One child, age ten, representatively proclaims that while it is fair to hit back an equal number of times, one should not seek revenge. It is not revenge but justice in the form of equality that the children who advocate hitting back in the stories are seeking. Reciprocity is the keynote. An arbitrary punishment not related to the act is deemed inappropriate. By age eleven or twelve, children begin to forego this crude equality to become more charitable and forgiving. Equality is transformed into equity, a more mature form of reciprocity predicated upon the maxim "Do as you would be done by." Equity takes into account personal and surrounding circumstances and, in effect, is equalitarianism elevated toward relativity. Piaget comments upon equity as follows:

Equalitarianism makes way for a more subtle conception of justice which we may call "equity," and which consists in never defining equality without taking account of the way in which each individual is situated. In the domain of retributive justice, equity consists in determining what are the attenuating circumstances, and we have seen that this consideration enters very late into children's judgments. In the domain of distributive justice, equity consists in taking account of age, of previous services rendered, etc.; in short, in establishing shades of equality. (1932/1965b:285)

Thus, Piaget generalizes three stages of distributive justice. In the first of these, retributive justice outweighs distributive justice. The "just" is conceived of as the adult's command. Expiation, related to heteronomy or constraint, is predominant and linked to an excessive reverence for law. In the second stage equalitarianism emerges fully and distributive justice is supreme. Punishment and obedience no longer hold sway. Subordination to authority declines in favor of autonomy of moral thought. The growing child dissociates the "just" from adult command and simultaneously is developing mutual respect among peers. Younger children tend to view punishment as a moral necessity, and they advocate more severity than older children. Their thought is characterized by what Piaget calls immanent justice, a belief that punishment for transgressions is inherent in nature and will follow automatically. It is not surprising that young children believe in automatic punishment, as their egocentric world is permeated by a sense of life and purpose. For them, objects are governed by moral law and not chance occurrences. As children grow older, expiatory punishment gives way to their seeking to convey to the violator that the bond of solidarity has been ruptured and to generate a sense of the need for restoration of the balance that was upset by the transgression. The criterion for a sound punishment is its efficacy in prevention and not the harm or pain it imposes. The decrease of expiatory punishment in favor of a more enlightened, ideally reciprocal form of justice is gradual, and during the second stage, from seven to ten years, the stark reciprocity of equalitarianism reigns. In the third stage, at around eleven or twelve, equity tends to predominate among the children.

It is important to keep in mind that Piaget does not claim these "stages" have the same rigorously structural character as do the stages he describes in general cognitive development. Even among the more advanced children, responses reflecting primitive moral thought can be found, and, similarly, the younger children do at times give evidence of the mature responses. It is a matter of the proportion of responses, with primitive moral thought gradually decreasing over time as mature moral thought concomitantly increases.

The reader is cautioned to not lose sight of the fact that Piaget's study emphasizes moral judgment and not behavior. There are many instances of developmental lags between the two. Often a child will make verbal judgments of retributive justice, but will demonstrate more charitable and generous behavior in a real-life situation among friends. It is only later that his conceptualization will capture what is implied in his behavior. Sometimes the lag is in the reverse order, as when a child might verbalize a respect for the rules in the game of marbles, yet break the rules at every turn in playing the game. This is because his articulated respect is externally based on authority and not yet upon a genuine interiorized understanding that the rules are made and can be changed through a process of mutual cooperation, that the rules are not immutable and handed down from above, but rather are made by and exist for the players. Paradoxically, when he grasps this, he will volitionally abide by them in action, while recognizing that through mutual and reciprocal dialogue they can be changed.

Since the time of its first publication in 1932, Piaget's only major work on moral development has stimulated an enormous amount of replicated and related studies. The weight of evidence largely supports the early findings, although this is certainly not the case in every detail. Breger (1974) offers a broad summary of the findings, indicating that the heteronomous characterization of the young child's morality by Piaget has been validated, including such elements as expiative punishment, objective responsibility, immanent justice, and the sanctity of authority. Autonomous morality, however, is later in arriving, develops over a longer period of time, and is constituted by more stages than originally postulated. Peer group interaction, although important to the decline of egocentrism, does not exercise a significant role in moral development until adolescence and early youth. For further reviews on Piagetian-based moral research, the reader may also wish to consult Hoffman (1970) and Lickona (1976).

An issue of central importance that has been confirmed by Lee (1971) is the role of cognition in moral development. Piaget contends that, while logic is the morality of thought, we may view morality as the logic of action. In a less cryptic view, Piaget maintains that the role of moral development depends on the role of cognitive development. Lee (1971) posited and confirmed the hypothesis through his own research that there is a progressive sequence in which authority-oriented responses predominate at the preoperational period, while cooperation and reciprocity responses prevail during the concrete operational period. Progression to the period of formal operational thought reveals moral judgment based on ideological and idealistic considerations.

In a more recent work Piaget (1964/1968) identifies will as a regulator of energy and compares it to the operation in cognition. Emotions becoming organized have will as their ultimate form of equilibrium. Will comes into play to resolve tension, such as when pleasure and duty conflict. If, for example, pleasure is the stronger but inferior component, will exerts a force on behalf of duty as the weaker but superior element. In general, Piaget comments, "Thus affectivity from seven to twelve years is characterized by the appearance of new moral feelings and, above all, by an organization of will, which culminates in a better integration of the self and a more effective regulation of affective life"(1964/1968:55).

The Moral World of Lawrence Kohlberg. Kohlberg's stage theory of moral development is founded upon Piaget's early work on the subject, but represents a considerable extension and refinement. Kohlberg posits six stages of moral development. It appears that the first four are characterized to varying degrees by the morality of heteronomy, and stages 2 to 6 are characterized to varying degrees by the morality of autonomy (Breger 1974). Piaget's version of autonomous morality coincides with stage 3 in Kohlberg's paradigm. Like Piaget, Kohlberg rejects a maturational explanation, believing that the evidence does not support a view of the stages automatically unfolding as neurological structures appear. He believes that social interaction within the matrix of institutional arrangements, such as family and school, promotes role-taking activities, which in turn stimulate moral development. New cognitive structures are necessary for advanced moral judgment and behavior, although their appearance does not assure a higher morality. They serve as a necessary, but not sufficient, condition for the corresponding moral stage.

The six stages of moral development identified by Kohlberg are said to emerge in an unvarying sequence regardless of class or cultural variables (Kohlberg 1969; Walker 1982). However, these variables do seem to influence the rate of development and the ultimate level which a given individual will attain. It is not the case that each person will go through all of the stages, and, in fact, relatively few people ever arrive at stages 5 and 6. Prime examples of stage 6 achievers are such historical figures as Socrates, Jesus, and Martin Luther King, Jr. In recent years, Kohlberg has conceded that there is no solid data base to sustantiate an empirical stage 6, unlike the other stages, which have received consistent cross-cultural validation. Stage 6 is now generally viewed as Kohlberg's own preferred philosophical and ideological orientation, which is shared by many liberals in the tradition of Western civilization.

Kohlberg assesses level of moral development by the formal character of the judgment rather than the content involved. Emphasis is placed on the mode of reasoning exercised in arriving at a position, as opposed to the specific position actually adopted. There are structural dimensions within the social sphere pertaining to the moral arena in a fashion analogous to the physical dimensions pertaining to the cognitive arena. These dimensions are universal and more important in moral development than the internalization of the particular rules and taboos of any culture. They encompass such issues as punishment and guilt, property rights, personal roles of affection, authority and governance, laws and rules, value of life, liberty and civil rights, distributive justice, truth, and sexual values. At each stage of development a growing youngster will conceive of these universal societal issues in different ways. They are analogous to such categories as space, time, and causality in the physical world.

Kohlberg's theory of moral development is the dominating paradigm in the field. It is not only the most conceptually sophisticated, but is based upon an impressive longitudinal study exceeding twenty years. The study began in 1958, Kohlberg's youngest subjects then being only ten years old and the oldest sixteen. Many of the subjects have been followed through college and some of them into their thirties. Throughout the years, Kohlberg has refined his theories to fit the emerging data and revised his scoring manual, making it consistently more sensitive to discerning structure over content. As did Piaget, Kohlberg elicited his subjects' responses by posing moral dilemmas to them and then probing to discover not only their resolutions, but the reasoning process underlying them. Kohlberg's stories are more tightly organized than Piaget's, explicitly placing into conflict either the individual and society or the rights of two individuals. An example is the famous Heinz dilemma, in which Heinz's wife is dying of cancer. A local druggist has discovered a medicine that can cure her, but he will only sell it at an exorbitant price, which places it out of Heinz's reach. The question is whether or not Heinz should break in and steal the drug.

Kohlberg (1963a and b, 1969, 1971a, 1981) has presented his stage theory in a variety of journals and chapters in books over the years. The following exposition has been drawn from several of these sources. The six stages are organized into three levels. Level 1 is comprised of stages 1 and 2. It is called Preconventional or Pre-moral and is characterized by a conceptualizing of morality as obeying the law. However, the law is external to the self and the emphasis is upon obedience. The child has adopted a concrete individual perspective. At this level, children, while responsive to notions of good and bad or right and wrong as prescribed by the culture, make moral judgments based on pleasurable and unpleasurable consequences. Personal interests are paramount. Children under nine years are usually at this level. At Level 2, the Conventional Level, we find conformity and fidelity to what is expected by others and the social order. The majority of people are at this level. They adopt a member-of-society perspective and identify with prevailing law, which they no longer experience as being imposed from an external source or authority. Emphasis is upon maintaining the law, for that which "is," is construed as that which "ought" to be. Immediate consequences are of less concern than meeting the expectations of one's family, group, and country. Both adolescents and adults are to be found in abundance at this level. While stages 3 and 4 comprise the Conventional Level, stages 5 and 6 constitute the Postconventional or Principled Level. This level is based upon a principled morality of universal application which transcends the authority and rules prevailing in the individual's personal life and general culture. The individual adopts a prior-to-society perspective from which he can evaluate whether any given law is moral and accords with principles of justice and respect for individual rights. Unlike the conservative character of Level 2, the Level 3 individual stands ready to seek change in those laws that are deemed to be unjust. The self is now differentiated from both rules and expectations. It is not before age twenty that the relatively small number of people who progress to Level 3 begin to manifest such moral reasoning.

Stage 1 is founded upon an orientation to punishment and obedience. Although deference to authority is observed, one complies to avoid personal harm. There is no recognition of, or respect for, an underlying moral order from which punishment and authority stem. Basically, good and bad are determined by the anticipated application of reward or punishment. Although Kohlberg's description of stage 1 coincides with Piaget's heteronomous stage, there is a difference of interpretation, for Kohlberg rejects Piaget's emphasis upon the sacred character of rules and authority in the young child. Stage 2 is viewed as one of naive egoism or individualistic egoism. Like Piaget, Kohlberg finds the years from six to ten to be ones of reciprocity and mutual exchange. There is evidenced an increased equalitarianism over authority and an increased awareness of the relativity of values. Elements of autonomy as characterized by Piaget are beginning to appear. Nevertheless, the reciprocity involved in this stage is derived from one's own ego interests and not from a sense of obligation or respect for individual rights. Mutual respect is not central to it. Asked whether a man is right or wrong to steal a lifesaving drug for his dying wife from the local pharmacist who discovered it, but is charging a prohibitive cost, many youngsters at this stage will answer yes. However, when asked to support their position, they will frequently answer that if the wife dies there will be no one to cook the husband's meals. Another characteristic response to the stories which involve doing something for another is that at some future time help may be needed from that person. The hedonistic and reciprocal nature of such replies is obvious. It should not be overlooked, however, that a good deal of social exchange in adult life does indeed pivot around a stage 2 plane of development.

At stages 3 and 4 Kohlberg places special emphasis on the emergence of role-taking abilities. The preadolscent anticipates the way in which others might respond to his behavior and acts in such a way as to win approval and avoid disapproval. Obedience is not carried out merely for the sake of the rule or authority itself, but implies the attempt to attain certain social aims. The feelings of others are taken into account. Being of service to individuals and institutions takes on prominence. Stage 3 has been labeled "Good-boy Orientation" by Kohlberg, and, interestingly, in more recent years he has added the term "Nice-girl." The young person at this stage places a great emphasis upon affection and approval on the interpersonal level. The type of reciprocity exercised is not founded upon strict mathematical equivalence ("A blow for a blow"), but is predicated upon putting oneself in the other person's place to determine what is a just action toward him. In other words, Kohlberg maintains that at stage 3 one begins to demonstrate imaginative reciprocity, involving role taking, rather than engaging in an exact reciprocal exchange. Equity, taking into account individual circumstances, which Piaget has described, is found at this developmental stage. A significant limitation, however, is that the youngster's role-taking ability and concept of justice are confined primarily to the domain of his own concrete personal relationships with friends and family. At stage 4 there is a shift in emphasis from a concept of justice applied mainly between individuals to a focus of justice between the individual and the community or social system. The prevailing notion of justice is grounded in maintaining the social order. Patterns of behavior and relationship should remain within the existing rules and social structure. This law and order orientation has been found to be the dominant one among adults in all societies studied by Kohlberg. He stresses that this stage, which emphasizes the maintenance of rules and laws, is morally more advanced and based on a higher level of rational attainment than the earlier stage of obedience to rules found at stage 1. Stage 4 is only arrived at after the previous stages are passed through and a capacity for role taking which goes beyond one's immediate milieu to encompass the community has emerged. "Law and order" rhetoric that does not reflect this societal system perspective is below a stage 4 attainment.

Stages 5 and 6 witness the emergence of principled thinking. Stage 5 is based on the democratic process, has a legalistic character to it, and revolves around the social contract. Although moral judgment recommends working within the confines of the current social order, emphasis is upon engaging in the appropriate legal procedures to change laws when they are unjust. The rights of individuals become of paramount importance. The insistence upon maintaining the social order evidenced in stage 4 ceases to play a dominant role. Laws are conceived of as instruments for promoting individual rights and social welfare. Although laws are not seen as sacred, the stage 5 person will, in the conduct of day-by-day affairs, advocate observing them and will refer to them to define what is right. At the same time, a person at this stage will recognize the possibility of conflict between a legal or rational societal right and the right of an individual. Kohlberg illustrates this by citing a typical response to the Heinz dilemma. Many youngsters at this stage simultaneously suggest that the husband would be wrong to steal from the standpoint of society and the law, but right from a personal standpoint. Even though the act may be "just" from an individual viewpoint, a judge would be legaly proper, because of the social contract, to sentence the husband.

At stage 4 the person seems more concerned with protecting the collective or average citizen from law violations by others. The stage 5 person's concern for individual rights will extend to wanting to assure due process for the accused and convicted, as well as for the average citizen. The stage 5 person is interested in the preservation and protection of individual rights, while at the same time he emphasizes the making of laws which would promote and maximize social welfare. The methodology of implementing the democratic process is of greater importance to the stage 5 person than are the concrete rules and their enforcement. The reason is that the principles of democracy are said to be based upon certain natural rights which antecede the specific laws that obtain. The notion of justice with respect to adhering to a social contract at stage 5 is defined by a mutuality or reciprocity of consent on the part of the individuals, as in marriage, in contrast to merely obeying to preserve the social order. In succinctly formulating the two defining aspects of stage 5, Kohlberg and Elfenbein have written, "The stage 5 effort to make more universal judgments can take two forms. One is the principle of utility or welfare maximization. The other is the concept of human rights and the social contract—the idea that individuals have rights that are prior to society, and that the powers of the state are limited to those which are protective of or at least compatible with those rights" (1975:31). Most people do not arrive at the principled level even though the United States was founded upon democratic principles. In Kohlberg's view, it is obvious that merely acquiring experiences of responsibility, since most people do eventually have such experiences, is not sufficient to facilitate an advance to stage 5. He states, "Personal experiences of choice involving questioning with commitment, in some sort of integration with stimulation to cognitive-moral reflection, seemed required for movement from conventional to principled thoughts" (1973:41).

Stage 6 is presented as the highest attainment of moral reasoning. It has already been observed that Kohlberg does not claim to have empirical validation of stage 6 as a natural stage. Nevertheless, as it reflects Kohlberg's position on what does constitute the highest moral vision, we shall examine it. Both stages 5 and 6 are based on principles as opposed to rules. Rules offer concrete indications of specific actions to be carried out or refrained from. Principles are absolute, universal, and admit of no exceptions. They take into account the respective claims of all parties involved in a conflict and offer general guides to resolutions. Kohlberg uses a principle not as a rule to action but as a guide to choice; it is what he calls a metarule as opposed to a mere concrete rule. Principled justice, according to Kohlberg (1971a), signifies the resolution of diverse and competing claims. It calls for dealing with each person equally in the realm of distributive justice, without taking into consideration the vested interests of individuals. Rawls (1971) has devised an approach to achieving this, which he calls the "original position." In his approach, a concept of justice is arrived at by imaginatively contemplating a hypothetical society in which one's own role(s) is unknown. In this manner, a "veil of ignorance" precludes a judgment from being based upon vested interests, as one attempts to construct just laws to govern the society.

Kohlberg points out that stage 5 does not offer an adequate guide to when it is proper to violate the law. Stage 6 would prescribe that civil disobedience is appropriate in response to an unjust law, one which violates basic human rights, but under no other circumstances. Increasingly as the person moves from stage 5 to stage 6, he takes a perspective outside of society and identifies with the just claims of the individuals involved regardless of specific laws that have been enacted. At stage 6, morality is viewed as conscience in the form of self-chosen ethical principles based on a universal, consistent, and comprehensive concept of justice. Such a concept of justice allows for judgments that are without internal conflict or inconsistency, cover all conceivable contingencies, and are applicable across the board to all individuals regardless of status. Kohlberg believes that Rawls' "original position" exercise, in which the moral actor can take each person's role alternately, without being tainted by a knowledge of vested interests, will facilitate arriving at a just resolution that will satisfy and command consensus from all fully rational persons. Engaging in this "ideal role-taking" activity and being willing to assume any position in a situation under the rules or laws generated by it is a manifestation of completely reversible moral thought which, in Kohlberg's view, is the apex of moral development. Further, reversible thinking in the moral domain is predicated upon a reciprocal relationship between duties and rights. If one person is said to have a right, this implies that another person has a duty in relation to that right. If one person has a duty, then another person has a right in relation to that duty. A stage 6 person can assume reversible positions in a conflict situation, acknowledging rights and duties which are coordinated to reach an equilibrated ethical resolution to the dilemma.

The two major universal principles which Kohlberg proclaims are based upon Kant's two moral axioms. The first is to act in such a way that the maxim guiding your own behavior would be willed by you to become a universal law. The second is to treat each person as an end in himself and not as a means to an end.

When contemplating Kohlberg's moral stage theory, it is important to keep in mind that two individuals of the same stage could have opposing resolutions to a dilemma from the standpoint of content. It is only essential that the structure of their reasoning be the same. Thus, for example, one child may advocate stealing and another be against it as in the Heinz dilemma and still both be at stage 2, as long as their conceptual justifications reflect a concern with their own hedonistic self-interests. It is only at stage 6 that all rational thinkers will not only share in structure, but will agree in content also. It is also possible to have six individuals, each at a different moral stage, yet each advocating the same resolution to a dilemma. In such a case, however, probing for the underlying justification of each individual would disclose six different forms of moral reasoning.

The relationship between cognitive-structural development and moral stages is such that the former is a necessary, but not sufficient, condition for the latter. Unless the individual reaches the concrete operational period, he will not go beyond stage 1. Formal operations are necessary for principled moral reasoning. Fully consolidated stage 4 reasoning requires at least the early phases of formal operations. The incipient phase of stage 4 reasoning is possible without formal operations; however, without going beyond concrete operations, it would not be possible to exceed early stage 4 reasoning. Kuhn, Langer, Kohlberg, and Haan (1977) provide an excellent empirically based discussion of this topic.

The question of whether there is a consistency between moral thought and behavior is a multifaceted one. There does seem to be some basis for accepting the cognitive-developmentalist position that there is a congruence between moral stage and action (Haan, Smith, and Block 1968; Kohlberg 1971b; Krebs and Rosenwald 1977). However, it is certain that thought and action do not exist in a one-to-one correspondence. Many variables other than one's moral stage may influence behavior. These variables are as follows: motivation, affect, situation, group pressure, self-interests, and personality. Furthermore, since the same moral stage can generate opposing behavioral prescriptions, it should be recognized that the clue to whether a behavior is congruent with moral stage is the meaning of the behavior to the actor carrying it out and not the behavior itself. Blasi, after an extensive review of the literature, concludes that "the body of research reviewed here seems to offer considerable support for the hypothesis that moral reasoning and moral action are statistically related" (1980:37). However, he follows this statement by citing several reservations and the usual plea for the utilization of increased methodological sophistication, which he believes is likely to demonstrate an even greater degree of consistency than has thus far been demonstrated.

Kohlberg's work is certainly not without its critics. Simpson (1974) views Kohlberg's formulations as being culture bound. Kurtines and Grief (1974) are critical of the measurement scale utilized, Gibbs (1977) questions whether either stage 5 or stage 6 is a natural stage of development, Gilligan (1982b) flaws the theory for being derived from a study of males only, and Carter (1980) and Locke (1980) criticize Kohlberg on philosophical grounds. The process is a dialectical one, however, with periodic rejoinders by Kohlberg and his colleagues, as well as responsive theoretical revisions and methodological refinements. It has already been noted that Kohlberg (1978) has acknowledged that stage 6 lacks empirical verification, and he now suggests that it be viewed as a theoretical construction rather than a separate developmental attainment to be found in morally advanced individuals. The highest level of moral development from an empirical standpoint is now held to be stage 5B. As Colby reports, each stage has been found to consist of types A and B. She states, "In a sense 5B substage is a consolidation or equilibration of the social perspective first elaborated at the A substage. It is as if a new social contract (involving a new level of perspective) were negotiated at each A substage. At the B substage this new social contract is made more general, reciprocal, and reversible: it reaches a more stable equilibrium" (1978:94).

A three-volume work containing the papers of Lawrence Kohlberg is presently being prepared. The entire set is entitled *Essays on Moral Development*. The first volume (Kohlberg 1981) has already been published, and its focus is on philosophy and the concept of justice. The second will emphasize the psychological aspects of moral development, and the final volume is to concentrate upon the practical application of the moral stage theory to educational settings. A full-length exposition of Kohlberg's work can be found in Rosen (1980).

Separating Conventional and Moral Domains. Turiel (1983) has advanced the thesis that social knowledge can be categorized into separate domains. He focuses specifically upon conventional and moral domains. Convention is defined as arbitrary and tied to particular social contexts. It is through direct participation in social systems that children construct concepts promoting their understanding of conventional rules that they and others are expected to abide by and that regulate reciprocal interactions. Morality, on the other hand, is not bound to societal contexts, but is universally prescriptive and is conceived of as being inherent in the nature of social relationships. It is concerned with issues of fairness and justice and provides guidelines for how people necessarily "ought" to coordinate their relations with one another.

Based on research that he and his colleagues have conducted, Turiel maintains that children as young as three to four years of age differentiate accurately between issues of social convention and morality. Despite this early capability to distinguish between the two domains, a considerable amount of development within each domain does occur through childhood and adolescence to young adulthood. Turiel critiques the moral developmental theories of Piaget and Kohlberg from this standpoint. Piaget emphasizes the child's unilateral respect toward authority and an attitude toward rules as sacred, as characterizing the child's early conceptions of morality. Kohlberg disagrees with Piaget on this point. Moral conceptions in early development prescribe obedience in order to avoid punishment from adult power holders. By stage 4, conformity to law is advocated because what is law must necessarily be right. Yet for both Piaget and Kohlberg, later autonomous morality is an outgrowth of the child's sense of social convention. Turiel's analysis suggests that this proposed sequence of development inappropriately fuses conventional and moral domains, each of which have their own separate developmental sequences. A consequence of this is that the early child's capacity for differentiating between distinctively moral and conventional issues is overlooked. Turiel states pointedly, "Noninstrumental moral conceptions are evident in early childhood and are based on inferences about interpersonal relations, especially those pertaining to harm and unequal treatments" (1983:157). He cites the work of Damon (1977) as exemplifying this position.

The Co-Construction of Social Knowledge. Damon (1977, 1983a and b) has explored the nature of children's social conceptions and their transformation with age progression. His interest has been in the structural organization and evolving reorganization of social knowledge. The specific focus of his studies has been upon four areas, which are: authority and friendship, both forms of social relations;

and justice and social rules, both of which seem to regulate social relations. Because it is most germane to the thematic content of Kohlberg's work, we will single out Damon's findings on justice for special attention. Children's reasoning in response to hypothetical dilemmas involving distributive justice were sought, and they were also engaged in real-life situations to observe the degree of consistency between moral thought and behavior. The story structure was deliberately simple and relevant to children's everyday lives. Participating children were middle-class and between the ages of four and ten. The findings of the study have since been replicated among diverse populations (Damon 1980, 1981).

Six levels of early positive justice concepts were formulated from these studies. A central defining issue was the balance struck in reciprocal action regulating individual claims to a share of the available resources and the actual rewards or punishments to which each individual was deemed deserving. All social interaction, for Damon, is essentially characterized by one form or another of reciprocity. It is these social interactions with their reciprocal activity that social concepts deal with. At Level 0-A the only justification advanced for receiving goods is the wish to have them or to see someone the child favors have them. Level 0-B is but a slight progression in which desire remains paramount, but external reasons pertaining to self are cited. An example might be, "We should get more because we're bigger." Level 1-A advocates absolute equality. The reasoning is that everyone should get the identical amount in order to avoid disharmony. Justifications based on merit are presented at Level 1-B. Individuals should receive what they have earned by their efforts. Level 2-A manifests a recognition of competing claims, with some priority given to those individuals who may not have been able to contribute to a group effort because of being disadvantaged. Merit as a basis for receiving a proportion of the goods available now must compete with need as a worthy criterion. There is an attempt to quantify or rank the various criteria. Finally, at Level 2-B, the various types of claims are coordinated with one another, and this is done in relation to each particular situation. Although each person should get what he is deserving of, the situation will be weighed in determining this so that sometimes there will be equality of distribution and at other times there will be uneven distribution. Each new level signifies not a quantitative increase of reciprocity, but a fundamental reorganization in the form the reciprocity takes.

Regarding the congruence between verbal reasoning about hypothetical stories and actual moral behavior, Damon found a complicated picture. There was, in fact, a significant amount of coherence between verbal and behavioral planes, but also a good deal of discrepancy. Self-interest in real-life situations seemed to be the dominant factor in impeding a just distribution of goods. This was most prevalent among the youngest children and diminished with age progression, but its influence was never completely absent at any level.

Damon, like Turiel, has been in the forefront of those cognitive-developmentalists researching children's construction of social knowledge. He has emphasized in his work that all we need to know about social cognition cannot be derived from studying how knowledge of the physical world is constructed. The need to coordinate mutual interactions between intentional beings distinguishes social relations and is a major focus of social cognition as opposed to the relationship between the individual and nonsocial objects. Further, Damon has proposed a view of *all* knowledge as social in character. Observe his comments on this theme:

If one begins with the assumption that all human knowledge is fundamentally social in nature, and that all subsequent restructuring of children's knowledge proceeds under the past or present influence of social interaction in some form, then one is left with a model that envisions social experience as an integral part of the developmental process. Rather than the view that the subject discovers properties of an external object, sometimes with the aid of social feedback, this alternative approach presents the view that knowledge is from the start motivated, organized, and communicated in the course of social interaction. It is co-constructed, rather than unilaterally constructed. (1983b:131)

In a recent study of children from ages five to nine, Damon and Killen (1982) sought to determine whether the children's level of positive justice concepts could be developed through peer group social interaction. In groups of three the children were assigned the task of discussing a real-life situation involving the sharing and distribution of candy bars. It was found that children whose participation was characterized by rejection and persistent disagreement did not make any gains. Damon and Killen interpreted this as signifying that conflict actually impeded development. A distinction was made, however, between this type of social conflict and the cognitive conflict of Piagetian tradition, in which a single individual is aware of internal contradiction. Among the children in the experiment who started out at lower levels of positive justice development, those who made gains were observed to have been accepting of the others' ideas, willing to engage in compromise, and also to extend and elaborate upon their peers' points of view. It was not clear what accounted for gains of the children who scored at a relatively high level of positive justice at the pretest; it was clear that they also did not number among those who created an atmosphere of social conflict, however. Commenting upon those children who started out at low levels of positive justice and did show signs of developmental progress, Damon and Killen stated, "The reciprocally accepting or transforming nature of these children's interactions with peers implies an orientation toward co-construction and conciliation rather than towards either argumentation or passive withdrawal" (1982:365).

This emphasis upon cooperation and the co-construction of social knowledge is also to be found in the work of Youniss (1980) and within all probability reflects a growing trend in the field. The co-construction of knowledge through social interaction has similarly been a focal point of investigations conducted by Doise and his colleagues in Geneva (Doise and Mugny 1979; Mugny and Doise 1978). In their work cognitive conflict has assumed a significant role; however, the knowledge constructed has been of the physical world and not that of social concepts.

Care As the Moral Imperative. In the very act of delivering criticism against the limitations of Kohlberg's moral stage theory, Gilligan (1977, 1982a and b) advances a complementary developmental theory. Kohlberg's stages were initially formulated on the basis of research conducted with young males. Subsequently, in exploring the moral developmental level of females, women were measured against the standard of a male derived theory. As a consequence of this artificial condition, the distinctive moral voice of women was masked. Women tended to be scored at stage 3 and considered morally below males, who generally ranked higher. Although coming from a different theoretical orientation, it is well known that Freud has made much the same claim about women's alleged moral inferiority. Gilligan (1982b) studied both male and female college students, as well as a heterogeneous group of women ranging in age from fifteen to thirty-three who were pregnant and considering abortion. Her main claim is that women tend to conceptualize moral conflicts in terms of an ethic of care and responsibility with emphasis upon communication, relationship, and avoiding harm to others. Men, in contrast, construe moral conflict in terms of impersonal considerations of fairness, justice, and law. For women it is the way of attachment and connectedness; for men it is the way of separateness and individualism.

Gilligan views these two orientations to moral conflict and resolution neither as one of them being lower than the other in a sequential hierarchy nor as both of them in opposition, but rather as complementary to one another. Although empirically her investigations have disclosed women and men to conceptualize moral dilemmas as she has described them, Gilligan emphasizes that both descriptions should be viewed as themes which are not absolutely or necessarily linked to one sex or the other. Indeed, a fully mature moral vision requires an appreciation of both modes of conceptualizing experience. Gilligan informs us, "Thus, starting from very different points, from the different ideologies of justice and care, the men and women in the study come, in the course of becoming adult, to a greater understanding of both points of view and thus to a greater convergence in judgment" (1982a:167).

As a caveat, it should be noted that in a lengthy review of Gilligan's work, Colby and Damon (1983) assert that recent literature reviews (Rest, in press; Walker, in press) reveal no difference in moral stage scores regarding the sex variable, once subjects' education and career are controlled.

TAKING ANOTHER'S PERSPECTIVE

There are three types of perspective taking: visual, affective, and cognitive. Perspective taking is the activity of decentering one's own point of view and inferring the perspective of another person, when that person's viewpoint differs from one's own. As development occurs, the individual becomes increasingly more able to coordinate the other person's viewpoint with his own and ultimately to take a systems perspective beyond the immediate context. Thus, at a more advanced level, an individual cannot only take the perspective of his own nation, but can coordinate it with the perspective of other nations. Whether at a dyadic microlevel or an international macrolevel, the ability for multiperspective activity is a highly adaptive social function.

Piaget and Inhelder (1948/1967) provided a starting point for a considerable amount of subsequent attempts by others to explore the child's growing ability to decenter from his own perspective and to see things from another's point of view. Utilizing a cardboard apparatus simulating three mountains, they explored children's perspective-taking ability to reconstruct varying perspectives of position rotating around the mountains. Piaget and Inhelder have observed that children from four to twelve undergo a developmental progression from egocentrism during the earlier years to a complete relativity of perspectives in which their own views are coordinated with the various alternate possibilities. Fishbein, Lewis, and Keiffer have identified the coordination of perspectives in its broadest sense as "The *knowledge* that the appearance of objects is a function of the spatial position from which they are viewed, and . . . the *ability* to determine what the appearance will be for any specific viewing position" (1972:21). There is a decisive pattern of age-related development with the child generally arriving at the ability to decenter from his own viewpoint, reconstruct alternate perspectives, and coordinate these various possible perspectives at approximately ten years of age. Masangkay, McCluskey, McIntyre, Sims-Knight, Vaughan, and Flavell (1974) conducted research which led them to conclude that some ability at spatial perspective taking is present in children from two to three years of age, whereas Laurendeau and Pinard (1970) carried out research in which the majority of youngsters did not achieve high-level visual perspective taking until several years after age ten.

The critical variable seems to be task complexity. The very young children in the experiment by Masangkay et. al. (1974) were presented with a very streamlined, simple task. To the contrary, the subjects in the experiment by Laurendeau and Pinard (1970) were confronted with a task that placed even more stringent demands upon them than the one utilized by Piaget and Inhelder (1948/1967). Laurendeau and Pinard caution against construing egocentrism as being found exclusively in one period followed by its absence. The relative complexity of the tests utilized may invoke egocentrism even at more advanced developmental levels. Flavell (1974) offers an interesting developmental model to explain the primitive role-taking capacity cited by Masangkay and his colleagues in their subjects.

In an extensive survey of the literature on role taking or perspectivism, as it is sometimes alternately called, Shantz (1975) sharply differentiates it from what social psychologists generally mean by role. It does not refer to role enactment, in which a person assumes the postures or gestures of another person, nor does it signify the traits expected to be observed in such designations as occupational or sex role. Rather, it is a set of cognitive skills which enable one person to infer something about another person's thoughts and feelings. It takes place in greater proportion as egocentrism declines, which facilitates the individual's ability not only to take the perspective of another, but to coordinate that with his own. As Shantz points out, role-taking capacities are often employed as a means to an end, as in efforts to persuade, playing a game to win, and resolving social conflict. Since both people in an interpersonal dyad have some degree of role-taking abilities, there is a reciprocal and cooperative character to it.

Pioneering work in this area has been carried out by Feffer (1959), Feffer and Gourevitch (1960), and Feffer and Suchotliff (1966). Feffer's aim in this series of projects was to redirect the concept of decentration, so vital in Piaget's view on constructing knowledge in the physical world, to the social dimension. A central hypothesis was that effective interpersonal behavior derives from an individual's ability to consider multiple perspectives simultaneously with respect to his own behavior. It is emphasized that centration on one's own viewpoint leads to distortion and that only a partial correction of the distortion is achieved when the individual engages in decentration of a successive nature, that is, shifting sequentially from one part of the perceptual field to another. It is in simultaneous decentering, taking into account a number of facets of a situation at one time in relation to one another, that distortions are more completely corrected. Individuals who centrate on their own viewpoint will encounter difficulty in appropriately modifying their responses to suit the interpersonal dynamics of a situation. In effective social interaction, the individual can assess his intended behavior from the standpoint of what he would anticipate the other person's reaction would be to that behavior, were it to be carried out. The skill involved in performing this cognitive act entails keeping one's own perspective in mind while simultaneously taking into account the perspective of the other. In so doing, a distortion that may derive from exclusively centering or fucusing upon one's own outlook in a situation can be corrected for by adjusting this in relation to the other's outlook. For example, a young man who has been overlooked at a time of year when pay raises are issued is angered and contemplates storming into the boss's office to demand an explanation. However, upon placing himself in the role of the boss, he anticipates that the boss will counter with even greater anger at this unbridled display of impulsivity and hostility. Therefore, having anticipated an undesirable reaction to his intended behavior, our young man modifies that behavior without having carried it out. Instead, he selects an approach which is more likely to lead to a desirable outcome. Hence, we see that a balanced decentration, in which correction is made for the maladaptive behavior that would have occurred had he centrated exclusively on his initially intended behavior, leads to more effective social interaction.

This exposition deals only with the decentering ability of a single individual decentering. Feffer's work gets progressively more complex as he examines the reciprocal decentering capacities of two interacting individuals, confirming the hypotheses that when two individuals are able to simultaneously consider their behavior from alternate viewpoints, ther is likely to be more effective social interaction between them (Feffer and Suchotliff 1966). Feffer (1967) has attempted to show how primitive social interaction, in contrast to balanced decentrations, can be utilized to explain symptom expression.

Flavell, Botkin, Fry, Wright, and Jarvis (1968) have presented an interesting series of studies on role taking, which revolve around guessing games, recounting stories to another person, communication tasks, and persuasion activities. The work of Flavell et al. (1968) constitutes a most ambitious effort. It traces developmental ability in recursive thinking such as "I think he thinks that I think . . . " Expanding recursive thought leads to increasingly more complex and subtle game playing, as well as interpersonal relationships. In one project children ranging from second grade through eighth grade, thus spanning middle childhood and early adolescence, are expected to state the next move which an opponent will make in a game and to explain their reasons for their predictions. The opponent's goal is to select between two cups that are upside down, only one of which conceals either one nickel or two nickels. In the initial condition of the experiment, one cup had one nickel underneath it and a second had two nickels underneath it. On the bottoms of the cups, which are visible because they are turned upside down, there is stuck either one or two coins, the amount corresponding to what is underneath. However, when the opponent is out of the room, the child is instructed to remove the amount from whichever of the two cups he predicts the opponent will select when reentering the room. The opponent's goal is to select that cup which he thinks will still have the money underneath it. The child is reminded that the opponent is aware that the child will be attempting to fool him.

The results reveal a progression of age-related responses characterized by increasingly more subtlety and complexity. Flavell identifies four strategies. In strategy o the child either refuses to make predictions of if he does, he fails to provide an explanation for his choice. Strategy A is a class of responses in which the child fails to take into account the possibility that the opponent migh have some thoughts about the child's own behavior. Explanations focus on the cups and coins. In other words, the child would commonly predict that the opponent would choose the cup with two nickels displayed on it because, he would explain, the opponent would get more money that way if the coins turn out to be under the cup. In strategy B the child evidences a rationale for his selection which anticipates that the opponent is thinking about what the child is thinking about. In effect, the child of strategy B is reasoning, "I think he thinks that I think he will pick the two-coined cup. Therefore, I predict he will pick the one-coined cup." Strategy C proves to be extremely rare and involves one more loop in this recursive thinking. We will confine our analysis to the process of shifting from strategy A to B, as this is the most critical phase emphasized by Flavell.

The subject must first come to realize not only that the other person can have thoughts about things external to the subject, but that he can also think about the subject himself. Flavell believes that this step is preceded by the subject recognizing that the other person can have thoughts about inanimate objects and people in general. The child next advances to a realization that not only may the other person think about him, but that the other person can think about what it is the child is thinking. In other words, the other person has a cognitive domain which can encompass the child both as an object and also as an object with a subjective component, about which the other person makes inferences. These two steps are considered absolutely necessary for the transition from strategy A to strategy B to occur. Despite the considerably greater complexity of strategy B, Flavell stresses that even strategy A is a form of role taking, for it does entail ascribing certain attributes or motives to the other person (i.e., "He'll choose that one because there is more money under it"). In fact, he suggests that a great deal of the "genuine interactions with peers, marked by efforts at cooperation, compromise, real argument, and other characteristics which reflect some awareness of the other's point of view" (Flavell et al. 1968:54) is predicated upon the "nascent role-taking activity" of strategy A. As the child moves from middle childhood into preadolescence and adolescence, an increasing use of strategy B characterizes social interaction. Flavell et al. refer to Sullivan (1953) in commenting that

the child is now prone to develop intimate interpersonal relationships with a same-sex chum, relationships in which meticulous attention is given to the careful gauging of thoughts and feelings of the other (especially toward oneself), of comparing and contrasting his perceptions of the world with one's own, and the like. And this sort of thing certainly continues with a vengeance during adolescence, to the child's profit and pain, with reference to others of both sexes: "Does she think I'm good looking?" "How will they take it if I do such-and-such?" etc. could scarcely be called atypical cognitions for this age group. (1968:54)

The child who does not undergo the appropriate advances in developmental strategies of role taking will certainly suffer the consequences of arrested interpersonal relationships.

In her review on social cognition, Shantz (1975) distinguishes within the realm of affective role taking between a child's ability to understand what another is feeling (Borke 1971) and feeling an appropriate response within oneself in relation to another's plight (Feshbach and Roe 1968). Borke (1973) found that children as young as four years old could identify happy responses of others in simple situations. Further, between ages four and seven, children show a progressive capacity for correctly labeling such negative feelings as fear, sadness, and anger in others. Feshbach and Roe (1968), in addition to exploring how well children from six to seven years old could identify how another feels, also investigated the extent to which the children could empathically experience a vicarious affect based on another's plight. They concluded that understanding what the other is feeling is a precondition for "affective empathy," but that such social understanding of another's affect does not rely on actually feeling what the other is feeling. Shantz suggests that the ability in early childhood to identify another's feeling in a given situation is not based upon role-taking skills. If it is, the form it has taken is at a most rudimentary level. At best, the ability being displayed by these very young children may be tantamount to merely describing themselves based on similar past experiences. They are in effect simply attributing responses to the other which they themselves had previously experienced in similar situations. If so, this does not meet the hallmark of role-taking: the cognitive capacity to infer the perspective of another when that perspective differs from one's own (Chandler and Greenspan 1972). Thus we see that inference and decentration are essential to genuine role taking. Nevertheless, the significance of knowing what another is feeling by identifying with it should not be minimized. It reflects an ability, however primitive, which not only has intrinsic value and utility, but which may well serve as a bridge to advanced affective role taking.

In summarizing her review of literature in this area, Shantz comments, "Overall, these studies suggest that accurate empathy concerning simple emotions is achieved by preschool children when the situation the other person is in is familiar to the child and/or the other person is substantially similar to the child. Accurate understanding of these same emotions is not usually attained until middle or late childhood when the situations and people judged have low similarity and low familiarity to the child" (1975:281). Hoffman (1983) has pointed out that by the time of late childhood or early adolsecence, youngsters have begun to attribute to others both personal identities and life experiences extending beyond the situational context in which they are immediately known. As a result of this cognitive advance, one's empathic capacity for others takes on greater complexity, stability, and duration.

A fruitful formulation of interpersonal perspective taking and social reasoning has been advanced by Selman (1971a, 1971b, 1976, 1980), Selman and Byrne (1974), and Selman, Schorin, Stone, and Phelps (1983). It is one which Loevinger (1976) finds similar and congenial to the conception of ego development elaborated upon in her latest work. In his own words, Selman has utilized the "Piagetian structuralist-developmental approach" in exploring the ontogenesis of social role taking. He cautions that one should not look to a social-cognitive analysis to provide causal explanations of behavior. Instead, it serves as a means for describing and organizing behavior and in turn leads to strategies of intervention to help the child improve his social reasoning and functioning. The approach in clinical practice derived from a social-cognitive model would not be a "cold-blooded" one, but rather a highly individualized one which makes every attempt to accurately diagnose the child's cognitive level of stage development in order to comprehend how he is construing his social world. For example, it may be discovered that the child who acts hostilely and persists in fighting whenever a peer accidentally bumps into him may not yet have developed to the stage of differentiation between intentions and objective consequences.

In addition to working in the Piagetian tradition, Selman has also been influenced by Feffer (1959, 1970) and Flavell et al. (1968), both Piagetian-derived theorists themselves. Selman has largely focused upon applying his own interpersonal model to the moral sphere and in so doing has drawn heavily upon the Kohlbergian dilemmas while utilizing the clinical method in pursuing children's responses to them.

The stages presented by Selman (1976) range from 0 to 4. Below is a characterization of these developmental stages. The ages cited are suggestive, based on current research.

Stage 0: *Egocentric Role Taking (Ages Three to Six)*
The child does differentiate between self and others but fails to do so specifically with respect to their ponts of view. Emphasis is given to overt appearances as opposed to internal psychological states. No capacity is demonstrated to assess a person's actions on the basis of his underlying reasons. Alternate perspectives of differing participants in a situation cannot be related. As Loevinger (1976) points out in commenting on Selman's stage 0, either physical terms or egocentric wishes are criteria exercised in characterizing interpersonal relations.

Hence, a child may construe a friend as a person who lives close to him or as someone who possesses desirable toys.

Stage 1: *Social-Informational Role Taking (Ages Six to Eight)*
The child views himself and the other as having essentially different points of view about the same social situation. Access to different information is believed to lead to alternate views. People may also be in different situations and, as a result, think or feel differently. Now the child has a grasp of the subjectivity of persons other than himself, but he does not yet realize that another can consider him as a subject. He cannot place himself in the role of the other, while at the same time maintaining his own perspective. There is a shift from stage 0, where others are merely seen as collectors of social data that are visibly manifest, to seeing them as capable of processing information as well. Persons, therefore, are capable of evaluating as well as collecting information. Reasons are now understood to serve as internal mediators which cause behavior.

Stage 2: *Self-Reflective Role Taking (Ages Eight to Ten)*
It is now comprehended that each individual has a unique set of values and purposes and that these govern how one thinks and feels. The child's role-taking capacities are still rooted in the dyadic or two-person context, but he has now acquired the ability to take the perspective of another. Furthermore, he grasps that the other person can perform similarly; that is, he realizes the other person can figuratively enter his shoes, and this enables the child to reciprocally anticipate how the other will respond to the child's own thoughts and feelings. The sort of recursive thought processes developing here are dealt with at length in Miller, Kessel, and Flavell (1970), who have adopted for their paper the highly indicative title "Thinking About People Thinking About People Thinking About . . . : A Study of Social Cognitive Development." A striking advance in this stage is the child's awareness that others may be multimotivated and, hence, that either another person or the child himself may be in conflict between altruistic and self-interested concerns or between any two conflicting feelings. Reciprocity of a quid pro quo nature is especially characteristic of this stage.

Stage 3: *Mutual Role Taking (Ages Ten to Twelve)*
At this level of development the child can adopt a disinterested

perspective, as if he were a spectator overlooking the dyadic situation. He can now adopt a view as taken by a generalized or average member of a group, differentiated from the perspective of his own self. Whereas in stage 2, perspective taking is successive and not simultaneous, the child at stage 3 "discovers that both self and other can consider each party's point of view simultaneously and mutually. Each can put himself in the other's place and view himself from that vantage before deciding how to react (the Golden Rule)" (Selman 1976:305). In addition to this simultaneity of role-taking, each child can rotate from participant to participant and assume a perspective from the point of view of a third party, who holds a coordinated and impartial perspective. Friendship at this stage is seen as going beyond mere "reciprocal back scratching" that takes place in the immediate present, but assumes a mutual character of an enduring nature which is not vulnerable to the vicissitudes of temporal quarrels or fleeting ruptures. A friend is no longer simply one who does a favor or acts in a generally benign manner from one's own perspective, as in stage 2. Selman states, "Thus mutuality at Stage 3 is evidenced in both structure (a simultaneous coordination of perspectives) and concept of the person (the understanding that both self and other hold mutual expectations)" (1976:306).

Stage 4: *Social and Conventional System Role Taking (Ages Twelve to Fifteen Plus)*

At this stage the youngster transcends the dyadic situation. He can not only adopt the viewpoint of a single impartial observer, as in stage 3, but now he conceives of a *generalized other* which is representative of the social system. It is recognized that each self in an interpersonal relationship shares the view of the group or generalized other, representing an integration of the prevailing conventions and mores of the society. There now exists for the youngster a group perspective embodying social custom and laws of the society. He is able to stand outside of himself and adopt that perspective. Loevinger (1976) points out that in adopting the viewpoint of society or the legal system, the youngster at stage 4 has entered a hypothetical or abstract realm. She stresses that at this stage in Selman's model there is a conception of persons and human relationship that is both very deep and complex. The beliefs, attitudes, and values of another person are now recognized as being elements that are developing in that person and that comprise a complex intrapsychic matrix. These evolving internal components are now recognized as predictive of an individual's future behavior and instrumental in understanding his past performances.

In relating the stages of his own model to research findings, Selman (1976) suggests that social role-taking skills are necessary, but not sufficient, for corresponding moral judgment. He sees role taking as being at the midpoint between logical and moral thought. Each stage in Kohlberg's developmental scheme requires the appropriate stage in role taking ability as a necessary condition. Although Selman has only carried his work up to the fourth stage, Byrne (1975) has forged out stages 5 and 6. Citing various empirical findings, including his own, Selman underscores the discovery that there usually exists a parallel between stage of role taking and moral development or that, at the most, in normal populations role-taking ability is only one stage beyond the moral stage. In contrast, role-taking skills have been found to be two or more stages above those of the moral stages in a group of young adult delinquents. This particular study (Hickey 1972) with delinquents makes it clear that a much higher level of social reasoning than moral thinking can obtain in a single individual. There is clearly a potential danger to others in such circumstances, since it offers fertile grounds for antisocial behavior.

In general, of the studies surveyed by Selman, while it was sometimes found to be the case that a subject's role-taking ability was above the corresponding level of moral development, there were no instances in which moral reasoning exceeded social or role-taking reasoning. As he points out, it would seem that in order to have a mature power to reconcile conflicting claims in the moral domain, one must first have ascended the developmental scale of social reasoning. When a child's stages of both moral and social reasoning appear to be lagging significantly, it would seem that the first approach might well be to focus on promoting role-taking skills. If this does not succeed in stimulating the growth of moral reasoning, as it may or may not, training designed to directly effect moral development could be instituted next. Given the prior necessity of role-taking structures in resolving moral dilemmas, this would have merit as the more parsimonious and logical intervention strategy. However, it is certainly conceivable that attempting to stimulate moral development directly at the outset may lead to a simultaneous surge of both social and moral reasoning.

Selman illustrates diagnosis and intervention based on social reasoning levels with the case of Tommy. Although eight years old, Tommy was at stage o. He, therefore, was performing on an egocentric basis, which is typical of children at ages four and five. Natural observation of him interacting in the environment with others such as peers, teacher, and diagnostician revealed that he did not differentiate between his own and others' feelings. Grossly deficient in role taking abilities, his relationships were fragmented and temporal, indicating no sense of reciprocity whatever. Good and bad were defined in terms of his own desires. Failure to meet his needs without delay or question meant that the nonrespondent hated him. It is obvious from this description that his relationships must have been dysfunctional and were destined to deteriorate in time. The prescription for treatment was to enroll Tommy in a therapeutic camp in which great emphasis was placed upon explaining constantly to him the reasons for social rules, games, and behavior. The underlying motives of others at the camp, peers and counselors alike, were articulated for him. The normal and reasonable expectations which others would have of him were disclosed continuously. In brief, the therapeutic efforts were geared to assisting Tommy in the task of differentiating his own thoughts and feelings from those of others, learning to seek internal causes of behavior, and taking the role of others so that he would understand their perspective. In the span of eight weeks Tommy shifted from stage o to stage 1. He acquired many new friends, despite being extremely disliked at the beginning of the summer, and his notion of friendship evidenced progress. In conclusion, Selman stresses that he is not advocating traditional diagnostic approaches be replaced by a cognitive-developmental one, but rather that the latter should be added to those already in use.

Thus far our discussion has assumed that role taking is a developmental phenomenon which undergoes changes or transformations with age progression. This assumption has not gone unchallenged. In the view of Turiel (1983), role taking does not constitute an "organized transformational system," hence a stage analysis of it would be inappropriate. Role taking is seen as a method for gathering information. It undergoes quantitative change, not qualitative, in the sense that with the passage of age the role-taking function acquires the capacity to encompass more and more information. For Turiel, "The use of role taking in a given situation is dependent on the individual's level of conceptual knowledge in the domain with which the role-taking activity is associated" (1983:73). He offers an interesting illustration pertaining to a hypothetical situation in which three- and four-year-old children are asked to predict how a ten-year-old child would respond to a conservation task involving continuous quantities. Chances are that the younger children would predict that the older child would cite the tall, thin beaker as containing more liquid than the shorter and wider beaker once the pouring has occurred. The children would be incorrect in their prediction, but not because of a role-taking deficiency. Lacking an understanding of conservation, they are constrained from exercising their role-taking ability by a conceptual limitation. Once they understand conservation they would be able to make accurate predictions in this type of situation. However, it is not their role-taking skill that has developed, but rather it is their knowledge of an aspect of the physical world that has shown development. Therefore, it is the nature of the conceptual domain and the child's developmental level in that area that will determine the utilization and accuracy of role-taking skills. Noting that research has reflected such disparate results as findings of children first manifesting role taking at ages ranging from three to sixteen in spatial perception tasks, Turiel remarks, "Those observed wide-ranging age discrepancies in performance are consistent with the distinction between the conceptual demands of the task and role taking as a method of information gathering. Inasmuch as the tasks entail *both* role-taking activities and conceptual activities on the part of the subject, role-taking performance is determined by whether or not the child has attained the level of spatial conceptualization required by the task" (1983:72). Turiel's conclusion is that role-taking skills are present as early as three and four years of age, they develop quantitatively but not qualitatively, and they demonstrate an increasing capacity to gather more and more information across and within knowledge domains.

Whether role taking undergoes continuous, quantitative changes only or is subject to discontinuous, qualitative changes undergirded by structural reorganization is as yet an unsettled question. Selman does caution against equating his social perspective-taking stages, an evolutionary series of self-other relationships, with role taking as narrowly defined in the literature. Perhaps we are dealing with two different types of phenomena. Certainly Selman's more mature perspective-taking stages transcend the narrow boundaries of role taking between people in an actual situation, as the stages emerge onto a plane of highly abstract systems of perspective taking. The same could be said of Kohlberg's levels of social perspective. At the same time, with respect to the particular areas he cites, Turiel has marshaled a cogent argument for his position. Whatever the explanation, as children grow older they unquestionably appear to exhibit more effective interpersonal strategies based on a changing capacity to make inferences about other people's feelings and thoughts. Yet there is ample evidence to restrain us from conceiving of development as a simple linear progression from egocentrism to perspectivism. The child's role-taking ability is at least to some extent subject to the vicissitudes of the natural environmental context and task specificity (Cox 1980; Damon 1983a). Regardless of how prevalent egocentric errors may appear to be in young children, we should be wary of making generalized judgments of child egocentrism. However, we must also guard against assuming that the child is exhibiting a higher level of role-taking competence than may actually be the case. Each situation demands a careful analysis in its own right and should not be judged with the absoluteness of prior theory.

ADAPTIVE COMMUNICATION

Speech as we know it is certainly one of the most distinguishing characteristics of human beings. The effectiveness with which it is commanded in interpersonal exchanges will in large mearsure determine the quality of our personal relationships in work, play, and love. The social matrix places constant demands upon us for acts of negotiation, compromise, persuasion, and cooperation. All of these are significantly influenced by communication skills of a wide variety, including the capacity to take the perspective of the listener, on the part of the speaker, and the capacity to convey the inadequacy of messages received, on the part of the listener. Of course, in real-life contexts each individual generally shifts back and forth between speaker and listener roles, hence for maximum effective communication each individual would ideally possess the attributes desired to be a good speaker and listener. The acquisition of language itself, although an epochal achievement, does not assure that the child's verbal productions will effectively transmit the intended meaning to the receiver. There is even the question of whether the child's early speech is intended to be communicative.

The first book written by Piaget (1923/1955) was devoted to the child's shift from egocentric to socialized speech. It has served as a seminal work which has been the springboard to a recent surge of effort by many to further explore its implications for adaptive communication. Piaget's material on this topic was introduced in chapter 2 of this book. After a few amplifying comments we shall proceed to more contemporary formulations.

In discussing the functions of language, Piaget identifies two major categories. The first is egocentric speech, which is so-called partly because the child speaks mainly of himself, but primarily because he does not take the viewpoint of his listener in the communication process. He is not motivated to convey information nor to persuade the listener of anything. The three classes of egocentric speech are repetition (echolalia), monologue, and dual or collective monologue. In the first of these the child repeats words and syllables for his own pleasure with no intent to communicate. In a monologue the child does not direct his comments to anyone, giving the impression that he is simply thinking aloud. In a collective monologue the other person serves as a stimulus to each child's verbal production, but there is no continuity of theme and each speaks only for himself without taking into account the other's interests.

Socialized speech is classified into five types. The first of these is adapted information. In such speech the response of one child is appropriately related to what the other has just said. There may be argument or collaboration manifest in the speech utilized, but in either case the intent is social in that an interpersonal exchange is taking place. The child may even be talking about himself, but as long as he is supplying relevant content to the other, the message qualifies as adapted information. The remaining forms of socialized speech will not be elaborated upon here, but they are as follows: criticism, commands, requests, and threats, questions, and answers. At around seven or eight, children shift significantly in the direction of seeking greater comprehension of each other and increased effectiveness in exchanging their thoughts. Before that time the child's speech is characterized by Piaget in the following manner:

Although he talks almost incessantly to his neighbors, he rarely places himself at their point of view. He speaks to them for the most part as if he were alone, and as if he were thinking aloud. He speaks, therefore, in a language which disregards the precise shade of meaning in things and ignores the particular angle from which they are viewed, and which above all is always making assertions, even in argument, instead of justifying them. (1923/ 1955:60)

Piaget investigated the question of whether children actually understand each other when they assemble and talk. On the basis of over 100 experiments, he concluded that children do not understand each other any better than they understand adults. To begin with, they do not attempt to adapt the information to the perspective of the listener. Furthermore, the listener does not attempt to adapt what he hears, but instead extrapolates from the content what appeals to him most and encodes that material in terms of his preconceptions. Significantly, Piaget observed that a crucial reason why children do not understand one another is precisely that they believe they do. Making the assumption that the other will understand, or perhaps that he already understands, eliminates the necessity of even attempting to communicate with exactitude and clarity. He stresses that young children have around them daily adults whose knowledge far exceeds theirs—people who require little effort from the child before understanding his needs and wishes. Specifically, in offering explanations to peers in the studies, the speaker often left out any reference by name to the objects he was talking about. Furthermore, the speaker would tend not to provide adequate reasons for events, and causal links were either omitted or not placed in an order signifying causality. The child, already believing that he would be understood, perceived no need to be concerned with syntactical ordering. Piaget cites excerpts from the protocol of one egocentric speaker, as an illustration, in which the words "and then" are repeatedly used to signify neither causal nor logical relations, but merely idiosyncratic connections between ideas as they surface in the speaker's mind.

The deficiency of order in communication is pronounced at six to seven years of age, in contrast to seven to eight years of age when it appears infrequently. The egocentric child seems to disregard the "how" of natural and mechanical events when he explains things to others. Unrelated components may be juxtaposed without really explaining "how" the speaker will produce an "effect" in his explanation. Piaget maintains that in thinking to ourselves we do not bother to detail the exactitude of various cause-and-effect phenomena. However, in socialized speech, the personal fantasy that allows us to overlook the "how" of events must yield to the demands of adaptive communication. The egocentric speaker fails to make the necessary shift from the network of his own imagination to meeting the requirements of the listener's informational needs. His expositions are fraught with a lack of coherence and a series of juxtaposed sentences bearing no evidence of grasping causal relations. The word "and" may replace "because," and the sequence of thought readily reverses cause and effect to effect and cause. The child may just as well say either "The car will not go and the gas tank is empty" or "The gas tank is empty and the car will not go."

It is striking that despite the obscurity of the messages arciculated by the speaker in Piaget's investigations, there were rarely any protestations from the listeners. The subject's assurance of being understood on the part of the speaker had its mirror image in the listener, whose own egocentrism provided him with the assurance that he, in fact, was understanding. The youngest children seemed the most content in this respect, for it was in the age range of seven to eight where the few objections that were registered originated. In the main, egocentric listeners would simply assimilate what they heard into preexisting schemes without any accompanying effort at accommodation. If there are previous commonalities of schemas between speaker and listener, there may occur some accidental understanding.

Piaget emphasizes that the emergence of a desire to communicate and be understood arises at about seven to eight years of age. It is at this time that the child demonstrates a concern and awareness regarding the objectivity of his statements to others. Prior to this age, children who do not understand what they hear will invent stories or explanations when asked to reproduce the information. They evidence no awareness that their romancing, as Piaget calls it, issues from their own imagination. Children at seven or eight years of age rarely romance, and, contrary to younger children, they can distinguish when they are doing it. Primarily, however, they are more concerned with the fidelity to fact of their accounts, and they genuinely strive to achieve objective communication. Hence, the egocentrism that radically limits effective communication has sharply declined by seven or eight years of age, when a pattern of socialized speech begins to show increasing evidence of appearance.

Piaget's position on the predominance of egocentric speech during the preoperational period has not gone unchallenged. Brainerd (1978a) concluded from a meta-analysis of research articles on the subject that while young children do engage in differing proportions of egocentric speech, the amounts never reach 50 percent. Hence, Brainerd maintains that for even the youngest of children more than half of their language is socialized and intended to be communicative. It should not be overlooked, however, that desiring to communicate is conceptually distinct from possessing the role-taking skills to effectively do so. Futhermore, we should not overlook the fact that many adults, at various times, seem to engage in what resembles egocentric speech; a fact that is frequently the source of dysfunctional interpersonal relationships. Brainerd (1978a and b), incidentally, is a severe critic of Piaget's theory of intelligence, and a reading of his work is likely to prevent even the enthusiastic Piagetian scholar from becoming a cultist.

An exploration of the significance of role-taking skills in the transmission and receiving of information has largely taken place in studies on a subfield known as referential communication (Dickson 1981; Glucksberg, Krauss and Higgins 1975). The following exposition is a summary from a portion of an excellent literature survey by Glucksberg et al. (1975). Communicating effectively depends upon the speaker's ability to utilize words in a referential manner. A distinction is made between denotative and referential meaning. In defining referential meaning the specific context is essential. It pertains to that which is being referred to in particular, as opposed to a generic or abstract meaning regardless of context. An example is given using the words "Mars" and "planet." In a specific communication the speaker can request that the listener either look at Mars or look at the planet up there. In such a context both "Mars" and "planet" may be used inter-chageably as a referent for the identical object. Yet, in general, on a denotative level, the two words actually have different meanings. Since most words do not have a univocal meaning, there exist grounds for ambiguity and confusion in communication. The task of the speaker is to choose from the total range of his vocabulary that word or phrase which best conveys the meaning he intends. Words may in fact be much too general, even if utilized correctly, to be of any help in effective communication. Telling someone, whom you have never met before, over the telephone that you will be wearing clothes when you wait for him or her in front of the opera house will be accurate but useless information. Unless, of course, you are residents of a nudist colony. In that case, telling the listener that you will be clothed is an excellent referent because it discriminates between how you will appear in contrast to all others present. The essential point is that it provides the listener with the information that is needed to pick you out from among everyone else. The use of referential communication, particularly in ambiguous situations, is not innate or the immediate accompaniment of vocabulary accretion. It is a developmental phenomenon which gradually emerges with age and does not match adult levels of attainment until early adolescence (Flavell et al. 1968).

Glucksberg et al. (1975) collate four fundamental processes that thread their way through the literature on referential communication. The first is "sensitivity to the referent-nonreferent array." It is the ability to accurately select the referent which will distinguish the object or event under discussion from a spectrum of nonreferents which would only confuse the listener. For example, two children separated by an opaque screen each have on a table in front of them a set of varied red geometric forms. If the speaker tells the listener to pick up a red object when he actually wants him to pick up the triangular object in the set, then "red" is a poor referent. The second process is "sensitivity to characteristics of the listener and the listener's situation," On constructing a message it is essential for maximum adaptive communication to take into account both what the listener already knows and what he needs to know. The speaker must be able to discriminate between knowledge which the listener holds in common with him and knowledge which he, the speaker, possesses exclusively, in relation to the listener. The third is "sensitivity to the listener's feed-back." Very young children are either silent or repetitive when confronted with feedback requesting more information or voicing confusion. Older children and adults will tend to alter the message or reconstruct a new one (Glucksberg and Krauss 1967). The fourth deals with the listener's assessment of the message. A listener may detect the deficiencies in a message, may possibly make these known to the speaker, and may even go so far as to convey what additional information he requires to comprehend the message. Although conceptually distinct, these strands are intertwined in real-life situations, and current research underscores the importance of actively cooperative interaction between speaker and listener for maximum referential communication (Patterson and Kister 1981).

Some of the leading early work on referential communication is that of Alvy (1968), Cohen and Klein (1968), Fishbein and Osborne (1971), and Glucksberg and Krauss (1967). Flavell et al. (1968) in a most ambitious study have extended the work of Piaget by tracing the contribution of role taking to adaptive communication through adolescence. Although much of the early work relied heavily upon Piaget's views on egocentrism and role taking, it has become increasingly more evident that while they may play a significant part in the process, they do not offer a sufficient explanation accounting for referential communication. It must be kept in mind that an individual may not be egocentric yet communicate poorly in a referential task for other reasons, such as limited vocabulary, lack of skill in discriminating referential attributes, and simply not realizing that the task requires identifying and conveying differences (Whitehurst and Sonnenschein 1981). Shantz (1981) has pointed out that a speaker may appear to be speaking egocentrically, but that this may be misleading, for he may have made an erroneous assumption that he and the listener share a greater fund of common knowledge than is actually the case. If the false inference he has made is cleared up, then such a speaker will make the necessary adjustment to the listener's needs. Reviews of correlational studies between role-taking skills and communication have revealed mixed findings. Both role taking and communication skills show progress with age increase, but the actual correlation between the two frequently shows up as being low or, at best, moderate (see Asher and Wigfield 1981; Shantz 1981 for further discussion on these findings). In contrast, Roberts and Patterson have established a strong relationship between role taking and referential communication. Their contention is that studies finding low correlation have treated egocentrism as a globular concept and assessed the subjects' role-taking abilities in contexts unrelated to referential communication activities. In the words of Roberts and Patterson, "A child's perspective-taking skills should be assessed *within the specific context* in which it is assumed to be relevant" (1983:1006). Crafting a methodological strategy based on that premise, their results were significantly positive.

There is evidence of nonegocentric communication among preoperational children, which runs sharply counter to the Piagetian tradition (Maratsos 1973; Menig-Peterson 1975; Shatz and Gelman 1973). Maratsos (1973) reported that children as young as three years of age adapted their communications differentially between sighted and nonsighted listeners. Yet Flavell et al. (1968) reported that children in the second grade did not do this, whereas eighth grade children did. Flavell (1977) has attempted to resolve this puzzling discrepancy by offering some explanations, as he has so thoughtfully done on numerous other occasions. He suggests that the tasks where children show some listener-adapted speech are of a much simpler variety than those which do not find listener-adapted speech until much later. The "information processing demands" of the latter type make it extremely difficult for the youngster to keep his listener's needs in mind when his own are under stress. Further, more recent studies showing earlier role-taking skills in communication seem to utilize situations that would seem more natural and familiar to the child, which would tap into his potential more readily. Finally, in a speculative vein, Flavell suggests that those studies finding listener-adapted communication at later ages may require a capacity for "metacommunication," which he defines as the capability to think about and analyze a verbal message. The skill of reflecting upon one's own communications calls upon an abstract capacity which is a relatively mature cognitive development, and would not be available to the younger children, whose simpler tasks in the studies where they were successful did not require it.

Early training studies, in which the goal was to foster referential communication by enhancing role-taking skills, have been conducted by Chandler, Greenspan, and Barenboim (1974), Fry (1966, 1969), and Shantz and Wilson (1972). The Fry study was unsuccessful, but several methodological weaknesses could readily account for the poor outcome. The Shantz and Wilson study improved upon the Fry design and did yield a modest improvement in referential communication performance among the participating children, ages seven and eight. There was also some evidence of generalization to similar type tasks as those used in the study. Unfortunately, the research design did not make it possible to identify precisely what intervention accounted for the gains. The Chander, Greenspan, and Barenboim study bears special attention for several reasons, one of which is the fact that its subjects were emotionally disturbed children from two residential settings. Despite a diversity of admitting diagnoses, most all of the subjects were described as antisocial and socially incompetent. They manifested low communication performances prior to intervention and were significantly behind developmental levels generally reported for normal subjects of the same age in the task areas under examination. Subjects' ages ranged from nine to fourteen years.

The design called for three groups: training in role taking, training directly in referential communication, and no training. Training in role taking exposed the subjects to experiences in video filming which required that they alternate in portraying various dramatic characters. The rationale, of course, was that by deliberately assuming another's role the subjects would automatically be practicing the taking of perspectives other than their own. In referential communication training a heavy emphasis was placed on offering subjects feedback in order to induce cognitive conflict when confronted with information about their own inadequate communication. It was expected that this would facilitate a process of equilibration, which would lead to the construction of increasingly more adequate messages. The experimenters encouraged subjects to compare their messages with peers, and to play back tape recordings of their statements for self-evaluations. However, the experimenters did not directly criticize the messages of the subjects. Training, therefore, pursued a philosophy of promoting self-correcting action as opposed to content-oriented teaching by another person. Role reversal between speaker and listener was also employed in the referential communication group.

Results of the study substantiated significant postintervention improvement in both experimental groups as compared with the control group. However, while the subjects trained in referential communication demonstrated marked gains in both that area and role-taking tasks, those trained in role-taking tasks exhibited improvement only in the area that they trained in. Chandler et al. suggest that this is possibly due to the fact that the opportunity to acquire skill in applying inferences made about another's attributes to nonegocentric verbal communications is afforded by training in referential communication but not by the training given in role taking. Alternately, they propose that role taking may be viewed as a necessary, but not sufficient, condition for competent referential communication. Regarding the extension of Piagetian sociocognitive concepts to the psychopathological sphere, Chandler et al. state, "Taken in combination these findings lend additional weight to the initial orienting assumptions that constructs and methods originally developed for the normative study of sociocognitive development may be usefully transported into the study and possible amelioration of serious social and emotional disorders of childhood" (1974:552).

Asher and Wigfield (1981) in a state of the art analysis recommend that perhaps both role taking and referential communication training can best be promoted by utilizing methods of direct instruction on what is entailed in the processes and precise feedback on prior inadequacies accompanied by what is needed to make corrections. They also argue against the globular approach to egocentrism, urging that the role-taking process be analyzed into its component parts (Flavell 1974) for the purposes of training. This position dovetails with that of Roberts and Patterson (1983), who found a strong positive relationship between role taking and referential communciation, when aspects of the former that were pertinent to the specific demands of the communciation task in context were taken into consideration.

CONCLUSION

The present chapter has examined the construction of social knowledge and the role of the social matrix in this developmental process. Special emphasis has been given to moral reasoning, perspective taking, and adaptive communciation. Piaget's seminal views in these areas have been described, as well as more contemporary positions, some of which are within the Piagetian tradition and others of which tend to run counter to it. Although not beyond dispute, more recent findings suggest that the child's sociomoral knowledge, at least when the tasks and situations are simple enough, is manifest earlier than Piaget indicated. Other findings suggest that sociomoral knowledge continues developing with even greater complexity and adaptiveness beyond the ages reflected in Piaget's studies. Important distinctions such as those between conventional and moral domains, as well as male and female issues in moral reasoning, have been made. The growing emphasis upon the co-construction of knowledge has been emphasized, along with an inquiry into the roles of cooperation and conflict in the development of knowledge. Perspective taking and adaptive communication, both so critical in achieving and maintaining effective interpersonal relationships, have been presented and explored at length. Their essential nature and relationship to one another were elaborated upon.

There is good reason to believe that there will be a continued and accelerated effort within the field of cognitive development to expand upon the current thoeretical and empirical foundation pertaining to the construction of social knowledge and the role of the social matrix in the construction of both physical and social concepts. This is bound to be a most welcome trend to clinicians, with their interest in social competence and interpersonal dysfunction.

CHAPTER 5

Cognitive-Developmental
Psychopathology

There does not exist at present a systematically integrated body of knowledge based on an application of the work of the Geneva School to the field of psychopathology. Piaget himself, although a student of the subject as a youth, chose to consistently explore the normal evolution of intelligence. He informs us in his autobiography of the following:

Indeed, I have always detested any departure from reality, an attitude which I related to . . . my mother's poor mental health; it was this disturbing factor which at the beginning of my studies in Psychology made me intensely interested in questions of psychoanalysis and pathological psychology . . . I have never felt any desire to involve myself deeper in that particular direction, always much preferring the study of normalcy and of the workings of the intellect to that of the tricks of the unconscious. (1976c:116)

Nevertheless, despite his own lack of concentration in this area throughout a long, prodigious, and brilliant career, Piaget (1975) has recently stated that he sees on the horizon a new interdisciplinary science grappling to pull together a synthesis of knowledge to be known as *Developmental Psychopathology*. Although seemingly optimistic, he does not hesitate to assert that before this can be done an enormous amount of creative effort must be brought to bear in the face of many obstacles. In this chapter, I propose to make a modest attempt to survey some of the literature that has been appearing in journals and, on occasion, in books over the last couple of decades.

As a prelude to embarking upon an exploration of the literature on cognitive-developmental psychopathology, the reader may be alerted to a conceptual classification which should prove useful. Briefly, there are four basic approaches employed either separately or in combination, which will be encountered. They are, in random order, as follows:

1. *Assimilation-Accommodation.* Adaptation requires an appropriate balance of these two processes. An excessive predominance of one over the other, unless corrected by an equilibrating or auto-regulative process, can result in grossly dysfunctional behavior.
2. *Egocentrism-Decentration.* A developmental failure to appropriately differentiate between subject and object prevents one from achieving a genuine grasp of reality and precludes mature interpersonal relationships.
3. *Stage Arrest.* Some psychopathological manifestations can be directly related to subjects not having progressed normally through age-appropriate stages and periods of cognitive development.
4. *Preoperational Characteristics.* A good deal of the unrealistic and magical thinking typical of many abnormal subjects represents more than an average amount of adherence to such preoperational aspects of thought as animism, realism, and participation.

It should be obvious that these categories are not mutually exclusive and that they are highly interrelated. Often, in fact, the same phenomenon could be examined through the prism of any one of them, the difference being primarily a matter of emphasis.

EGOCENTRISM AND SCHIZOPHRENIA

Lidz (1973) has produced a major attempt at explaining schizophrenia in adolescence through Piaget's concept of egocentrism. An exposition of his work will be presented here. Schizophrenia, for Lidz, is not a disease possessed by the patient, but the result of a process of enculturation within a family, which trains the child in irrationality through the influence of language and parental roles. It is a form of egocentrism in the parents which prevents the child from learning through the family matrix the meaning system subscribed to in the broader culture outside of the home. Parental egocentrism further blocks the child, once he becomes an adolescent, from successfully navigating through the developmental stages necessary to mature adulthood. When this occurs, the result is cognitive regression and schizophrenia.

Lidz conceptualizes the family of an adolescent schizophrenic into either one of two types—the skewed or the schismatic. The skewed family appears harmonious at first glance, but further familiarity reveals that the apparent harmony is won at the expense of one of the spouses living in compliance to the will of the other. The ideas of the dominant spouse are characterized as often being bizarre and strange. It is generally the mother who carries this role. The schizophrenogenic mother is insensitive to her spouse and children as individuals with needs and wishes that exist independently of her own. In relation to her son, who becomes the patient, she constantly probes into his world and seeks fulfillment through him. She monitors all of his activities and manages to get across to him that he is central to her existence, which would be futile without him. His attempts toward independence are blocked by her and he senses this. The son is not permitted to individualize his own feelings and claim them as separate from the mother's. Those of his feelings which are not congenial to the mother's security are ignored or distorted by her. The father is an inadequate husband and parent who offers the son little in the way of coping skills.

In the schismatic family there is found a network of relationships in open conflict. Parental discord is compounded by the fact that both parents belittle each other to the children and seek to rally the children's support for themselves. The schizophrenic adolescent in this family is usually a female. Both parents have low self-esteem and have little emotional sustenance to offer their children. The female patient receives a message from the mother signifying the futility of life. Deprived of maternal attention when she was a child herself, the mother now has little warmth to extend to her own daughter. She becomes preoccupied with her daughter's adolescent sexual attitudes and activities. The father in such a family is inflexible, disturbed, distrustful, and seeks emotional gratification from his daughter rather than his wife. The adolescent daughter cannot resolve the conflict between her parents, and should she attempt to favor or meet the needs of either one, she runs the risk of alienating the other. In the schismatic family egocentrism is an attribute of both parents, who fail to perceive the separate needs of their daughter and strive to have her conform to their own needs. The schizophrenic adolescent then has either one or two egocentric parents. He or she becomes parent centered, "viewing the world according to the parents' feelings, needs, and defenses, and living to protect and complete the lives of persons from whom he has not properly differentiated" (Lidz 1973:48).

In Lidz's view, the peculiar, nonshared meanings and reasoning adopted by the schizophrenic represent his attempt at escaping the situation imposed upon him by an untenable family system. In doing this, however, he forgoes cooperative social life and effective adaptation to the environment at large. The patient not only fails to surmount the egocentrism specific to adolescence, but actually undergoes a cognitive, as well as emotional, regression to forms of egocentrism especially characteristic of the preoperational period. Egocentric is used in a strictly Piagetian sense here and does not connote selfishness or narcissism. The schizophrenic is said to be overinclusive in an egocentric manner in that he does not accommodate to reality, but instead assimilates and distorts it to meet his own needs. Passing and incidental comments by others are perceived as related to him. Events accidental to his experience are construed as integrally associated with him. We see this in paranoia, in which the patient may think that the FBI or an agent of that organization is diabolically engaged in activities designed to destroy him. On the other hand, Lidz points out that there is the catatonic patient who remains absolutely rigid, for fear that any shift in his body will adversely affect the world.

Lidz reviews the process through which language is acquired, stressing how the child moves from using words in a subjective, private way to employing them in terms of their public meaning. In families of schizophrenic patients, however, the meanings of words are not properly taught. The words are contorted to meet the needs of the parent(s), and the child is unclear as to which are his own needs and which are his parents'. The normally responsive mother is aware of the needs of the two-year-old who uses words subjectively, and she verbalizes the appropriate, that is, the publicly shared vocabulary and syntax when he does not. Gradually the child acquires language and meaning which have been adopted by the sociocultural environment outside the family boundaries. The schizophrenogenic mother is not fully capable of this because of her own egocentrism. In general, the parent(s) lacks a capacity to maintain ego boundaries and denies realistic facets of the environment in order to maintain internal security. The child is trapped in the net of the parents' diffuse ego boundaries and is constrained to invalidate his own perceptions of reality in order to preserve the parents' security.

Lidz states that most adult schizophrenics attain completely the level of concrete operational development, and some even become completely formal operational with highly sophisticated abilities at abstraction. They do, however, have trouble in the struggle for separation and independence, feeling that success would be destructive to their parent(s). It is the egocentrism, developmentally speaking, that emerges at adolescence which Lidz sees as crucial to a sounder understanding of the schizophrenic. At this time the young person acquires second order operations. He can think about his own thought. He is no longer limited to applying operational thought to concrete or familiar objects, but can now reason about the many possible alternatives in the universe. Ideals and utopias are mentally generated with great gusto. In the first blush of this new form of egocentrism, the adolescent is unperturbed by the constraints of social and physical reality, often becoming visibly annoyed and impatient with those who do not share his vision. Decentration and the accompanying decline of this egocentrism come from renewed social interaction in which one's ideas are repeatedly challenged, as well as from the environmental demands of the work world which the young person must ultimately enter.

Lidz observes, however, that "The period contains the particular danger that the youth can get lost in mental operations, fantasying potential futures for himself and the world without becoming involved in the tangible measures required to make them become real" (1973:78). The young person who becomes schizophrenic fails to negotiate the developmental hurdles involved in separation and attaining autonomy, which most adolescents succeed in doing. Rather than moving naturally in the direction of decentration, the preschizophrenic becomes increasingly and excessively egocentric. External events are inappropriately referred to the self. Blocked from going beyond adolescent egocentrism, the young person cognitively regresses to preoperational forms of it. Chance occurrences are not recognized as such, but are seen as meaningful events. Desire and reality are not differentiated. The word and the object are once again confused. It is once more believed that one's own thoughts can influence external and even distant things. Thinking may revert to a preconceptual level and show evidence of syncretism, in which a string of thoughts are woven together in a tangled conglomerate.

The above picture is, perhaps, overdrawn. Lidz emphasizes that the schizophrenic does not lose whatever former cognitive gains he had made before the regression. The issue, he suggests, is not whether the individual any longer has a conceptual ability, but rather under what circumstances he uses it as opposed to what circumstances induce overinclusive egocentrism in his thinking.

It has perhaps been observed in the above review of the work by Lidz that the four classifications involving egocentrism, adaptation, stages, and preoperational characteristics have already become intertwined, as indeed they would be difficult to separate in any such discussion. They will appear later in a similar medley.

THE CONCEPTUAL DEFICIT

Schizophrenia is commonly viewed as a thought disorder. The exact nature of the conceptual deficit involved, however, has not met with common agreement, and various hypotheses have been advanced to explain it. Cameron (1938, 1939a and b, 1944) maintained that the thinking of schizophrenics tended to be overinclusive. In examining the language of schizophrenic patients, he noted the propensity to eschew an organization of content based on logical and causal grounds. Instead, material that was meaningful only in terms of the patient's private associations would be included in his verbal productions. The inappropriate content could be drawn from perceived objects in the environment that have no bearing on the theme, or from objects in the patient's own past that are equally irrelevant. Goldstein (1936, 1944, 1959) has maintained that the schizophrenic's thinking is deficient primarily in that his capacity for abstraction has been impaired, which results in his functioning at a concrete level. The ability to consistently classify objects in an accurate fashion would consequently be absent, as this activity requires abstracting a common element which is then applied uniformly across all objects to be classified which conform to the abstracted attribute. (The reader is cautioned here not to equate the use of the word "concrete" as employed by Goldstein with the use of the term by Piaget in referring to the concrete operational period. Remember that classification is precisely one of the major achievements of that period.) Cameron argued that if sufficient care is taken in working with the schizophrenic patient, it will be demonstrated that he has not lost the ability to function at an abstract level.

Shimkunas in summarizing the literature on the subject has the following to say: "The bulk of this research has indicated that schizophrenics are not abnormally concrete, but that they verbalize peculiar and idiosyncratic concepts" (1972:149). Shimkunas reinterprets Goldstein, and while rejecting the notion that a deficit in abstraction leads to thinking in concrete concepts, he holds that there is an impairment in the capacity to abstract, which results in overabstraction. Although we shall not delve further into the formulation by Shimkunas, it should be noted that he believes that through an extension of the abstraction capacity, idiosyncratic and autistic thinking is introduced.

A position advanced by Von Domarus (1944) and elaborated upon by Arieti (1955) which has merited a considerable amount of discussion states that schizophrenic thinking is paralogical. Such thought processes are said to contain an abundance of logical flaws in that they deviate from the canons of formal Aristotelian logic. In interpreting the Von Domarus principle, Arieti has called it paleologic, suggesting a profound regression to the type of thought characteristic of primitive peoples and children. In the Von Domarus–Arieti view, the schizophrenic will go so far in his thinking as to equate objects on the basis of having only some attributes in common. What is involved here is not simply erroneously including an object in an array of objects being classified, but actually regarding two partially similar objects as being identical. The paralogic hypothesis by Von Domarus has been criticized, not because schizophrenics do not deviate from the laws governing formal logic in their thinking, but because of the prevalence of such deviations even among normal populations. Mahler (1966) stresses that research continues to validate that personal affective material will influence the thinking of individuals, but that this is true for both schizophrenic and normal people. A careful analysis of the actual thinking process of the schizophrenic person, however, does not support the Von Domarus position, he contends.

The brief summary above was based on traditional research literature. Presently we shall examine a few attempts at understanding the thinking of schizophrenics through the application of Piagetian tasks. In effect, these efforts have been aimed at a cognitive-developmental diagnosis and comparison between subgroups of schizophrenics or between schizophrenics and other groups, such as children and normal adults. An aspect of testing which proves to be illuminating is not only the developmental level of the testee, but also the manner in which he relates to the testing situation.

Trunnell (1964, 1965) has reported two attempts at examining the developmental level of schizophrenic patients, the first being a pilot study and the second a replication study. Three groups were used in each study, including adult schizophrenics, children, and normal adults. A variety of Piagetian tasks were employed, primarily involving classification and seriation tasks. We shall discuss three of them here. One is a similarities test in which the subjects were required to determine whether, out of a large arrary of stimuli, groups of three, two, or no objects could be classed together. For example, could the subject select car, bicycle, and train to be grouped together, based on the common element of transportation? In all of the tasks administered, the experimenter was as interested in the subject's reasons for his conclusion as in the conclusions themselves.

A second task involved cross multiplication or conjunctive classes. For example, a task taken directly from Piaget's early work is as follows. An animal with long ears may be either a mule or a donkey. An animal with a thick tail may be either a mule or a horse. Now think of an animal with long ears and a thick tail. Is it a horse, donkey, or mule? Note that a conjunction represents two statements connected by "and." Therefore, the statement "A mule has long ears and a thick tail" is a conjunctive one.

A third type of task involved seriation or ordering of elements by intensity. Again drawing from Piaget, the subject was asked such questions as Edith is fairer than Susan who is darker than Lily; which of the three is darkest? It was predicted that in the similarities test schizophrenics and children would be likely to select either two elements or none for classification, whereas the normal adults would more frequently select an appropriate grouping of three elements based on a common attribute. Trunnell anticipated that the schizophrenics and children would center on partial aspects of objects in the stimulus arrary and that they would be riveted to specific physical characteristics of the objects. It was further anticipated that even when they selected the three appropriate objects that would go together, they would provide different explanations for having done so than would the normal adults, hence indicating a difference in thought processes behind their performance. It was predicted that adult normals would offer more correct answers and that their explanations would be more logically complete. Both cross multiplication and seriation require that the subject be able to effectively decenter and, thereby, maintain two characteristics of the objects in mind simultaneously. Therefore, Trunnell anticipated that schizophrenics and children would focus more on one attribute of an object or relationship. Even in the case of having guessed correctly that the imaginary animal is a mule, as in the previously described task, the schizophrenic or child may say that the fact of the animal having a thick tail is the reason he made this particular selection. The explanation, of course, does not supply an adequate rationale, as an animal with a thick tail may be either a mule or a horse. A sufficient explanation must cite both the thick tail and long ears, which would then include only the mule but would exclude the horse and donkey. In fact, all of the normal adult subjects cited both attributes in naming the mule as the solution to the problem.

The schizophrenic population in the replicated study numbered twenty-four; twelve females and twelve males. Diagnostic criteria utilized relied essentially upon the traditional features of autism, ambivalence, association, and effect. All subjects in this group had some college education, most were in ongoing psychotherapy, and the majority were described as being well integrated at the time of the study on a behavioral plane. In general, the hypotheses formulated by Trunnel were confirmed. It was possible to distinguish a group of twenty-four schizophrenic patients from a group of twenty-four controls comprised of normal adults matched on dimensions of education, sex, and age. The distinguishing criteria were based on test performances and explanations derived from Piagetian cognitive tasks. In addition, there were significant similarities between task performance and underlying thought mechanisms of adult schizophrenics and children. There were also, however, important differences. The children involved ranged in age from six to eleven years, were twenty-four in number, and were also divided into twelve females and twelve males. The schizophrenics did perform in a superior manner to children on tests requiring verbal responses because of their more extensive language experience, although the actual quality of cognitive thought was not at a level comparable to that of the adult control group. In the tasks requiring the sorting of objects into classes and in combinatorial analysis, neither of which requires verbal responses and both of which are more complex logically than the tasks requiring verbal responses, there were no differences between schizophrenics and children in performance.

Trunnell speculates that a child growing up in a family in which viewpoints of one or both parents are inconsistent and ambiguous would have great difficulty in learning to decenter from his own viewpoint and, therefore, in coordinating his own viewpoint with those of others. Since conjunctive thinking involves joining two attributes of an object or relation, Trunnel suggests that the interpersonal deficit which the schizophrenic experienced as a child with his parent(s) would possibly lead to a deficiency in thinking conjunctively. Poor communication models in the family can lead to very specific types of cognitive limitations. Furthermore, social interaction is usually accelerated as the child enters the concrete operational period, for it is then that he begins his school career. The child whose propensity for such interaction is markedly diminished will not be as likely to engage with peers in activities which would promote being able to handle two attributes or multiple perspectives simultaneously.

It should be noted, however, that Trunnell discounts the possibility that responses of the schizophrenics could be based on social withdrawal characteristic of their condition. There is, first of all, the specificity of one type of response over another. That is, in the similarities test there was a consistency in linking two rather than three congenial items, or rather than a blatant negativism rejecting the task or stating that none of the items go together. The patients voiced opinions that the tasks were preferable to work on rather than submit to the usual hospital routine, and they seemed very involved in trying to effect a solution to the problems.

Trunnell has commented on the characteristics of the schizophrenic patients in attempting to handle the problems. He states, "One is impressed with non sequiturs, inappropriate responses, personalized reasons, and figural configurations which usually accompanied the more sophisticated response in the schizophrenic" (1965:14). In contrast to the control group, the schizophrenics took about one half hour longer, on the average, to complete the tasks. The schizophrenic tends to center on his own personal past experiences, and, hence, his responses are often idiosyncratic and poorly adapted to the reality of the test material. While he still may have some tendencies toward centration, the child is clearly going through a more balanced process of assimilation and accommodation, as he concentrates more on the physical properties of the materials utilized for the test.

Attitudinal differences while being tested appear strikingly significant. The children were indifferent to success or failure, whereas the schizophrenics were preoccupied with the outcome. They made constant inquiries about the consequences for them of either succeeding or failing, although they had previously been informed that their performances would have no bearing on their hospitalization and that the outcome would not be conveyed to the administration. In contrast, the focus of the children's concerns was interpersonal. In essence, the children seemed to want to satisfy the experimenter and to be perceived as a good boy or girl.

In making some general comments, Trunnel stresses that development may very readily derive from poor communication patterns within the family matrix. However, the specificity of interaction between child and parent from one family to another may vary considerably. For example, in one family a child faced with confusing and unclear parental communications may react passively, whereas in another family a child may assertively persist in attempting to improve communication, thereby minimizing his own chances of growing up with gross cognitive deficiencies. Many other permutations of communication patterns are possible with different cognitive-developmental consequences. Trunnell is especially sensitized to the perennial problem of dichotomizing thought and feeling in psychological circles. He suggests, "The disturbance in schizophrenic thinking may be neither primary nor secondary to the emotional conflicts and intrapsychic dynamics. Both contribute to the essence of what constitues schizophrenia" (1965:16).

Lerner, Bie, and Lehrer (1972), investigating a group of hospitalized mentally disturbed youths ranging between the ages of fifteen and twenty-three, similarly reported their subjects to be significantly below normal populations in cognitive development. Kilburg and Siegel (1976) hypothesized that schizophrenic patients would not perform as well in formal operational tasks as normal adults and that process schizophrenics would not perform as well as reactive schizophrenics. Hospitalized subjects between the ages of twenty-one and fifty were compared with normal adults drawn from a local trade union. Utilizing the Lunzer Analogies Test, designed to test formal operational reasoning, the predicted direction of scores was confirmed. The normal adult group outperformed the reactive schizophrenic group which, in turn, outperformed the process schizophrenics.

A question that arises frequently in discussions on the cognitive deficit in schizophrenia is whether there is a particular kind of cognitive flaw which is specific to that diagnosis. Strauss (1967) has argued that excessive concreteness is responsible for the basic intellectual impairment in schizophrenic functioning, but that the phenomenon has its roots in normal development, and, although present in exaggerated form among some schizophrenics, it is not unique to them. Utilizing three Piagetian tests and one non-Piagetian test, he based his conclusions on a study of both acute and chronic schizophrenic patients and a comparative control group of normal adults. It was not only the case that Strauss found no type of reasoning to be specific to the patient populations, but it was also the case that some of the schizophrenics in the sample did not demonstrate the cognitive impairment that was found in varying degrees across all groups. The aim of the tests was to explore how the excessive concreteness of the schizophrenic, so often reported in the literature, affects the capacity to infer causal and explanatory aspects of phenomena. The capacity for complex thinking involving acquisition of knowledge through integrating perceived variables is what was tested.

There proved to be few differences in performances between the acute schizophrenic patients and the control group. The chronic schizophrenics made a significantly greater number of concretistic errors, failing to make abstract inferences going beyond the perceived variables of the task materials. However, these errors were found among members in all three groups, and there was no type of error found exclusively among schizophrenics.

Strauss views the excessive concreteness or attention to a single perceptual variable, one of the types of errors he detected, to be in some ways diametrically opposed to the overinclusion said to be characteristic of schizophrenic thinking. However, he believes that both excessive concreteness, as seen in his own subjects, and over inclusion, as described by Cameron (1939a and b), are marked by a focusing impairment. The problem is in the individual's incapacity to derive complex ideas from an appropriate selection and coordination of available perceived data. Since the chronic schizophrenic group manifested significantly more errors, as opposed to the acute and control groups, Strauss emphasizes the importance of research ventures which differentiate within patient populations, to avoid overgeneralization. Strauss notes that the errors of excessive attention to a single perceptual variable are also characteristic of young children in the preoperational period. Nevertheless, he goes on to urge exploration which will attempt to discern whether there may not be qualitative differences between these thinking errors as observed predominantly among the chronic schizophrenics and the manner in which the limitation is to be found in young children. Regarding the chronic population, he suggests that that the subjects' tendency to commit these errors could be either derived from prolonged hospitalization or are possibly indicative of chronic schizophrenia being a separate illness and not merely the end result of chronic hospitalization for acute schizophrenia.

Piaget has maintained that in normal development there exists a functional but not a structural relationship between cognition and affect. In other words, affect does not influence the nature of cognitive structures or the invariant sequence through which they develop. Affect does have a dynamic role to play, however, with respect to the pace of structural development and the selection of what will be learned. Voyat (1980) has made a contribution to our understanding of cognitive psychopathology bearing upon this view of affect. He studied ten schizophrenic children between eight and ten years of age, finding 20 percent of them to be at the concrete operational period, 50 percent to be at a transitional level, and 30 percent to be purely preoperational. Most of his subjects gave egocentric responses to conventional Piagetian tasks, did not demonstrate a grasp of logical necessity, and did not follow the expected sequences of development. Their responses to the tasks were characterized by a highly individualistic approach which Voyat describes as a "logic of the self" substituting for a genuinely logical justification. Further, in some instances the children gave explanations which described powers outside the logical realm to the experimenter. In some instances the subjects demonstrated competence at a later task while not demonstrating competence at a task usually understood earlier in development. These findings, in Voyat's interpretation, reflect not regression but structural disorganization. The schizophrenic children do not present a picture simply of normal development that is structurally younger than their actual age. Rather they present a developmental picture which basically deviates from normal cognitive organization. There appears to be a disruption of an assimilative-accommodative equilibrium, with assimilation predominating. Accommodation seems not to be playing its natural part, and an intensification of affect seems to cause the assimilative aspect of adaptation to work overtime.

Voyat observes that unlike normal egocentric children, his schizophrenic subjects experienced anxiety because they were aware that they lacked logical explanations. Voyat states, "They seemed to experience the need for logic without the mechanism—or structure—of logic. As a result, they have unusual responses" (1980:111). A final difference proffered by Voyat is that in schizophrenic children, cognitive operations exist in isolation from one another and, hence, are not part of an integrated cognitive system, as is the case in normal concrete operational development. Suggesting that his may be due to affective elements, he goes on to conclude that in the case of schizophrenic children, affect does influence structural development beyond the pace and content of learning.

SENSORIMOTOR ROOTS

This section will present material selectively from the sensorimotor period with reference to both normalcy and pathology in development. Practical intelligence is developed on a behavioral level throughout this period, which ultimately culminates in the acquisition of a capacity for symbolic thought at one and a half to two years of age. Gains made on a behavioral level will later have to be reconstructed on a conceptual level. For example, the child who learns to navigate competently on a physical plane in his environment needs to develop more complex cognitive structures before he can symbolically recreate that environment in the form of a map. The child's integrated comprehension of reality is constructed in such areas as time, space, causality, intention, object permanence, play, and imitation. In this section special attention will be given to causality and object permanence.

The normal route of development in the sphere of causality will be offered here because of its central role in adaptive living. Many adults identified as dysfunctional or mentally ill lack an appropriate sense of the source of causality in the world. They may either fail to see themselves as the locus of causality when it is appropriate to do so or see themselves as a cause agent influencing events over which they have no control at all. Either or both of these errors will result in grossly maladapted behavior. Yet it is developmentally in the sensorimotor period that the child first organizes his activities in relation to the world so that he learns to distinguish between things and events which he can influence and those which he cannot.

Piaget (1936/1971a) in stages 1 and 2 characterizes primitive causality as a fusion of efficacy and phenomenalism. During these first two stages, the infant's behavior revolves around looking, grasping, and sucking reflexively, as well as the primary circular reactions of these reflexes. In a primary circular reaction, the activity is repeated by the presence of a stimulus accidentally come upon. A child sucks from the nipple, swallows, then has the sucking mechanism triggered off again by the presence of the nipple. In this way there is strengthening of the response and a beginning accommodation to reality. At the same time that the accommodation is occurring, the child is, of course, assimilating the external world, which he does not perceive as such, into his reflex schemas. The external world upon which he acts at this stage is experienced as an extension of his own activity. The infant experiences a diffuse sense of efficacy, but this feeling is not of himself as a separate entity. Piaget states, "Primitive causality may therefore be conceived as a sort of efficiency or efficacy linked with acts as such, always with the reservation that such feelings are not considered by the subject as coming from himself but are localized in perceptual aggregates constituting the point of departure for objects in general or for the body itself" (1936/1971a:257). Eventually the efficacy will become a clear internal sense of the self's own power, and the phenomenalistic aspect becomes a full realization of the external world as separate from the self and as constituting a network of independent causality. In brief, efficacy becomes psychological causality and phenomenalism becomes physical causality.

In the third stage the infant makes some progress but remains characterized by what Piaget calls "Magico-Phenomenalistic efficacy." The essence of this is the child's sense of his own movements being the cause that creates effects even of events residing at some distance from his body. There are three main areas that the child observes—movement of his own body, effects in the external world which depend on his own actions, and movement in the external world which is not dependent on his activities. In the previous two stages, cause and effect were differentiated but experienced together in a single perceived act. However, from the third stage onward the child internalizes the sense of his causal efficacy, and the effect is externalized when he acts. The flaw in his behavior is in attempting to produce the sound of his rattle by merely waving his hand, having previously triggered off the sound when his hand had accidentally come in contact with the rattle. The child can be obsessed with looking at his own hand under these circumstances, with a studied expression as if his hand movements should be the sole source of causing the rattle to effect a sound. On some vague level the child is becoming conscious of purposefulness. He is beginning in the third stage to perform what Piaget calls secondary circular reactions. When his own actions accidentally trigger off an interesting sight or sound, the child will reproduce the action to make the interesting spectacle last. However, he does not necessarily bother to make spatial contact and, therefore, is not always successful. Thus efficacy and phenomenalism are still not completely differentiated at this magico-phenomenalistic stage. The secondary circular reaction reflects a movement away from the body toward things in the external world, whereas the primary circular reaction involves body-centered activities. The child still does not have a sense of self as separate from the rest of the world, however.

Piaget raises an interesting question in attempting to determine whether the child at stage 3 has as yet developed a recognition of objects outside of himself as a source of independent causality. Supposing A is observed causing B. Will the child who wishes to continue experiencing the effect B attempt to act on A by touching or pushing it once it stops causing B? Piaget set up circumstnaces in which this could be observed, and he concluded that the child does not. For example, if the experimenter swings an object several times and then stops, the child may revert to magico-phenomenalistic actions such as arching his back or swinging his hand at the air while looking at the object as if to see it repeat its former effect. Alternately, the child may direct his attention to the experimenter's hand, possibly only striking it and then looking to see if the object is again repeating the effect. However, he does not make any attempt to steer the experimenter's hand toward the object so that it may perform causally. The hand is simply not viewed by the child as an independent causal agent, but merely as causally subordinate to the child's own efficacy. Regarding the movement of the child's own body, generally, the actions of his body directly upon other objects, and the action of an external object upon another, Piaget comments, "In these three cases it is to the dynamism of his own activity that the child attributes all causal efficacy, and the phenomenon outside, however removed it may be from his own body, is conceived only as a simple result of his own actions" (1936/1971a:281).

It is perhaps plausible at this juncture to entertain the notion that schizophrenic persons who have an unreal sense of omnipotence with respect to their control over the universe may have become arrested developmentally at stage 3 in the area of causality, or may have regressed to it. There are also features of this in the ontological egocentrism of the preoperational period, and where one is to pinpoint the arrest or regression would depend on the degree of primitiveness of the belief. Since the areas of development in the sensorimotor period are interdependent aspects of the same growing person, it is likely that any such arrest or regression would not be limited to a single area. For example, the schizophrenic person who is functioning at least partially in stage 3 of causality is also likely to have a grossly deficient concept of object permanence.

Piaget has made some particularly interesting remarks about the role of the person in the child's environment at this stage. In Piaget's view another person in the environment is subject to the same attitude and behavior in the realm of causality as are inanimate objects. There is a reality in the child's life which lends some credence to such a relation to the person, for the child has often only to cry or perform other acts and the other person's behavior is fairly predictable. An adult or older sibling will frequently comply with the child's attempts to get him to do its bidding. There is an essential method, however, which is unique to how the child may attempt to produce an effect in the other person through imitation. In the third stage the child can only imitate behaviors which are already in his behavioral repertoire. When he imitates the other person with the intention of producing a repetition of the same act in that person, he merely experiences the other person's actions as an extension of his own performance. In general, throughout development during the sensorimotor period, Piaget places great importance upon the role of the person in fostering the child's cognitive growth. He notes that the child is more animated in the presence of other people and states "Contact with persons plays an essential role in the processes of objectification and externalization: the person constitutes the primary object and the most external of the objects in motion through space" (1936/1971a:285). It is the person who represents the most prominent and dominant locus of causality outside of the child, and, therefore, constant interaction with the other person facilitates the child's detachment from causality as inhering only in his own activity.

In the fourth stage the child does in fact dissociate causality in his own actions. The two are no longer inseparable. External objects are viewed as being a source of independent causality, yet are in some way still congingent on the child's activities. Another person can act as an independent causal agent, but requires the action of the child to set him in motion. Therefore, while external objects have now acquired partial objectification and spatilization, they require the intervention of the child's actions to be put in motion as causal agents. The child is now observed taking another's hand and placing it by a toy to be swung, even going on to attempt to get the exact action desired by manipulating the person's fingers to provide momentum. Note that, while this still provides a significant role to the child in activating the other's causality, it is an important advance over the previous stage when he would simply strike the other's hand as if this would make the toy swing. Similarly, in the fourth stage the child relates to inanimate objects in the same way. He will give them a push or strike them and then wait to see them go into action.

The fifth stage ushers in a total objectification and spatialization of causality in the external world. The child after the first year of life no longer acts as if animate or inanimate objects in his world are links to his actions before performing causally. External objects are seen as being independent sources of causality. The child is now observed placing a ball at the top of an incline, then allowing it to act in accord with its own nature. Piaget observes about his own daughter's behavior in this stage while playing with a toy, "Jacqueline, instead of pushing the object or even giving it a shake by a simple touch, makes every effort to put it down as rapidly as possible and to let go of it immediately, as though her intervention would impede the toy's spontaneous movement instead of aiding them!" (1936/1971a:309). The source of causality now inheres in the object. The same shift, of course, is seen in relation to people. For example, when Jacqueline wants her father to resume blowing in her hair after he has stopped, she merely places her head next to his lips and awaits expectantly for him to initiate the action. Pervious to this stage she would literally manipulate his lips, as if her own action were necessary before he could blow on her again.

Two major achievements arise during the fifth stage which have great bearing on the furthering of the causal notion. They are the tertiary circular reaction and the invention of new means through active experimentation. In the tertiary circular reaction the child searches for the novel and shows an objective interest in exploring the properties of objects as they exist independently of himself. This forces a greater accommodation to objective reality than previously experienced. In the process of inventing the new means, the child gropes with the object through a series of trial and error behaviors, but the groping is goal directed and not merely random. The child has increasingly come to recognize that there is a world of cause and effect independent of himself and that maximum adaptation requires of him a certain amount of submission to these phenomena. Piaget asserts: "Whereas up to now the child has commanded nature, he now begins to do so only by 'obeying it' " (1936/1971a:330). It is worth noting here that obeying nature is not to be enslaved by it, but by understanding its laws one gains a greater command over it. There now exists a reciprocal relationship in which the child is acted upon by external causes and also acts upon those causes in the objective world, as well. He comprehends himself behaviorally as one of a series of causes existing in the world.

In the sixth stage the child acquires representation in causality. He no longer is solely reliant upon direct perception, but can now infer causes from observed effects and conversely can anticipate the effect of a contemplated causal action derived from an object in the environment. The emergence of the capacity for symbolic thought gives rise to causal deduction, which frees the child from the sensorimotor limits of direct perception. As in all stage phenomena, it should be realized that limitation of former stages persist, despite the capacity to perform at the symbolic level. They may be especially manifest in the face of problems that are more than moderately novel and that pose exceptional difficulty.

Goulet (1974) has researched the causal development of the very young child in relation to his reaction to strangers. He points out that while there is general agreement on the observation that sometime during the second year, the child begins to manifest a fear reaction in the presence of a stranger, disagreement revolves around how to understand the meaning of this event. Tracing the development of the causal concept, Goulet pauses at the fifth stage to emphasize that Piaget suggested that at this stage the child will regard objects with an apprehensive expression because he no longer thinks they are predictable. He now has a greater tendency to take note of the novel in his environment. Goulet speculates that prior to this stage of causal development, fear of new or strange aspects of the environment is not likely. A scale of causalty was constructed to diagnose the child's causal level based on Piaget's work. There were thirty-two subjects, eight in each of the following age groups: thirty-two weeks, forty weeks, forty-eight weeks, and fifty-six weeks. The mother was present and visually accessible throughout the experiment, although she remained inactive. The stranger, the experimenter, acted in a normal manner while moving through a series of graded steps to bring him into closer contact with the infant. The subject's reactions were observed in terms of facial expression, motor activity, and vocal sounds. Basically, reactions could be classified as positive, negative, or neutral.

One facet of the findings was that from among the oldest infants (fifty-six weeks) there were only two of the eight who showed positive reactions. In the other three groups, a majority of the infants responded positively. In general, when comparing responses across age groups in relaton to certain positive and negative reactions, there were twice as many infants behaving negatively in the oldest age category that in the other three groups. Negative behavior included such reactions as attempts to avoid contact, crying, or even striking out at the approaching stranger. The oldest infants were also ranked at the highest level of causal development, as one would expect. Nevertheless, when the sample was analyzed from the standpoint of specific causal stages for each subject in relation to whether the global score of responses in the presence of a stranger was positive, negative, or neutral, it was found that there was no correlation. Hence, Goulet concluded that the infants' stages of causal development did not correspond with their affective reaction to the presence of a stranger.

The findings convey that for an infant to express fear of a stranger it is not necessary that he be at high level of causal development, as fear of a stranger was found in a few infants who were only at stage 3. These results were not expected. In analyzing the data further, Goulet discovered that there is, however, a unique role played by stage 5 development. Some subjects seemed positive when the stranger was present but at a distance, and shifted to an intesively negative reaction when being approached or touched by the stranger. All of these subjects were at stage 5 or 6, although not all subjects at stage 5 or 6 reacted negatively to such stranger behavior. Goulet puts it succinctly; "approach or contact would constitute an inherent threat in the eyes of the child only if he has acquired a thoroughly objectified and spatialized concept of causality" (1974:93). Goulet theorizes that viewing objects as capable of autonomous causal action, independent of the child's own activity, is responsible for his fear as the stranger approaches or touches him. While motionless at a distance, the stranger poses no threat. It is not his presence but his behavior that produces anxiety in these infants. The behavior is a necessary, but not a sufficient, condition, for not all infants at stage 5 or 6 will react apprehensively in these circumstances. However, only infants who reach stage 5 will show a capability for such a response under the conditions described.

Brossard (1974) has conducted a study similar to Goulet's, in which he sought to discover whether there is correspondence between the infant's development in object permanence and his response to strangers. The reader will recall that for the youngest infant there exists no concept of a permanent object which is independent and durable irrespective of the infant's own perception and actions. It is only through gradual stage transitions that he can finally deal with complex, invisible displacements of an object. His ability to deal with invisible displacements is due to the development of representation, which enables him to make deductions about the object even though he, himself, is neither perceiving nor acting upon the object. Brossard stresses that the problem he is researching is an interpersonal one, because the stranger is, in fact, an animate and not an inanimate object. The distinction is a developmentally important one for, as Piaget has noted, there is a décalage in which children will be observed to arrive at stage 6 in relation to the substantiation or permanence of a person before they arrive at an object concept for inanimate objects.

The scoring of positive and negative reactions utilized by Brossard was the same as that utilized by Goulet. Both research attempts were part of a larger project and were presented in a volume by Décarie (1974). Brossard found no correlation between the infants' affective reaction to the presence of a stranger and their stage of object permanence with a person. However, further analysis reveals that of a total of thirty-two subjects, there were sixteen who changed affective tone when the stranger moved toward them and/or touched them. Further, fourteen of the sixteen proved to be at stages 5 or 6 in object permanence in relation to a person. There was also a marked tendency for those who did not show an affective change to be in the lower levels of object permanence development. Those who shifted in affect almost invariably changed in the direction of a negative response, hence signifying that the situation was being interpreted as a threatening one.

Décarie (1974) dares to speculate upon the findings of Goulet. She points out that only two of the subjects who manifested a change in affective tone from positive to negative were at stage 5 in relation to attributing causality to inanimate objects. The other three subjects who manifested this behavior were already at stage 6. Since an infant will experience a décalage in development, first acquiring a causal concept in relation to persons and later acquiring it in relation to inanimate objects, Décarie sugests that it is entirely possible that the two subjects at stage 5 in relation to objects may already be at stage 6 with regard to persons. If this should be the case, all five subjects who changed from reacting positively when the stranger remained at a distance to reacting negatively when he moved toward them or actually touched them would be at stage 6 in relation to attributing causality to persons. More specifically, this would mean that they had reached the stage of representative thought and were conceptually capable of anticipating and making inferences that would take them beyond the immediately perceivable. At a distance, the stranger is merely an unfamiliar but interesting sight, which poses no threat. Upon approaching the infant at stage 6, the stranger may trigger off an anticipation of a fearful event. The infant at a stage prior to the sixth does not have the capacity to imagine such an event. The infant at stage 6 may infer that the stranger is about to pick him up and that this will cause the mother to leave, or he may infer that the stranger is going to pick him up because his mother is planning to leave. Décarie emphasizes that either interpretation of the event will very likely stimulate anxiety in the child. She points out that this imagined sequence is not at all uncommon for infants to have experienced, as when a baby-sitter arrives, picks up the child, and then the mother leaves.

PERSON AND OBJECT PERMANENCE

The phenomenon of a décalage in development regarding object permanence has been carefully studied by Bell (1970), who has indicated some diagnostic significance to it. An earlier attempt at researching Piaget's hypothesis that person permanence would precede inanimate object permanence was conducted by Saint-Pierre (1962), who found a confirmation in twenty-three of thirty infants studied. There were cases, however, in which either no décalage occured or where the sequence was reversed. Recognizing the mother as central to the infant's interaction with his environment, Bell sought to examine her role in relation to the child's development of the object concept. In particular she wished to ascertain whether the nature of the child's attachment to his mother exercised any influence over the sequence with which person permanence and object permanence appeared. Bell worked with a population of twelve females and twenty-one males, totaling thirty-three infants, of middle-class background. Each was measured on developmental level in relation to object permanence and separately in relation to person permanence. The sample was divided into three groups, designated positive décalage, negative décalage, and no décalage. If an infant evidenced a décalage favoring person permanence, it was considered in the positive group, and in the negative group if it favored object permanence. Attachment to the mother was determined by structuring situations in which the infant would be separated from the mother for several minutes and then brought back to her. Behavior of the infant would be observed and scored. It should be noted that, during the separations, the infant would be in an unfamiliar situation in the presence of a stranger. There were basically three groups of children, classified according to their tendencies to explore the surroundings during the phases of the study and to seek closeness to the mother. Interviews were held with the mothers to obtain data about their attitudes and activities with the children.

In accord with Piaget's previous observations, a majority of the subjects evidenced positive décalage. There were twenty-three infants who were more advanced in person permanence than in object permanence. The negative décalage category had seven subjects, and for three subjects no décalage was found. Each of the infants was tested three times between the ages of eight and one-half and eleven months, and a portion of them were tested once again at thirteen months. The décalage for those favoring person permanence was relatively constant over the testing period and was not eliminated until both person and object permanence reached the most advanced level sometime after the experiment. Infants with a negative décalage, however, moved more rapidly in closing the gap, so that by the time of the third testing session all but two subjects had eliminated the discrepancy. Therefore, Bell points out, being scored as having no décalage may simply signify that the infant is being tested at a particular point in development when that condition obtains, but it does not signify that there has never been a décalage.

What can be said of the relationship between mother attachment and object concept? There were twenty-four infants assigned to group B, which was characterized by the subjects' ability to use the mother as an anchor point of security in order to venture forth to explore the environment prior to the brief separation phase of the study. Further, infants so classified displayed clear attempts to interact and gain closeness with the mother once reunited. Of these twenty-four subjects, Bell reports that twenty-three were scored as having a positive décalage and one had no décalage. Group A contained five infants. Their characteristic behavior was to avoid person contact and to focus upon interaction with objects in the environment. The negative décalage classification claimed four of these subjects and one exhibited no décalage. In group C there were four children who showed maladaptive coping behavior in the unfamiliar situation and were ambivalent toward the mother in her presence. All four scored a negative décalage. One of them had registered no décalage until tested at thirteen and one-half months, at which time the negative décalage was apparent. Significantly, the only subjects who demostrated a positive décalage were those who had a close attachment to the mother, but who also felt secure in leaving her side to explore their surroundings.

A comparative analysis was also performed in relation to the developmental level of object permanence for both the positive décalage group and those with either negative or no décalage combined together. In general, by the age of thirteen and a half months it appears that infants in the positive décalage group have also acquired a concept of object permanence which is more advanced than that of those infants in the negative décalage group. Bell asserts that the quality of interaction between mother and child during the first months of life will directly influence the nature of attachment and development of person permanence. She has made some general comments based on the interviews with the subjects' mothers which are worth quoting at length.

Mothers of babies in the positive décalage group tended to go on frequent outings with their babies and to avoid even brief daily separations from them. They tended to comment only on the baby's positive features, and never showed physical rejection or mistreated the infant in front of the observer. Mothers of negative décalage infants instead were significantly rejecting . . . they were prone to express disapproval and rejection through inappropriate use of physical punishment, refusal to establish contact with the baby, or abrupt interference with his ongoing activity. (1970:309)

Bell has highlighted through her impressive study the singular importance of a good mother-child interaction in contributing to adaptive cognitive functioning and the development of symbolic activity. (Read Clarke-Stewart 1973, for a well-documented review of the influence of mother-child interaction upon the child's cognitive functioning.) The child who has a negative décalage will also be observed to have a less sound structure of object permanence than the child with a positive décalage. Recent evidence presented by Chazan (1981) confirms the pattern of positive décalage as related to the nature and quality of maternal interaction with the infant. Specifically, mothers who engaged in enhancing communication and stimulating active achievement were those whose children were most likely to experience positive décalage.

We shall now turn to a developmental issue of the sensorimotor period bearing on mental representation as defined by Piaget and to the early hallucinatory experience as described by psychoanalytic theorists. Piaget's findings on the construction of the object concept have been confirmed independently by Décarie (1965) and Escalona (1968). What seems to be a subject of debate is whether the early hallucinatory image is a phenomenon of true mental representation, given that its appearance is posited by most psychoanalysts at a time in development prior to the time that Piaget claims for the emergence of genuine representation. Vitally linked to this problem is the relationship between the psychoanalytic concept of object constancy, first introduced by Hartmann (1964) and the Geneva School's concept of object permanence introduced by Piaget (1936/1971a). Major attempts have been made by Décarie (1965) and Fraiberg (1969) to place the psychoanalytic and Genevan positions into a conceptually consistent framework. The following formulation will rely heavily upon their insightful efforts.

It would seem that depending upon whose definition and understanding of the concept is being honored, object constancy may generally be found to first appear anywhere between five months and thirty-six months (Kaplan 1972). The nature of object constancy will vary depending upon which theorist is being accepted. The issue is whether object constancy requires object permanence in the Piagetian sense or whether it may predate Piaget's concept. Anna Freud has not used the concept of object constancy in the cognitive sense to denote the capacity to evoke absent objects, on a symbolic plane, which have substantial existence independently of the child. Her emphasis is on the stability of the emotional attachment or libidinal cathexis of the child for the mother. Prior to object constancy the child undergoes a "need-satisfying" phase during which the object is cathected only in times of need and frustration. During this period the object has no existence when there is no need. Further, cathexis is withdrawn from the disappointing or thwarting object. In the subsequent period of object constancy the cathexis is maintained regardless of the child's need state or the frustrating actions of the mother. The emphasis is upon libidinal attachment throughout and not upon the separate existence of the loved object as an independent entity in itself. According to Décarie's interpretation of Anna Freud, the first appearance of object love, but not object constancy itself, appears between five and six months. From then on there is a gradual progression toward object constancy. Décarie states, "The kind of object constancy which is implied in the continued cathexis of the absent object does not really appear before the beginning of the third year" (1965:116).

On the other hand, Spitz (1957, 1965) specifically relates object constancy to mental representation in the strict cognitive sense. (Colbiner, in the appendix to Spitz 1965, presents an extended discussion from the psychoanalytic perspective.) He pinpoints stranger anxiety at eight months and explains it through mental representation. The stranger's face is compared to the infant's internal image of the absent mother. Recognition that the stranger is not his mother and that she is not presently available to him produces anxiety. Fraiberg (1969) reports that through an exchange of correspondence, she received confirmation from Spitz that he views object constancy as present in the infant by eight months and that he intends to assert that the child of that age has the capacity to evoke an image of the object not present to him. However, Spitz acknowledges in the correspondence that the object involved here is specifically the mother and that the circumstances are especially stressful for the infant. Whether the infant could perform similarly with consistency and under less stressful conditions remains a moot question for him. Nevertheless, it should be apparent that placing mental representation at eight months of age poses a problem when examined in the light of Piaget's position, confirmed by subsequent researchers, that this capacity appears between eighteen months and two years of age. It is true that Piaget holds that person permanence appears prior to the permanence of inanimate objects, but one would not expect a time lag of such proportions.

Mahler, Pine, and Bergman (1975) clearly link object constancy to mental representation, but do not see it as fully developing until between twenty-five and thirty-six months. Because of the special nature of the interaction between the child and his mother, as opposed to the interaction between the child and less emotionally charged objects, the mental representation of the mother may occur more swiftly, but may be less stabilized at first than is the case with inanimate objects (Pine 1974). The stringent position adopted by Mahler et al. is reflected in their own words:

It is only after object constancy is well on its way, which according to our conceptualization does not seem to occur before the third year . . . that the mother during her physical absence can be substituted for, at least in part, by the presence of a reliable internal image that remains relatively stable irrespective of the state of instinctual need or inner discomfort. (1975:110)

Fraiberg (1969) suggests that theorists who date object constancy from eight months to eighteen months are construing libidinal cathexis in terms of some form of mental representation. When object constancy is seen as emerging at eighteen months, Piaget's stage 6 criterion for mental representation is invoked. In the case of Mahler, who does not place object constancy before twenty-five months, Fraiberg states that even more restraining criteria are being utilized to account for the sustained image of the mother which the child can manage even in the face of internal disruption. It is precisely the meaning of the term "mental representation" in psychoanalytic usage which remains variable and vague in the literature.

Fraiberg sets out to clarify matters by offering a distinction between the terms "recognition memory" and "evocative memory." Recognition memory is triggered by the sight of some sign which, in turn, points to further detail that is recalled. For example, seeing an old friend may bring to mind a series of past experiences which one might not have otherwise imagined. However, representing these events in the total absence of any triggering stimulus would be an example of evocative memory. Fraiberg cogently argues that the anxiety Spitz observed in the infants he studied at eight months can be explained by recognition memory and need not invoke an interpretation of evocative memory. Responding to Spitz's comment that the mother is felt to be "lost" to the child when he fails to find her upon comparing her image with the stranger's face, Fraiberg states, "On the contrary, if a mother is 'lost' when she is not perceived, this may be taken as evidence that the mental image of the mother is still unstable, is not independent of perception, requires affirmation from visual experience" (1969:24). In the child's visual experience there is a repeated presentation of the joyous sight of the mother. When the "expectation" of still another repetition is disconfirmed for the eight-month-old child, this could produce an unsettling effect. The expectation need not be predicated upon evocative memory at all. Further, Fraiberg asserts, "The child who is capable of evocative memory can sustain the image of the mother *not* present in perception which should theoretically diminish the disturbing effect of a strange face" (p. 24). She then predicts that, in fact, one would find a corresponding basis in cognitive development that would account for diminishing stranger anxiety at about twelve to thirteen months old, which she suggests is supported by Piaget's observations and theories. In her argument, Fraiberg emphasizes the possibility that the very absence of a stable and well-developed mental representation is the source of anxiety for the child who has become so libidinally cathected to the mother. Its presence would offer a sense of security.

What of the image in relation to the early hallucinatory experience which gratifies an intense need or wish? Is this a genuine case of mental representation? The child in the absence of food and in a state of intense hunger may hallucinate the breast, taking it to be the real object. There follows at least partial gratification. Décarie (1965) adopts the position that this hallucinatory event is not to be equated with full mental representation of stage 6 development in the object concept. In Fraiberg's terms it is recognition memory. It lacks the complete evocate character of Piaget's stage 6. Instead, it is more like stage 4 in which the screen behind which a ball may be hidden from a child is the sign that leads him to retrieve it. Even though the ball is no longer in sight, the child still depends on visual cues to locate it. When still at this stage, in fact, if the ball previously located at position A is seen being removed to position B, the child will only look for it where it had been previously found. He cannot as yet deal with either visible displacements (stage 5) or invisible displacements (stage 6). In referring to the hallucinatory image, Décarie contends, "This is not yet true representation but rather analogous to representation in stage 4, in which visceral hunger sensations play a role of perceptual indicators of a forthcoming feeding and lead the infant to believe that the object is already present." (1965:206). She further points out that the image in these circumstances is described by Rapaport (1954) as being vague, diffuse, and undifferentiated. Hence, it lacks the distinct and precisionlike form of mental representation as appearing at stage 6. It also lacks the independent, substantiated existence of an object in the Piagetian meaning of complete object permanence. To the contrary, its appearance is subjectively rooted in the temporal and sporadic need system of the infant rather than being grounded in external reality and accorded continuity of existence. To qualify as evocative memory, a more advanced form of mental representation, it must sunder its roots from the stimulus of need, just as the child eventually transcends his dependence on visual cues related to the external world. This is an essental point advanced by both Décarie (1965) and Fraiberg (1969).

Kaplan (1972) has advanced the observation that, despite the wide range along which the appearance of object constancy is placed by varying psychoanalytic theorists, there are many who view it as a gradually developing phenomenon. Elaborating upon this position, she has proposed that the development of object constancy can be followed through adolescence. Her contention is that the various phases can be understood in the light of stage properties and décalages as in Piaget's system. Achievements at one level are reconstructed at a later and more advanced level where they are integrated with the newly evolving structures of development. Kaplan concludes, "The process of new structure formation and reorganization of adolescence should modulate the intensity of libidinal ties and identifications of the past without eradicating them" (1972:333).

Taking this long-range view, Blatt (1974) has maintained that adult depression may have as its source the impairment of object constancy and mental representation at one of the earlier developmental stages. It is suggested by him that as long as the object is present in the individual's actual environment, the problem may not be apparent.

However, upon removal from or loss of the object, such as a parent, the flawed capacity for object representation fails to offer the needed internalized images for support. Absence of the cathected object on both an external and internal plane then produces fertile grounds for depression. Despite the more differentiated and discrete nature of the image at stage 6 of the sensorimotor period, it is not until the outset of formal operations, age eleven or twelve, that representation is comprised of a sharply etched image. Blatt points out that prior to this time, children have difficulty in recalling vividly even familiar faces and places. Once the individual moves into advanced levels of cognitive development, he has at his command a meaningful and broad repertoire of images and memories which he may evoke rather than become depressed. The type of depression, anaclitic or introjective, is said to be determined by the level of representational impairment.

Blatt and Wild (1976) have drawn heavily from Piaget in their developmental approach to schizophrenia in terms of boundary differentiations. Their concern is with the individual's capacity to differentiate between his own self and the external world, as well as between his internal representations and that which is represented. The individual who differentiates boundaries appropriately does not mistake the image or word for that which it signifies. Objects that are separate in reality are not fused in the mind. Boundary disturbances are likely to result in poor differentiation within the intrapsychic, cognitive, and interpersonal domains, according to Blatt and Wild. Yet these disturbances are not to be found in equal proportions among all schizophrenics. The authors' premise is that paranoid subgroups invoke defense strategies which are designed to combat boundary problems. Projection in particular is viewed by Blatt and Wild as a defense which serves to differentiate between self and object. In general, they have found that poor cognitive, perceptual, and interpersonal boundaries are maintained by chronic, undifferentiated, process schizophrenics. However, in contrast, Blatt and Wild assert, "The paranoid's hyper-alertness, overly focused attention and perception, fragmented thinking, extreme constriction, excessive autonomy and interpersonal distance, preoccupation with power and control, and guarded and suspicious behavior can all be understood, in part, as exaggerated defensive efforts to prevent the dissolution of boundaries and accompanying experiences of merging and fusing"

(1976:229). They believe, also, that the extent of boundary disturbance may serve as a measure of pathological severity. There is a positive correlation beween early disruption of interpersonal relationships and the maintenance of poor boundaries. Patients with such a history and current boundary problems will have a more difficult time sustaining personal relationships in the present. Among the more imparied schizophrenics, there is a greater likelihood of mothers having been either cold and distance or intrusive and enveloping from the patients' early life onward. The patients as children failed to differentiate between self and parent. They are marked by a desire to merge with the parent; a primitive struggle for separation ensues, which goes beyond the normal adolescents' struggle between independence and dependence.

The genesis of boundary disturbances is to be found in very early cognitive development. Radical egocentrism of the sensorimotor period is gradually surmounted through the infant's interaction with the environment. This interaction enables the child to defeat the most primitive boundary limitation of all, in which there is, in the beginning, no sense of either self or external world. Behavior suggesting that the infant construes the object as being a part of his own activity is finally surrendered, as the object is accorded an independent existence apart from the child's own activity or perception. It is the gradual construction of a stable mental representation which makes this possible. It is necessary, however, that the image or verbal signifier in representation be distinguished from that which it stands for, if genuine boundary differentiation is to be maintained. The infant progressively relinquishes behavior which expresses the self as the exclusive locus of causality. By the end of the sensorimotor period, the infant differentiates between causality residing in the self and that which derives from people and objects outside the self. A further distinction is made between cause and effect, as the infant by stage 6 can infer one from the other, going either from cause to effect or from effect to cause. Effectual parenting gives due recognition to the child's own feelings and promotes his capacity to differentiate between what he is feeling and desiring from that which the parent feels and wishes.

Blatt and Wild further emphasize that schizophrenics have great difficulty in maintaining a realistic time orientation. This is especially true of nonparanoid schizophrenics. They lack an appropriate sense of sequencing and of the relationship among past, present, and future.

The origins of a sense of time are to be found in the sensorimotor period, as Piaget (1936/1971a) has informed us. A primitive sense of time is related at first to the infant's own subjectivity in terms of his efforts, satisfaction, and expectations. By the end of the sensorimotor period, the infant's time sense has become spatialized and objectified. The development of a sense of objective duration, of the relationship among past, present, and future, is inseparable from isomorphic development in the spheres of causality, object permanence, and space.

Anthony (1956) cites his observations bearing on the sensorimotor roots of childhood psychosis. He tells of a severely disturbed child, mute and vegetative, who attempts to pick up pictures of food that appear in a journal. The effort is a serious one and the child exhibits frustration at his failure. Yet when the page is turned, thereby concealing the illustrations, he does not attempt to restore the previous situation. He obviously has an inadequate sense of the continued existence of the "food." In a similar observation, the child is playing aimlessly with two objects. The first two objects are removed and replaced by two other objects, with the identical activity persisting. When one of the second pair of objects is surreptitiously removed, the child evidences no sense of loss. He initiates no effort to seek the missing object. It is as if it had never existed. In still another observation the child, in a state of hunger, eagerly moves toward a piece of candy he spots on a table. Before he can reach it, however, a cloth is thrown over it so that it is no longer visible. Once the candy is out of sight he immediately stops moving in that direction and begins another activity. To test whether he was possibly inhibited from removing the cloth in the presence of the observer, he is left alone. Despite this, he makes no attempt to obtain the candy. In another situation, twelve pieces of candy are separately placed under twelve corresponding cups. As each cup is removed by the observer, the child will take the candy. He makes no attempt himself, however, to remove a cup. There appears to be no inference that the remaining cups may conceal a piece of candy. The impairment of object permanence and the ability to anticipate is clear in these examples. Confusion between what constitutes a two-dimensional image and a real object is also apparent. Anthony emphasizes that while there were varying degrees of a poor object concept among the psychotic children he observed, they were all rooted to the sensorimotor level.

Bettelheim (1967) observes that the autistic child is well known for his persistent efforts to keep the environment the same. Perhaps, Bettleheim urges, the austistic child has faulty object permanence development and is striving to achieve a level of constancy in the external world to compensate for his inability to maintain images internally. In fact, it does seem that objects exist for the austistic child only when visually perceived or found in customary surroundings. The infant at stage 4 equates the object with a place. Once having located it at a particular place, he will look for it there again, even if he has seen it displaced to another location. Bettelheim stresses that the autistic child must always have his familiar objects in the same location, as if "place" were a part of its definition and permanence. By insisting on constancy as he knows it, the autistic child is assuring his own security. Bettelheim cogently comments, "Through his insistence on sameness the autistic child makes his most immediate surroundings a bit predictable, but without any comprehension or belief in the permanence of objects. This eliminates the need to understand the nature of the object. If the object is an Object-in-a-certain-place I need not know its intrinsic nature to predict the vagaries of existence" (1967:449). He suggests that normally a child will have a wish for the mother to return when she is out of sight and that this wish eventually gives rise to the image which sustains him in her absence. The development of person permanence in this manner will soon extend to less significant objects in the environment. However, for the autistic child the mother does not generate secure feelings and is a threat. Therefore, he does not possess a wish for her to return when she is absent, for he is actually better off without her. There then exists no basis for the image to be constructed in the autistic child and he, consequently, lacks object permanence. Central to Bettelheim's view is that the autistic child refuses to interact normally with the environment, to assimilate and accommodate to it, because he finds it destructive in the form of his mother. Further, the child fails to interact beyond the sensorimotor period with others in the environment and, therefore, lacks the experience of testing out his perceptions and cognitions against those whose view of reality differs. Change does not occur. Development is impeded.

Freeman and McGhie have also reported from their studies of chronic and deteriorated schizophrenic patients that the psychopathology observed can largely be understood as an expression of a flawed sensorimotor development. They have made observations of hebephrenic adult patients who exhibit object concept development at the level of a very young infant. In the case of one patient, he would often ask for cigarettes, but whenever one would drop from his line of vision he made no attempt to retrieve it. Yet he had a strong desire for cigarettes, which were the only environmental objects he showed an interest in. If he placed a lighted cigarette off to the side on a table, he would request another shortly, but never think to go back to the original one. Freeman and McGhie state succinctly, "It appeared to us that, like the infant, once the object passed out of his immediate perceptual field it had disappeared" (1957:182). They note that the overt behavior of chronic schizophrenic patients reflects activity similar to the primary and secondary circular rections of the infant. It is the aspects of not having a goal in mind at the outset and of being influenced by chance happenings by which Piaget characterized primary and secondary circular reactions that seem to also describe much of the behavior of patients observed by Freeman and McGhie. They further report that many of their chronic schizophrenic patients do not clearly distinguish ear, mouth, and eye. The authors relate this to an early stage in the development of imitative capacities, in which Piaget (1946/1962a) points out that the infant can only imitate with parts of his body which he can see. There appears to be ample basis for acknowledging that the construction of reality by the child during the sensorimotor period serves as a foundation for normal adaptation to the environment. Impaired development in structures of space, time, causality, object concept, and person permanence can result in poor boundary differentiations and the painfully chaotic world in which the schizophrenic is so often found to live.

E. J. ANTHONY ON PSYCHOPATHOLOGY AND CHILDREN

A pioneering attempt, possibly the best available, to extend Piaget's system to a clinical understanding of children has been made by Anthony (1956). He characterizes Piaget's developmental psychology as an ego psychology dealing, as it does, with the conflict-free sphere. Although establishing the fact that for Piaget cognition and affect are indissociable, Anthony suggests that the ego ideal of the system might well be considered the "logical machine." The adaptive processes of assimilation and accommodation are presented as the dynamic structure of the system. An imbalance of these functions, in which assimilation predominates, could lead to fantasy, egocentrism, and autism. To the contrary, excessive accommodation could lead to undue lability with an ever-changing personality, always seeking to conform to something outside the self.

Anthony highlights the similarity between the syncretistic thinking of the preoperational child and the paranoid psychotic. Syncretistic thoughts fuses unrelated elements and subscribes to causal forces that are nonexistent. Connections and relationships are seen when only chance occurrences are operating. The tendency for transductive thinking, in which elements tend to be equated on the basis of predicates, has also been found in both children and schizophrenics. For example, if an avocado, which is green, is ripe, then a banana, which is green, must be ripe. The accidental attribute of green signifies an equation of ripeness in both foods. Transductive reasoning is especially prevalent just after the sensorimotor period and is a preconceptual phase which is conducive to syncretic thought, as it permits unrelated thoughts to be fused.

Anthony identifies the concept of immanent justice as one which persists longer and has greater intensity among subgroups of children. Immanent justice is the belief found among preoperational children that wrongdoing may be automatically punished by external forces inherent in nature. Children with phobias of paranoid content are especially vulnerable to this expectation, as are disturbed children who have difficulties with masturbation. One may also speculate that the paranoid expectations of some adults could be based on the persistence of the immanent justice notion, so that they expect retaliation from nature for a "sinful" deed or thought.

Animism is a powerful turn of thought in the young child's development, and Anthony suggests that for a time it protects him from facing the fact of death. The endowment of all things with at least potential life is characteristic of the very young child. As development progresses he gradually constricts the range of types of objects to which he is willing to ascribe life or its properties. Unclear at first about the nature of death, the child abandons animistic thinking at about ten or eleven years of age, and this sets the groundwork for a new kind of fear. The younger child, of course, is vulnerable to fearfulness of objects in his environment because he has unrealistically endowed them with life. For example, I am familiar with a young child who was terrified when in the presence of a loudly functioning old-fashioned vacuum cleaner. Given a dash of animism and a bit of imagination, the vacuum cleaner has all the makings of a first-rate monster.

Anthony believes that animism is largely responsible for many of the fears and fantasies of the child under seven years, whereas afterward the anxieties expressed seem to derive more from the social arena. In normal young children, Anthony's studies show, animism generally becomes prominent at night. The dream or nightmare is the bearer of many of these fantasies. It should be remembered that the preoperational child's thought is characterized by realism, in which psychic events are accorded external, substantial existence. Therefore, if in a dream the child may be prone to imbue an inanimate object with life, which might render it fearful, the child genuinely believes that it exists within the room and not in his head. Psychotic children were found by Anthony to show extensive animism in which objects such as the moon, lights, and shadows become feared. Clinically, Anthony has found that interpretations offering intellectual explanations are not useful if the child's fears derive from animism. The reader should not conclude from this discussion that fear responses are intrinsic to animism. Innumerable examples to the contrary can be cited. In one entertaining protocol, Piaget tells of a child observing a twisted string unwinding with a weight at the bottom. The child remarks that the string knows it is twisted and is deliberately unwinding itself.

Anthony dwells little upon the more logical and formalized components of Piaget's system. He does urge, however, that a systematic and penetrating developmental diagnosis of children's reasoning is useful, especially with those suffering from learning disabilities. He comments in closing, "Within the new discipline of *genetic epistemology* one must look more closely at the whole process of the acquisition of ideas. It is not sufficient to understand the dynamics of feeling; we must also understand the genetics of thinking, after which we may claim with greater truth that we really understand our patients" (Anthony 1956:34).

DECENTERING AND THE FEFFER MODEL

The interpersonal model advanced by Feffer has been extended by him to account for symptoms in psychopathological behavior. Feffer (1967) contends that, when sequential decentering prevails over simultaneous decentering, such characteristic manifestations of symptoms as "isolation, exaggeration, and fluctuation" will be evident. Sequential decentering offers only a partial correction of distortion, while simultaneous decentering provides complete correction of distortion. An example of this is seen in the Piagetian classification problem in which there are twelve wooden beads, ten of which are brown and two of which are white. The preoperational child can center on the total class and know that there are twelve wooden beads. He can also center on the two subclasses and know that there are more brown beads than white beads. However, when asked if there are more brown beads or more wooden beads, he cannot coordinate the decentration, simultaneously taking into account the relationship between part and whole, even though he has been able to shift sequentially from whole class to subclass. Instead, he centers on the perceptually salient aspect of the brown beads and claims that there are more of them than wooden beads.

Feffer believes that the same cognitive limitation inherent in this problem involving physical materials can also be applied to the interpersonal world to explain symptom behavior. The essence of this primitive form of cognition is that aspects of a reality are viewed in isolation, sequentially in time, without any reciprocal interaction coordinating the various aspects. Feffer, drawing upon a passage from Bleuler (1951), suggests that a lack of simultaneous coordination between means and end in striving to attain a goal would be indicative of immature cognitive functioning, and isolating the two so that neither can reciprocally modify the other leads to dysfunctional behavior. In the interpersonal realm, an individual can modify his own anticipated behavior by first taking the role of the other and assessing how that behavor would be reacted to by the other if carried out. Feffer, in analyzing a passage from Cameron (1951), attempts to further extend the decentering principle to symptom expression. He illustrates this by citing delusional thinking in which the schizophrenic patient imagines himself being the recipient of a hostile aggressor. In this hypothetical situation the patient is virtually assuming two roles in fantasy, those of the hostile aggressor and of the victim. Whereas in adaptive interpersonal relations the individual can view himself subjectively from his perspective and objectively from the perspective of the other, the delusional thinker isolates the various perspectives of victim and aggressor. This is true, even though both roles, those of victim and aggressor, are contained within the same person. The roles take on an exaggerated character because the isolation precludes modification or correction of distortion. The delusional person fluctuates between the two roles, never coordinating them through simultaneous decentering. The key to this condition is that the hostile role is one that is ego-alien and consequently externalized by projection. The patient must defensively isolate himself from it.

Defensive isolation from role-carrying attributes that are ego-dystonic has been studied at greater length by Lowenherz and Feffer (1969) in an ingenious experiment utilizing the Role Taking Test and Thematic Apperception Test. A comparison was made of cognitive levels, based on decentering capacity, between subjects' ability to role take in situations involving defensively isolated attributes as opposed to nonisolated attributes. It was found that when subjects were required to take the role of characters who had attributes which were not ego-syntonic to them, the subjects tended toward sequential decentering. Contrary to this, subjects role taking in situations where the attributes of the other were ego-syntonic tended toward simultaneous decentering. Specifically, where defensive isolation was not involved, a subject could invoke an internal orientation in describing one character of the story and coordinate this with an external orientation of another character. For example, the subject assuming the role of a wife in the story may describe her as angry because her husband came home late that evening and consequently the dinner was burned; while the same subject may, in assuming the role of the husband, describe him as realizing his wife is angry, but feeling he had no choice because of an emergency situation that developed at work at the last minute. In cases of defensive isolation, however, there was a higher incidence of responses favoring simple refocusing, in which the subject goes from the viewpoint of one character to the other's without preserving continuity or consistency. Hence, in the sample cited, the subject may describe the wife as angry when assuming that character's role, and when assuming the husband's role may describe him as viewing his wife as pleased. There is clearly no coordination between the internal and external perspective of the wife's behavior.

Feffer suggests that the notion of primitive decentering may also be applied to impulse and control behavior in the neurotic. An example may be an exaggerated impulse toward destructive or aggressive behavior which is countered by an equally exaggerated defense of reaction formation in which the neurotic adopts an excessively sweet and kindly attitude. Feffer cites the well-known example of the exaggerated impulse to soil, which is countered by an excessive control mechanism and cleanliness. In commenting generally on this phenomenon, he states simply, "The impulse and control are clearly separated: rather than serving to modulate each other, they are expressed as fluctuating polarities" (1967:24). Regardless of the etiology of the problem, it is the isolation precluding reciprocal modulation which is central to Feffer's position. Feffer seems willing to accept that the motivation to avoid anxiety stimulates defensive measures, but he holds that it is not the avoidance of anxiety that accounts for the exaggerated and fluctuating manifestations of symptomatology. Rather, it is the isolation of the subsystems that produces the symptom expression.

Feffer believes strongly that his formulation holds promise for bridging the gap between Piaget's essentially impersonal application of cognitive structures and his own interest in applying cognitive development to the interpersonal sphere. The concept of decentration is admirably suited to serve as a foundation for the bridge, as it is structurally isomorphic between physical and social domains. In an attempt to pursue that promise further, Suchotliff (1970) set out to discover whether the same construct, decentration, can contribute to an understanding of the schizophrenic's cognitive impairment in both social and nonsocial contexts. It was hypothesized that the forty schizophrenic patients would perform less adequately because of an apparent deficiency in decentering skills than a control group of twenty normal subjects. It was further hypothesized that, within the patient population, there would be a positive correlation between the low scores anticipated on both the socially oriented and the nonsocially oriented tasks. In other words, schizophrenics would be deficient in decentering when compared with normals, and the deficiency would constitute a formal property of their thought in all cognitive domains, whether social or nonsocial.

The social task involved communication in which a subject had to select a word from a list which would offer the recipient an associative cue to a target word which the donor knew but the recipient did not. The donor had to use the feedback from the recipient in order to make more effective selections of clue words on subsequent trials. Basically the task required that the donor decenter in order to simultaneously take into account the referent or target word, the clue word, and the feedback. By isolating these elements and focusing on only one of them, the subject would minimize his chances for effective communication. The schizophrenic patients did not adequately take into account differential feedback. They responded to feedback as if they were taking an individual word association test, reports Suchotliff, simply ignoring the referent word itself. In general, the hypotheses tested were confirmed. Decentering impairment cut across the communication and nonsocial tasks in the schizophrenic group, which in turn could not come up to the decentering competence demonstrated in the performance of the control group. Suchotliff's findings would seem to support Feffer's conviction about the vital importance of decentering in both personal and impersonal realms.

THE GENEVA SCHOOL

There has been a flurry of research activity over the last twenty years emanating directly from the Geneva School in Switzerland. Inhelder (1943/1968) has spearheaded this breakthrough with the publication of a major volume on retardation. Very little of what has been done, however, has yet been reported in English, and as far as I can ascertain, what has been studied is in a stage remote from any state of synthesis. What appears in this section represents merely a fleeting acquaintance with what, it is hoped, will eventually emerge as a comprehensive presentation of the Geneva School's findings on cognitive-developmental psychopathology. Much of the research (Inhelder 1966, 1971; Schmid-Kitsikis 1973) has been conducted through a collaborative effort with the staff of the Geneva University Psychiatric Clinic. Investigations have covered not only the mentally retarded, but also psychotic, dysphasic, and dyspraxic children. In addition, congenitally blind children were compared with those who were blinded four years or more after birth. Senile dementia and adult schizophrenia have been studied as well. Material in this section will be devoted exclusively to observations on the psychotic child.

Inhelder (1971) has described the results of studies conducted with a group of psychotic boys, ranging in age from ten to fifteen years, who had been in some form of treatment for approximately ten years. Types of tasks utilized tested the children on classification, conservation, and chance. A cognitive diagnosis placed the children along a continuum from a beginning state of concrete operations through a transitional phase to formal operations. The sample contained a small subgroup whose members seemed to be characterized by an integrated thought structure and who did not fall below expected developmental level for their age. The vast majority of the subjects, however, had incompletely integrated and unstable structures. In all cases subjects could not deal with tasks involving chance phenomena, the solutions to which would have required invoking probabilistic thinking. The children with integrated thought structures were insistent that causal laws were operative, and when they could not adequately explain what was happening through those laws, they shied away from the problem.

Inhelder's main point is that these particular children possess the necessary operations to resolve tasks involving chance, but this is their characteristic reaction when confronted with stark uncertainty. The bulk of the children, those with only partially integrated structures, fall back upon invoking magical explanations. Those who do not do so suggest that they have been deceived by the experimenter. Generally in normal development, it is the preoperational child who has no grasp of the differentiation between chance and nonchance. As Flavell points out, "Nothing is deductively certain and nothing is genuinely fortuitous for him; his thought is forever at midstream between these poles" (1963:342). The concrete operational child recognizes the differentiation between chance events and those determined by necssary causality, but cannot adequately bring to bear his rationality upon chance factors. It is at the time of formal operations when the adolescent develops operations of combinatorial analysis and proportionality that he can resolve chance problems. Flavell (1963) cites a simple task of this sort at which only the adolescent excels at attempting the prediction of the distribution of twenty pairs of marbles drawn randomly from a bag in which there are twenty red and twenty blue marbles. What are the probabilities of obtaining more homogenous pairs of one color or the other, or of obtaining more mixed pairs?

Inhelder reports further that the psychotic children with only impartially integrated structures did not perform as well in conservation of matter tasks as they did with those pertaining to logical inclusion. Such a décalage or lag in development is not generally found among normal populations. Also, the psychotic children seemed to revert back to nonconservation responses even after a time when it appeared, somewhat deceptively, that the ability to conserve had become crystallized. It is most unusual for this to occur normally, as logical certitude and stability are major criteria to genuine development. It is also noteworthy that psychotic children who seemed stabilized in their conservation responses relied almost exclusively on reasoning involving identity explanations. Inversion responses were rare occurrences and compensatory responses were never introduced.

The last major type of deficiency discussed by Inhelder is that of the psychotic child's inability to make an imaginative assumption which is socially shared. Granted that a child has a rich fantasy life, for the psychotic child it is encapsulated in his private world. To share a pretended experience with another is a social act which he has little capacity for. Inhelder believes that sharing a make-believe world involves the symbolic function, that is, the ability to differentiate between signified and signifier. However, it is precisely the ability to distinguish between reality and the symbol that represents it which is impaired in the psychotic child.

In summary, Inhelder suggests that a study of radically psychotic children can promote illumination of normal development, and, conversely, a knowledge of normalcy in cognitive development will shed light on pathological mechanisms and structures.

Elsa Schmid-Kitsikis (1973) has made a contribution to the understanding of psychotic children's thought mechanisms by analyzing the self-regulating or equilibrating process among them. Her sample was of fifty psychotic youngsters ranging from seven to twelve years of age, who were administered conservation, classification, and relation tasks.

A striking aspect of the psychotic child's reasoning is the coexistence of preoperational and operational responses to a variety of conservation tasks. These responses may be detected in sequential statements which contradict one another or they could actually be built into a single statement. Schmid-Kitsikis indicates that, in dealing with conservation of weight, some subjects were observed saying, "It's the same weight; it's thinner than the other so it weighs less." There was no apparent awareness of the contradiction inherent in the responses of these subjects, and the oscillation between the two levels of reasoning did not eventuate in a more stable equilibrium of operational explanations. She further observes that these children tended to seek homogeneity of the experimental materials. For example, after one of two balls of clay had been made into a sausage during a conservation of weight task, the children would often seek to have the remaining ball transformed into a sausage so that identically shaped elements could be compared. Schmid-Kitsikis cites a further example of this propensity to duplicate the model in a different type of task, and she stresses that when the children are not permitted to do as they wish in this area they become disturbed and often cannot succeed at performing the task. Still another tendency is the resistance to predicting the outcome, but instead insisting on the task being executed first in order that they may observe the results before commenting. In other words, in a conservation of weight task, for example, the psychotic child will frequently request that the two items simply be weighed, rather than anticipate which would weigh more if they were to be weighed. Schmid-Kitsikis sees in this an inclination toward avoiding conflict, as is also manifest in the children's observable attempts to alter the experimental conditions so that there is conformity to concrete reality as they imagine it. In characterizing the behavior of the psychotic children when facing the various Piagetian tasks, Schmid-Kitsikis states, "Thus it would be possible to interpret the basic avoidance and reality transformation mechanisms as a fundamentally affective need for noncontradiction by annulment of too obvious conflicts, which would lead to a more reasoning state" (1973:704).

AFFECTIVE REALISM

Odier (1956) has made one of the earliest attempts at an extensive application of the Piagetian system to the field of psychopathology. He had been a psychiatrist and psychoanalyst of French-Swiss background, whose untimely death prevented his work from reaching its final stage of evolution. Nevertheless, some of the speculative formulations introduced in his book will be presented below.

The concept of objective relativism, borrowed from Piaget, is seen as central to the psychoneurotic's thought pattern. The neurotic has not achieved objective relativism to the degree that the normal adult has, and, therefore, his thought is characterized by three basic limitations. One of these is his tendency to accord objective and external existence to some of his own private psychic events. Another is his propensity to make absolute his own viewpoint, failing to recognize that any other could exist. The third limitation is to imbue an absolute existence to aspects of reality which actually exist only by virtue of their relational nature or the perspective from which they are seen. In brief, the neurotic negates objectivity, reciprocity, and relativity in some areas of his thinking. This state is predicated upon infantile realism, and Odier comments upon it as follows: "The existence of several possibilities creates the necessity for hypotheses and a respect for objective proof, but infantile realism is by nature the enemy of hypotheses and experimentation as well as of relativity of thought" (1956:18).

Although Piaget's concept of realism emphasized intellectual aspects, such as reasoning and judgment, Odier stresses that the same principle can extend to the affective realm, covering needs, instincts, and feelings. In fact, he contends that affective realism lasts longer than intellectual realism and is an even more clear exemplar of adualism, the inability to differentiate between internal and external. The reader, of course, will immediately recognize the term "adualism" as synonymous with egocentrism. The main point is that even well-educated and intelligent adults, who have surmounted intellectual realism, may continue to be characterized by affective realism and the attendant immaturity that would go along with it. The decline of affective realism leads to a sense of internal security, self-value, and autonomy or independence. These three achievements signify a dualism or decentration in the psychic organizaton. Together they comprise the ego functions, in Odier's framework, and working in harmony they produce a sense of "ego well-being." Disharmony among these three spheres is responsible for the individual suffering a sense of inadequacy and inferiority. The neurosis in Odier's view is not a new experience for the person, but a reexperience of affective realism.

The distinction between intellectual realism and affective realism is central to the position Odier is expositing. He states, "As we know, adolescents become familiar first and most easily with the principles and laws of intellectual logic. The logic of interpersonal relationships, the necessity of applying this logic to family and social life, may escape them for a long time . . . the resulting lag remains the specific feature of many adult neuroses" (1956:29).

Odier's book contains many highways and byways. We will travel only one of them in the remainder of this section, however, hoping that perhaps the reader will wish to travel further on his own at some later time. The "neurosis of abandonment" is one to which Odier devotes lengthy consideration. An abandonee is a person who, although he has not usually experienced real abandonment, suffers from a subjective feeling of having been abandoned in a relationship with another person. Abandonism is in direct proportion to an internal sense of insecurity. The abandonee fears most of all that he will be rejected. Any omission of overt attention on the part of the other is interpreted as a lack of love by the abandonee. His fear in fact generates imagined rejections. He requires the certitude that he is loved in order to achieve or maintain any semblance of security. The obsessive thoughts of abandonment lead to many undesirable interpersonal dynamics, ranging from obsequiousness in order not to lose the other person to alienating the other by imputing to him motives of wishing to abandon. Odier goes into some detail to demonstrate that while the abandonee desires only security, his neurosis precipitates constant crises and conflicts in relationship with a spiraling effect of intensified insecurity. I will focus on one aspect of the problem here.

A characteristic line of reasoning pursued by the abandonee reveals the egocentric nature of his reasoning. A woman feels that since the man with whom she is involved does not have the kind of consideration for her that she expects, he cannot possibly love her any longer. A man who has not received a desired telephone call concludes that the woman from whom he expects it is detached. Another man reasons that the woman with whom he is involved did not come to visit him even though she knew he would be at home; therefore, he is now unimportant to her. In still another instance, the woman deduces that since the man forgot her birthday, he must be angry at her. Finally, a woman observes that the man was pleased when they were last together, but seemed displeased when he returned; therefore, she reasons that he is going to terminate the relationship. The general description of what is taking place is worth quoting at length.

Clearly the needs and demands, desires and fears of S are expected to magically dictate O's thoughts, words and acts. O has to partake in the affective life of S; this intimate participation arising intuitively between the two is the fundamental cause for their relationship. If S has a desire, O has to have it too. He must love or dislike the same things and the same people. Difference is confused with disagreement and the latter with disunion. Everything that threatens this participation produces a sudden decrease in S's feelings of value and security. (Odier 1956:226)

The three principles undergirding this type of egocentric reasoning pivot around the lack of objectivity, relativity, and reciprocity. The abandonee does not inquire into the objective reasons behind the other person's behavior. Difference or disagreement not being countenanced, the abandonee simply absolutizes his own conviction that he is in some way being abandoned. Further, his own needs and feelings are not seen as relative to another's in the relationship, hence there is no realization that there must be mutual regulation and adjustment between the two participants. Finally, the abandonee's own affectivity impedes him from taking the role of the other. The partner to the abandonee is not permitted to act either spontaneously or independently without being accused of indifference and unfaithfulness. In brief, the partner must fuse his emotions in conformity with those of the abandonee, a restraint having been placed on the differentiation of feelings. Odier believes that the mature choice of an appropriate partner proceeds from self-esteem and security. The abandonee reverses this process and hopes to achieve these attributes as end products of the relationship. Unfortunately, however, the developmental presence of affective realism, which prevents objective relativism in the emotional domain, does not allow this painfully sought goal to be obtained.

STRUCTURALISM AND AFFECT IN PSYCHOPATHOLOGY

Recently, Siomopoulos (1983) has attempted to systematically apply a structural approach to an understanding of psychopathology. His primary concern is to answer the question of how structure is related to psychopathology. Although he weaves ideas from Freud, Lacan, and Gestalt psychology into his theories, the Piagetian paradigm is paramount in his work. Despite Piaget's insistence upon the inseparability of cognition and affect, he emphasized the cognitive aspects of development in his work. Siomopoulos restores the balance by giving attention to the affective aspect of the mind's structures. Not only does the intellectual life of the individual undergo the process of structural adaptation and transformation, but so also is the individual's affective life subject to these processes. Hence, feeling states have an underlying structure which participates in assimilation and accommodation of encountered experiences and which is transformed over time. Siomopoulos, in contrasting his conceptualization to Aaron Beck's cognitive therapy model, states, "One may observe that Beck focuses on the structure of thought, not on the structure of affect—affects for him, are secondary products of cognitive evaluations. In contrast to this approach, affects in this book are viewed as structures with their own transformational laws and their own symbolizing function" (1983:29). It is upon this theoretical foundation that Siomopoulos proceeds to explain such mental phenomena as anxiety, depression, apathy, delusions, rage, panic, obsessions, and phobias.

CONCLUSION

There has been an increasing surge of interest and effort in the direction of organizing a science of developmental psychopathology over the last several years (Cicchetti 1984). Piaget's work on normal cognitive development and its heuristic capacity for generating new knowledge in the area of psychopathology are bound to make a major contribution to the progress of this interdisciplinary science as it continues to gain momentum. The complementarity, where such is the case, between Freud's and Piaget's systems is likely to receive mounting attention (Basch 1977, 1981; Greenspan 1979) while simultaneously others pursue theory building within the Piagetian paradigm (Kegan 1982). As Inhelder and others have observed, a better understanding of psychopathology will enhance our own understanding of normalcy, and, reciprocally, the reverse is also true.

CHAPTER 6

Piagetian Perspectives on Psychotherapy and Other Interventions

PATTERNS AND TRENDS IN CONTEMPORARY PSYCHOTHERAPY

Corsini (1981), citing a proliferation of psychotherapeutic systems and practices, has listed no less than 250 schools of psychotherapy. Elsewhere he contends, "If psychotherapy is essentially a matter of philosophy, then ultimately there will be an infinity of systems; if it is essentially a matter of science, then ultimately there will be one eclectic system" (1984:10). Indeed, despite the bewildering array of psychotherapies to choose from, converging trends are in evidence. There have been scholarly attempts at integrating psychodynamic and behavioral approaches (Marmor and Woods 1980; Wachtel 1977), and Goldfried (1982) has produced an anthology reflecting the current convergence of psychotherapeutic themes toward a more unified outlook. Three recent works signifying efforts at providing eclectic models of psychotherapy are to be found in Beutler (1983), Driscoll (1984), and Hart (1983). Yet at the same time we are on the threshold of an era that has begun to deliver manuals that delineate precise strategies and tactics for conducting highly differentiated types of psychotherapy. These manuals serve the purpose of training therapists for clinical practice and participation in research. The first of them has been by Beck, Rush, Shaw, and Emery (1979) on the application of cognitive therapy to the treatment of depression. Klerman, Weissman, Rounsaville, and Chevron (1984) have written such a manual for treating depression through an interpersonal therapy model. A manual on the untilization of psychoanalytic therapy has been prepared by Luborsky (1984), and there is one available on time-limited dynamic psychotherapy (Strupp and Binder 1984).

A significant debate in the field of psychotherapy is that of accounting for patient improvement while in treatment through the invocation of nonspecific or common aspects that cut across all therapies versus the specificity explanation, which attributes change to the distinguishing techniques characterizing any one school of psychotherapy. Proponents of the former (Frank 1961; Garfield 1980; Patterson 1980) identify such aspects as the patient's positive expectation for improvement, the therapist's conviction about his method, restoration of the patient's morale, emotional catharsis, encouragement and support in performing the desired behaviors, and several others. The nonspecific argument plays down the possible influence of any particular technique utilized during therapy. This position is bolstered by the fact that although there is strong evidence to support the contention that significant numbers of patients can and do improve while in therapy (Luborsky, Singer and Luborsky 1975; Meltzoff and Kornreich 1970; Smith and Glass 1977), there is no empirical foundation to support the assertion that one form of psychotherapy is uniformly and unequivocally superior to another (Strupp 1978). Research by Luborsky et al. (1975), and Sloane, Staples, Cristol, Yorkston, and Whipple (1975), in particular, would seem to bear this out. However, Kazdin and Wilson (1978) have argued persuasively that very specific behavioral therapy techniques have demostrated differential efficacy for a wide variety of problem areas including, but going beyond, neurotic and personality disorders.

As increasing refinement in research methodology occurs, the old question "Is psychotherapy effective?" is being discarded. Strupp states, "The problem of therapeutic outcomes must be reformulated as a standard scientific question: What specific therapeutic interventions produce specific changes in specific patients under specific conditions?" (1978:8). Pursuing this question clearly indicates some degree of conviction that a particular technique, despite the nonspecific features of all therapies, may be sufficiently potent in itself, under certain circumstances, to effect a positive change in the patient, which change would not have been forthcoming had the technique been withheld.

Assuming that a particular technique or procedure is found to be more efficacious than its alternatives, the question of arriving at a theoretical explanation for its effectiveness remains to be answered. This issue is illuminated especially well by the popular procedure of systematic desensitization introduced by Wolpe (1958) to eliminate neurotic anxiety and phobias. The procedure outlined by Wolpe has been extensively researched and few dispute its effectiveness, even though direct exposure to the feared object seems to be superior (Marks 1981) to Wolpe's imagistic approach.

Systematic desensitization involves the construction of a hierarchy of anxiety-producing scenes which are presented to the patient in order of intensity from least to most. The patient is instructed to imagine these scenes while he is in a state of deep relaxation, which he has been trained previously to achieve. Wolpe explains the success of this procedure through the principle of reciprocal inhibition, which posits that the two antagonistic states, relaxation and anxiety, cannot coexist. Hence, the associative bond between each scene (stimulus) and the anxiety (response) is broken by the gradual introduction to the hierarchical scenes during deep relaxation. However, other explanations accounting for the success of this phenomenon have been proffered, encompassing a compelling placebo effect (Franks and Wilson 1976), counterconditioning or nonreinforced exposure (Kazdin and Wilcoxon 1976), and an alteration in the client's belief in self-efficacy (Wilson and O'Leary 1980). Wolpe (1982) has come forth with a strong rejoinder reasserting his contention that reciprocal inhibition is the central element explaining the efficacy of systematic desensitization. Regardless of who may be right in the dispute, the point is that while there can be consensus about the successful outcome of a therapeutic procedure, or a system of psychotherapy, there can be disagreement simultaneously about the explanation of that success. This sometimes leads to a situation in which we have advocates of one school applying their theories to explain any apparent positive outcomes produced by alternate schools of therapy. Whether ultimately we will be witness to "an infinity of systems" or "one eclectic system" remains to be seen.

Amid the patterns and trends of contemporary psychotherapy we find attempts to integrate the Piagetian paradigm with particular existing schools of psychotherapy, efforts at applying concepts of Piagetian epistemology uniformly across all therapies, and distinctive interventions spawned by Piagetian principles.

GENERAL OBSERVATIONS ON PIAGETIAN IMPLICATIONS

Piaget's genetic epistemology does not constitute a new system of psychotherapy. Nevertheless, there is a growing trend toward attempting to extract from it principles and practices that may be useful in the course of clinical intervention. One approach to exploring Piagetian implications for therapeutic practice is to identify various aspects of the theory with the aim of exploring the extent to which they enhance or expand our understanding of preexisting systems of psychotherapy. This is a meta-theoretical approach. Concepts such as equilibration, assimilation, and accommodation lend themselves well to this endeavor. The notion of matching an intervention to an individual's cognitive-developmental stage is another which has utility across a broad range of psychotherapies. It should be noted that Piagetian implications for psychotherapeutic models apply to children, adolescents, and adults alike. Bear in mind that many adults are either not at the formal operational stage or, if they are, they are not beyond the early phase of formal operations. Further, although one may have developed to the stage of complete formal operational structures, it does not follow that the advantages of such advanced development will be utilized in all domains of one's life. It is precisely in the area of emotional and interpersonal functioning that a troubled person may not activate his full cognitive capabilities. A second approach to discovering the possible contribution of Piaget's work to the clinical field is to raise the question of whether it is itself generative of specific strategies and techniques that might be applied directly as therapeutic activities. A third alternative is to consider whether Piagetian psychology has anything to say about valid criteria for goal setting in psychotherapy. In the material that follows, these three issues will interweave their way throughout with varying degrees of emphases. The spirit of this chapter is suggestive and speculative rather than definitive; to approach the material otherwise would be premature at this stage and perhaps even presumptuous.

A recurrent theme in the Piagetian literature is that of equilibration. Indeed, equilibration is the critical factor in the theory that accounts for change and growth. With each newly achieved equilibrated balance a wider perspective is attained, the ability to coordinate more perspectives is possible, and a new view of the old perspective is acquired. Reequilibration occurs when the current structural organization is no longer adequate to a task it is facing. It cannot assimilate or resolve the problem at the current level of development. The individual is "stuck" and in moving beyond the impasse there will occur structural modification or the invention of new structures.

Let us take an excursion into a hypothetical, albeit unlikely, example for a moment. If witnesses to a robbery all agree that a particular man who has been apprehended is the culprit and another group of people claim that to be impossible because the same man was with them at a party during the time the crime was said to have been committed, then we are faced with a conflict and contradiction. In response to the ensuing disequilibrium we may at first resort to familiar ways of resolving the dilemma. We may, for example, attempt to discredit one set of witnesses or perhaps seek an explanation based on the malfunctioning of a clock that was used to fix the time of the crime. Yet what if these explanations are ruled out and nothing in our current knowledge organization enables us to resolve the problem? Now let us suppose, hypothetically, we are dealing with a society that has no prior experience with or concept of a "twin." We might then, with some degree of inventiveness, modify our scheme or concept of siblings to be inclusive of something called an "identical twin." This resolution solves the problem by breaking out of the old framework through the differentiation and integration of old and new schemes. The new cognitive organization is more adaptive in that it allows greater flexibility in solving a wider range of problems at the more highly equilibrated level. The process is similar to what Watzlawick, Weakland, and Fisch (1974) have written about in their work on alternative frames of reference in problem resolution. However, their philosophical underpinnings are very different as they are not addressing structural development with a clearly delineated adaptive direction.

A way of looking at patients in therapy from a Piagetian perspective is that they are stuck in a state of disequilibrium. The problem they are facing cannot be adequately assimilated and resolved at their present level of knowledge organization, but neither are they inventing new and more adaptive ways to handle the situation successfully. That is precisely why they have come into therapy. In effect, they lack a "twin" concept and are troubled in the struggle to develop one. A depressed person, for example, who is contemplating suicide lacks a "hope" concept. His phenomenological field simply does not include it. His is a poorly equilibrated system because the only solution he assimilates the problem to is a "suicide" schema[1] which if acted upon would eliminate life entirely and with it any potential for future enjoyment and growth. The therapist needs to assist him in reconceptualizing his dilemma so that he recognizes it as wanting not death but a cessation of pain. The task then becomes one of generating alternatives that will assist him in achieving his own goals while preserving life. It is naive, of course, to think that life will ever be without problems. The most we can expect is that the new problems the patient will experience during and after therapy will reflect the higher level of development. As Inhelder et al. (1974) have observed, the resolution of each disequilibrium poses new questions at the newly equilibrated level. We find this to be so even on a macroscale of societal systems. Conflict between labor and management, for example, led to the formation of unions empowering working people to organize and strike. This solved many problems, introducing a higher level of stability and adaptation. It afforded greater reciprocal interaction and avoided irreversible firings without recourse to appeal. Yet far from being a panacea, the newly equilibrated relationship between labor and management has gone on to produce new individual and social problems.

A natural question to raise is whether the direct stimulation of cognitive development is a valid goal from a therapeutic as opposed to purely educational standpoint. The answer can be in the affirmative if we take several factors into consideration. Higher-stage development is by definition more adaptive and, therefore, the further developed one is, the sharper and more effective will be his problem-solving skills. It is simply a fact that younger children use less efficient

---

1. Throughout this chapter the terms "schema" and "scheme" will be used interchangeably and are to be defined as meaning a cognitive structure.

problem-solving skills in handling tasks than do older ones. There is a definite progression of increased cognitive skills with age. Since competence in the real world has not only practical consequences, but is also linked to self-esteem, there is reason to value cognitive development as a therapeutic goal. Furthermore, it has been well established that cognitive-structural organization is a necessary precondition for the emergence of corresponding perspective-taking and moral reasoning abilities. The development of these abilities provides fertile ground for increased interpersonal effectiveness, fair play, prosocial behavior, and empathic sensitivities.

Finally, one simply cannot address cognitive development without, at least by implication, addressing emotion. Cognition gives structure to emotional experience and expression; therefore, the level of cognitive-structural organization will greatly influence the nature and range of one's emotional life (Piaget 1954/1981; Greenspan 1979; Cicchetti and Hesse 1982). Since in Piaget's view cognition and affect are inseparable, being two aspects of the same phenomenon, it would follow that what influences one would influence the other. Nevertheless, the reciprocal interaction may not be one of parity. It is beyond dispute that feelings can affect the individual's cognitive capacity. Anxiety can block the exercise of formal operations and determination can enhance it. However, the effect is not likely to be one of a qualitative change in cognitive organization. In contrast, a shift to the next cognitive stage can lead to a qualitatively different emotional organization. Cowan details the progression, pointing out that while the preoperational child is subject to fluctuating and unstable feelings, the concrete operational child acquires a conservation of feelings, which enhances the capacity for enduring relationships. Devotion to neighborhood, church, and school becomes manifest, but is confined to the concrete and familiar. By the time of formal operations, the adolescent becomes capable of affective ties to abstract social causes, political movements, universal institutions, and utopian ideas, all of which are beyond his immediate ken. Cowan cautions against prematurely concluding that the affect of cognitive progression upon emotions is necessarily positive and against minimizing the possible role of emotion in affecting cognitive structure. He suggests, "What we still need to know is how structural advances both facilitate and interfere with our comprehension of the social-emotional world—how the logic of things and the logic of feelings go together" (1982:76). Greenspan (1979), whose work is introduced below, attempts a further elaboration of this question. Chandler, reporting on research he participated in with others (Chandler, Paget, and Koch 1978; Koch, Harder, Chandler, and Paget 1979), strongly suggests the potentially positive effects upon emotional and social well-being of advancing cognitive development. They studied the relationship between cognitive maturity of children and the psychological defenses utilized by their parents. The first study revealed "clear relationship between children's level of cognitive developmental maturity and their ability to fathom various mechanisms of psychological defense" (1982:231). In the second study they focused specifically upon the children of psychiatric patients. In this study the researchers found that "children who, due to their relative cognitive immaturity, could not decode their parents' defensive strategies were rated by both their teachers and their peers as less socially and emotionally competent than children whose cognitive operational competency placed them in a position to decipher their parents' defenses" (232).

A problem which plagues all psychotherapies and broader intervention programs is that of the maintenance and generalization of gains. There is no assurance that gains made during the course of therapy will continue afterward or that they will be extended to additional sectors of the patient's life. In fact, Goldstein, Lopez, and Greenleaf (1979) claim, based on a survey of numerous outcome studies, that maintaining and transferring therapeutic gains is more the exception than the rule. This conclusion is applicable to all therapies: psychodynamic, existential, behavioral, and others. An analogue to this vital concern is the issue of whether, in the field of cognitive development, training studies are successful in obtaining a genuine conservation concept. Piaget (1964) proposes several criteria to assess whether this has been achieved. One is that of durability. Conservation predicated upon the invention by the child of appropriate operational structures should continue to be manifest in a posttest administered several weeks to several months later. A second criterion is generalizability. Training received successfully in one area of conservation, if built upon the construction of new structures, should be applicable to a wider range of related tasks which call upon the same structures. A third consideration, which logically follows from the above, is that training which results in true development should move the child from his original spontaneous operational level to a higher, more complex system of hierarchical operations.

In addition, Smedslund has repeatedly emphasized that genuine conservation should evidence resistance to efforts aimed at inducing extinction. In one experiment Smedslund (1961a) trained nonconservers through a stimulus-response method to verbalize conserving judgments, making them superficially indistinguishable from natural conservers. However, when they were tricked by the experimenter into challenging their own judgments, all of the children who had undergone the S-R learning reverted back to a nonconserving position, whereas half of those who had acquired conservation through natural development maintained their position. The natural conservers who did not revert to nonconservation sought rational explanations to explain the trick phenomenon. They exhibited a degree of logical certitude even in the face of the challenge, which none of the S-R trained conservers manifested. This experiment might be viewed as analogous to a patient having apparently achieved his goal in therapy only to regress under subsequent stresses, calling his gains into question.

Taking into account Piaget's criteria and Smedslund's experiment, the critical factor seems to be that of structural transformation as opposed to surface learning. It is the genuine development of the appropriate underlying structures that promotes the maintenance and generalization of conservation. Superficial learning without structural support does not signify a genuine comprehension of the conservation concept and remains vulnerable to extinction under stress. This would explain why certain forms of behavior therapy such as operant conditioning, a powerful behavioral change technology, have not been particularly successful in the maintenance and generalization of change (Kazdin 1978). Similarly with highly expressive therapies that rely heavily on emotional catharsis and the encounter groups so popular on the West Coast during the sixties. Participants would often feel very good immediately afterward, but any long-range benefit or transferability is highly questionable. The talking therapies, as is well known, are subject to being deceived by the patient who learns to verbalize all the correct ideas and sentiments, yet whose inner sense of well-being and behavioral performance do not seem congruent with his statements. In many cases behavior may change in the desired direction only to be discontinued once the therapy has ended. Yet this is certainly not a complete portrait of therapy outcomes, for there are not only genuine gains that are, in fact, made by many patients, but these gains are maintained, generalized, and even accelerated in some patients during the months that follow termination of the therapy.

What makes the difference? In Piagetian terms, genuine gains that will be maintained over time and generalized to other contexts are predicated upon a reorganization of knowledge structures. Furthermore, such a structural transformation provides a new foundation upon which to build the next evolutionary step, which would explain how it is that some people seem to continue growing after the formal therapy has ended. The larva that has emerged from the cocoon as a beautiful butterfly has not simply become a better larva, but has been transformed in its essential being and will never again be a larva.[2] This undoubtedly takes our discussion to lofty heights, and the practicing psychotherapist may have begun to wonder if this description resembles any patient in his own professional experience. Admittedly, confronted with severe psychopathology so much of the time, the transformational view may be only an ideal, or perhaps even an illusion, but in the words of T. S. Eliot, there is a time to pause for "vision and revision." In any event, cognitive development is not an illusion and each new stage does enable the individual to soar above the former stage.

We have seen that addressing deep structural change is one approach to the maintenance and generalization issue from a Piagetian perspective. Another is that of promoting more awareness in the patient of his own reasoning strategies and extrapolating general rules from a particular situation that can then be applied to a variety of other contexts. This is known as metacognition. Cohen and Schleser (1984) in reviewing a set of related experiments have found the capacity of metacognition in concrete operational children to be the critical variable accounting for why these children were able to demonstrate generalization of learned skills in self-instruction training programs (see also Kendall and Wilcox 1980). The research involved same-aged children who were determined to be either preoperational

2. I am indebted to Dr. L. Isobel Rigg for the use of this metaphor.

or concrete operational. The preoperational children generalized only when they rehearsed generalized self-instructions. They were not able to generalize when the self-instructions rehearsed were task specific, hence bound to the immediate context. However, they were not able to generalize even under the generalized self-instruction conditions when the method for arriving at the self-guiding instructions utilized was that of directed discovery, based on a Socratic dialogue with the experimenter, as the demands of this approach proved too discrepant from their cognitive stage. Contrary to this, concrete operational children were able to generalize their new skills to other tasks and contexts even under the self-instruction condition that was task specific. This was due to their capacity for reflexive abstraction that enabled them to construct a general plan or strategy from the specific context-bound, self-guiding statements involved, which the preoperational children, even though of the same age, could not do. Further, introducing the more demanding directed-discovery technique for arriving at generalized self-guiding instructions did not impede their capacity for generalization to other tasks, as it did with the preoperational children. The directed-discovery technique, although a challenge to them, was not too discrepant for their cognitive stage, as it had been for the preoperational children. In fact, by participating in the process of directed discovery they were able to benefit from the "strategy generation and application" qualities inherent in this method and by reflexive abstraction, once again, utilize what they learned from it beyond the immediate task at hand. We have seen a previous example of this type of abstraction in chapter 1 in the case of the young child who, when reflecting upon his own actions on a set of pebbles arranged in different formations, discovered that neither the order of the pebbles nor the order of his counting changed the number in the set. The rule that the sum is independent of order transcends the immediate context and can be transferred to other areas.

One message for the therapist in all of this is to design interventions that will maximize the metacognitive abilities of the patient and to explicitly discuss the transfer of abstracted knowledge on patterns and plans for use in other contexts and in the future. Arranging for this transfer of knowledge in the form of homework assignments may be very useful in helping the patient consolidate and extend his gains.

This therapeutic strategy is advocated whether working with children or adults. In summarizing the implications from a cognitive-developmental viewpoint of the research reported upon, Cohen and Schleser state, "Interventions should differ for children who lack a particular strategy and for children who have a particular strategy but fail to apply it. the developmental timetables for different strategies will vary as well. Thus, practitioners must be aware of the developmental implications of the strategies they are training in terms of the child's position both in the sequence of strategy use and with relation to other prerequisite skills and strategies" (1984:66). A clinical intervention is an external stimulus and, like all such stimuli, its meaning is relative to the cognitive-structural development of the individual to whom it is presented for assimilation. Addressing metacognition on a very practical plane, Borkowski and Kurtz state, "Training effects are often not durable because the child lacks an understanding of why the strategy should be employed. If the deliberate use of strategy results from a metacognitive understanding, adequate instruction must include an explanation of why the strategy is to be employed, repeated practice on its correct deployment, and feedback concerning the strategy's usefulness" (1984:209). Automatic maintenance and generalization while desirable where they occur are not to be assumed. It is frequently the case that a course of therapeutic activity while ostensibly successful from a short-range viewpoint has proven to be unsuccessful from a long-range perspective by ignoring this guideline.

Implications of Piagetian theory cut across all systems of psychotherapy. As we have already begun to see, if the therapist wishes to maximize his effectiveness, he would do well to structure communications and design strategies that take cognizance of his patient's cognitive-developmental stage and potentialities for stage growth. In working with delinquents and adult offenders, for example, it would be counterproductive to communicate in terms of Kohlbergian stage 4 concepts of duties, social order, and role fulfillment. Most of these subjects would more than likely hold a worldview expressive of stages 1 and 2, hence they would be preoccupied with issues of avoiding punishment and getting their needs met, respectively. A communication tailored to a stage 4 level would not have any meaning for them in its own right, but would be either ignored or distorted by assimilation to a lower stage. The more strategic approach in working with stage 2 offenders, for example, would be to design communications and programs which would both show a sensitivity to their stage 2 worldview and foster an evolutionary progression toward stage 3. This is exactly what Hickey and Scharf (1980) have done in a radically new therapy sometimes referred to as "Justice as treatment." Before delinquents and offenders can be expected to show concern for the social order at large, they must first undergo a hierarchical advance to a community concern with their peer group and with interpersonal issues that go beyond using others to get their own needs met. Any attempt at relationship therapy or couples counseling could benefit by an assessment and practice that takes into account the Piaget-Kohlberg paradigm. By extension, the same clinical principles would apply to group and family therapy as well.

Henggeler and Cohen (1984) have suggested differential treatment recommendations for sexually abused children based on whether they are preoperational or concrete operational. They point out that preoperational children who have been abused sexually are less likely to experience adverse consequences far into the future. Their comprehension of what has taken place and the accompanying fear will tend to be limited to the location where the act took place and to the person who performed it, When this is so, although emotional support is always desirable, the treatment package might usefully include behavioral therapy techniques. Concrete operational children who have been sexually abused, however, are more likely to suffer long-range adverse consequences. "Depression, guilt, low self-concept, and heterosexual problems, such as distrust of men and sexual dysfunction" are typical of the long-range difficulties that female concrete operational children are likely to experience, according to Henggeler and Cohen (1984:184). Because they are more cognizant of the social customs and prevailing mores, these children will suffer more intense and socially related guilt, possibly even becoming socially withdrawn. Therefore, they will require not only stronger emotional support, but also direct therapeutic effort to help them with the resolution of their intense feelings of guilt and to reestablish their sense of social connection. Henggeler and Cohen conclude with a concise statement of the main point, which is that "the individual's cognitive level dictates the person's comprehension of his or her own behavior, the operation of the system, and the intervention process"(188).

INTEGRATING PIAGET AND PSYCHOANALYSIS

There have been several previous attempts to interweave Piaget's genetic epistemology with psychoanalysis (Anthony 1956, 1957, 1976; Basch 1977; Colbiner 1967; Wolff 1960). The most comprehensive effort toward this goal can be found in the work of Greenspan (1979). Greenspan's primary aim has been to synthesize the two systems to form a unified model of human development, subsuming what he metaphorically refers to as an internal ego boundary and external ego boundary. The former is comprised of drives, wishes, feelings, internal representations, and affect-laden interpersonal relationshps; traditional interests of psychoanalysis. The latter is constituted by stimuli from the impersonal or physical world from which knowledge of reality is constructed; Piaget's major focus of attention. The model is proposed as one that can assist in comprehending both normal and psychopathological development, with ultimate utility for guiding the selection of clinical interventions.

Although structural development with regard to internal and external ego boundaries is said to be symmetrical, both being guided by the same basic processes, there may be differences in their rate of developmental progression and functional level. This is largely true because the internal ego boundary is subject to the vicissitudes of drives, affects, and relationships, hence is characterized by greater stimuli variability than the less variable impersonal stimuli of the external boundary.

The Piagetian view on the adaptive function of equilibrium plays a central role in Greenspan's attempt toward integration. At each succeeding level of equilibrium the individual achieves a greater mobility, stability, permanence, and field of application. At the highest level of equilibrium, that afforded by formal operations, new experiences are readily assimilated without disturbance or the need for further structural reorganization. Greenspan suggests that the equilibrium construct holds for the individual's emotional and interpersonal development, the realm of the internal ego boundary, as well as for his impersonal world. He thus links psychological maturity characterized by ego flexibility to the highly developed equilibrium state of cognitive structures in Piagetian terms. Despite the perturbations of strong impulses, intense affect, and disruptive interpersonal relationships, the ego flexibility of the psychologically mature person will succeed in restoring and maintaining psychic equilibrium. The optimal level of equilibrium characterizing formal operations is to be viewed more as an ideal for the emotional realm than as an achieveable goal, however. This is because of the aforementioned variability of drives, affect, and interpersonal relationships in sharp contrast to the relative immutability of the physical world. Further, since the internal ego boudnary is subject to ongoing changes throughout life, there is no closure on its psychological structures, which may continue to develop and mature. Throughout development there is a reciprocal interaction between the external and internal ego boundaries. Cognitive development provides structures and rules for emotional organization, whereas affects and drives influence the pace of cognitive development and may be instrumental in restricting the application of existing cognitive structures to particular domains in the external world.

Greenspan's formulations offer a fine-grained stage-by-stage analysis of the symmetrical and interactive development of both cognitive and emotional intelligence. A few aspects will be presented here for the purposes of illustration. With the advent of concrete operations, the latency child acquires cognitive structures for seriation, classification, and conservation. Reversible thinking, a hallmark of operational thought, is now available to him. The development of classification structures enables the child to order his feelings in a more coherent way. By being able to classify the objects of his feelings he can discriminate and generalize them more effectively. When angry at both mother and father, he knows he is angry at his parents. If he is also angry at his siblings, then he can know that he is angry at members of his family. Yet he can conceptually distinguish between family and friends, knowing that to be angry at his family members is not necessarily to be angry at nonfamily members. The classification structure also permits the child to recognize negative feelings for a family member as subordinate to the superordinate feeling of love and security reserved for the family as a whole. Thus the negative feeling does not predominate or disrupt the child's basic connection to the family unit. Seriation structures enable him to recognize relative degrees of feeling, knowing now that he may love someone more or less, rather than think in terms of absolutes such as either loving or hating someone. He may now also seriate his feelings toward a number of people, knowing that he cares for some more than others or that he dislikes some people less than he dislikes others. Especially important is the application of conservation to the latency child's object representations and interpersonal world. Greenspan comments, "Compared with his preoperational counterpart, one would expect him to have a more established concept of conservation in terms of the maintenance of stable object representations across the stresses and strains of interpersonal life. Extrapolating this principle in regard to his dealing with peers, we would expect him to feel stable, in the sense of having a more constant sense of identity across various peer relationships and across situations of peer and familial stress and separation" (1979:182). Reversible thinking enables the child to realize that hating someone today does not preclude liking or loving him at some other time. Although adults may be capable of reversible thinking about the physical world, as Greenspan points out, some of them are informed by their level of emotional intelligence that hating is forever, which is to say, that the feeling is irreversible.

Greenspan also illuminates our understanding of defenses by suggesting a hierarchy of defense mechanisms, each set emerging at the corresponding level of cognitive development. For example, he sees a distinct resemblance between reaction formation and reversibility. One child who hates another may unconsciously transform the feeling so that he consciously feels he loves that other person. Greenspan states, "This appears to be a type of reversibility by reciprocity, as if the equilibrium state of the ego can be maintained only by compensation for a powerful negative affect" (p. 181). Reciprocal action is also manifest in projection; for example, "I hate you" becomes "You hate me." In the defense of denial we see negation or inversion. "I hate you" becomes "I do not hate you." Hence, reversible thinking provides the structure for certain defense mechanisms at a particular level of complexity. Greenspan's unified model includes an informative explication of emerging defenses from the more primitive projection, denial, and ego splitting to the more advanced defenses of intellectualization and sublimation. Each emerging defense is linked to progressive cognitive transformations through successive stages of development.

As the latency child develops he begins to manifest a clear ability, in the realm of his internal ego boundary, to perceive connections between past events in his life and his current behavior. He also begins to see connections between his past and present emotional life and the events surrounding them. His capacity for grasping several variables either operating in the present or across time from his past to the present increases. At the latency stage, however, his ability to integrate multiple variables is limited, as is his ability to anticipate future possibilities. The emergence of formal operations during adolescence introduces hypothetical reasoning, combinatorial thinking, and higher-order reversible cognition, which integrates into one cognitive system both the inverse and the reciprocal. Greenspan develops the point of view that these attainments of impersonal intelligence potentially empower the internal ego boundary to achieve the same high-order equilibrium that it provides for the external ego boundary. In doing so it permits the adolescent entering the formal operational period a greater degree of self-awareness. Because the concrete operational child is more likely to construe his internal stirrings as real, they have the power to be more frightening. Therefore, the latency child invokes "a strict repressive barrier, reinforced by such defenses as reaction formation, denial, and isolation of affect" (p. 212). The formal operational thinker, in contrast to the latency child, is not confined to reasoning about what is real, but can open his thought up to an infinite variety of possibilities. Greenspan compares latency and adolescence:

The adolescent may need to disguise his internal world but not necessarily to repress it fully as does the latency child. He can view his internal world in a propositional sense and in a hypothetical sense; thus it is not necessarily real. Rage does not lead to killing; oedipal feelings do not lead to the act of incest; yearnings do not necesarily lead to fusion. The adolescent then, can scan his internal boundary with his new cognitive capacities. (pp. 212–213)

Greenspan demonstrates how the range and permutations of feelings are greatly increased in the adolescent with the advent of the INRC structure and combinatorial thinking. Emotional intelligence becomes increasingly more flexible in its growing ability to tolerate and balance many disparate variables, including oppositional feelings toward the same person and self-representations that are at variance with one another. The ego flexibility involved here is derived from the same transformational principles of equilibrium that govern cognition in the impersonal world.

The inability to integrate discordant elements is characteristic of a wide range of clinical patients. Greenspan is one of a pioneer group of professionals who are beginning to urge that clinical intervention start with an assessment of the patient's level of structural development. Following this, intervention designed and selected to supply or promote specifically what is needed should be implemented. His unifying concept of equilibrium cuts across therapeutic approaches, as one can assess equilibrium level both before and after intervention regardless of which method for helping is adopted, be it psychodynamic, behavioral, or cognitive.

INSIGHT AND THE GRASP OF CONSCIOUSNESS

In contrast to Greenspan's comprehensive approach to integrating Piaget and psychoanalysis, Tenzer (1983) has taken a limited, although vital, domain from psychoanalysis as a therapeutic method and has explored the extent to which it is similar to one of Piaget's more recently developed theoretical concepts. Specifically, she has advanced the premise that the very process of achieving insight during the analytic procedure is for the patient analogous to the developing child's grasp of consciousness, as studied by Piaget (1974/1976a). Questions are raised regarding whether Piaget's experiments on the grasp of consciousness can offer guidelines pertaining to the preconditions for insight and its actual facilitation in the process of psychoanalysis. Both insight and the grasp of consciousness are viewed as processes shifting the balance of psychic organization in a way that renders the unconscious conscious, followed by a reorganization and integration of the newly achieved consciousness in such a way that it expands the individual's autonomy. The attainment of insight is not automatic or instantaneous, but rather is isomorphic with the four stages leading to the grasp of consciousness, which Piaget has delineated with much greater precision than has psychoanalysis.

Tenzer suggests that as a precondition to insight there must be appropriate affect and readiness. It will be recalled that in Piagetian terms there is no cognition without affect, as the two are simply different aspects of the same phenomenon. Affect energizes the activation of cognition. The process derives impetus from interest and curiosity. Another source of the affective component is the disturbance experienced in the face of perceived incongruity or contradiction. The type of understanding attainable is dependent upon the level of readiness or cognitive maturity of the individual. Such activities as self-observation and reflective abstraction, to be discussed below, are contingent upon a certain degree of declining egocentrism and the form of logical reasoning respectively, which appear at about eleven or twelve years of age. A gross disparity between the individual's form of cognitive organization and an interpretation will prevent the interpretation from being effectively assimilated, regardless of how accurate it may be.

The four stages of insight in Tenzer's thesis, isomorphic to Piaget's stages in his research on the grasp of consciousness, are: unconscious behavior or behavioral change, the working-through process, the stimulation of self-observation, and ultimately integration and reorganization promoted by reflective abstraction. In a series of experiments, Piaget (1974/1976a) illustrates these stages very well. A given experiment would require that the child carry out an action and subsequently request that he provide a verbalization conceptualizing how he achieved the goal of the action. What became apparent in the course of these experiments was that children were able to successfully perform certain actions without being able to verbalize the reasoning strategy guiding their own activity. Hence, prior to one's conscious awareness of his own cognitive ability, there would appear to be knowledge outside of awareness guiding his behavior. This is true for adults, as well as for children. Of course, such a theme is not new in Piaget's work with its roots in the sensorimotor period where we observe practical intelligence as the forerunner to conceptual intelligence. However, in the recent experiments on the grasp of consciousness, Piaget demonstrates the unfolding of the stages in each individual child as he interacts with the experimenter, who encourages him to observe and reflect upon what he is doing. For Piaget, consciousness or cognizance is not merely a matter of casting light upon content lodged in an unconscious. In commenting upon the process of making the unconscious conscious, he states, "The passage from one to the other must require reconstructions and cannot be reduced simply to a process of illumination" (1974/1976a:332). In

Piaget's system the very process of becoming conscious transforms that which one becomes conscious of, and this in turn imparts more adaptiveness to the individual. However, first attempts at conceptualizing the knowledge implicit in one's action schemes are not necessarily successful. If what one observes contradicts preexisting belief schemes, then even accurate perceptions may be rejected and initial attempts at conceptualization may produce distortions and misunderstanding. Piaget compares this to a situation in which an unconscious desire clashes with the conscious demands of the superego and is, therefore, prevented from being integrated and organized within the conscious system.

Let us now examine the particular Piagetian experiment that Tenzer has selected to illustrate the four stages leading to consciousness and the connections she draws to insight in the psychoanalytic process. Children of varying ages were asked to swing around a ball from a string attached to it. Their task was to release the ball on the string so that it would land in a box that was located directly before them. The task was repeated several times and the children were asked to notice at which point they had to release the ball for it to fall into the box. They were requested to convey their observations to the experimenter. Children below seven years of age, even when successful at getting the ball into the box, were essentially egocentric in their responses, emphasizing their own positions and personal force rather than the direction the ball was being rotated and the release point in space. Further, there was no uniformity in their responses. Children at ages seven and eight were consistent in getting the ball to land in the box. Behaviorally, they were releasing the ball at an angle so that it traveled through an arc to reach its destination. Nevertheless, they not only reported that they had released the ball at a point directly in front of the box, but they insisted on this explanation even after making correct observations in subsequent attempts. In other words, when what they saw was contradicted by what they believed, they rejected what they saw. Nevertheless, their unconscious action schemes continued to correctly guide their behavior. When the experimenter carried out the action, the children were sometimes able to accurately identify the release point, even though they could not verbalize the correct explanation when they carried out the action. Children from eight to ten began to manifest a dawning awareness of the correct conceptualization for the task. At least some of these children began to acknowledge that perhaps the ball was not being released from directly in front of the box. Yet when the experimenter would seek greater precision by suggesting that the ball had been released at a forty-five-degree angle which he indicated in space, while some children initially agreed, they swiftly went back to their original interpretation. The regressive pull of their strong preexisting notion was still too great for the children to cope with the evidence of their own self-observations on the suggestion of the experimenter. By eleven to twelve years of age the children either immediately verbalized the explanation correctly by virtue of their capacity at inference or they quickly revised their formulation to a more accurate one after only a few repetitions accompanied by self-observation. The contradiction between prior belief and self-observation, which had previously led to maintaining a false belief, no longer existed. In drawing attention to the greater difficulty in achieving consciousness of this experiment over another not involving a preconceived belief, Tenzer comments:

It was harder because of the overwhelming need to fit new experience in with prior expectations, to pattern it, to make sense of it. It is clear from this experiment how strong this need for organization is and how strong a hold it has in the face of contradictory evidence. What does not make sense in terms of a current belief system is selectively inattended or repressed. (1983:326)

In the final stage of the experiment completely integrated consciousness was achieved through reflective abstraction. As Tenzer points out, the youngsters at stage 4 had not only to describe their actions correctly, but also to employ reasoning that invoked the concept of throwing at an angle so that the ball would follow the trajectory of an arc. The reasoning process imbues the situation with new meaning and leads to the revision of a prior, but false, belief scheme.

Drawing upon Piaget's research on consciousness, Tenzer forges out her view of the four stages leading to insight. Starting with the stage of unconscious behavior, she adopts the Piagetian position that there is a logic of action not yet known to consciousness and that the road to consciousness involves a series of reconstructions at successively higher planes. The unconscious behavior of psychoanalysis in which there is implicit knowledge includes "free association, dreams, parapraxes, and other acts" (p. 330). The second stage of "working through" is founded upon the belief of both Freud and Piaget that there are degrees of consciousness, but it especially emphasizes Piaget's interactive process of reconstruction. There occurs transient glimpses of the unconscious "through an enlarging of intrapsychic and interpersonal frames of reference" (p. 330). The patient, however, must be highly motivated and determined to pursue the analytic process, for as we have seen in Piaget's work, the strength of prior belief will at first lead to a swift rejection of the newly glimpsed knowledge. The third stage of "self-observation" witnesses the ability to obtain a greater hold in consciousness of emerging structures, but is primarily limited to the individual's increased awareness of his own behavior. This is a prelude to the final stage of "reflective abstraction," in which the capacity for meta-reflection on one's own behavior produces a high order of abstract, conscious knowledge that is organized and integrated in such a way as to lend increased adaptiveness and meaning to the total system. The attainment of insight at this level, in Tenzer's formulation, permits the individual a wider range of choice and generalization.

It is Tenzer's conviction that Piaget's work suggests that a relatively active role on the part of the therapist would be more efficacious than a passive one. She concludes this on the basis of the facilitating activities of the experimenter in the Piagetian studies on the child's grasp of consciousness. Analyst and experimenter are likened to one another in that both are endeavoring to foster accommodation of patient and subject to new knowledge or experience and do so by highlighting the many inconsistencies that characterize his existence. Briefly, in Tenzer's own words, "Piaget's work thus lends support to the view that gaining insight requires the active involvement of both patient and analyst, especially with respect to analysis of the transference" (p. 334). Voyat (1983) suggests that the interaction between patient and analyst may be subject to the same principles of equilibration, with its self-regulating characteristics, as is true for the individual patient in the process of acquiring insight. Both Tenzer and Voyat discuss the question of the relative developmental levels between patient and analyst in the psychoanalytic process. While it is important for the analyst to be at a higher level than the patient, it is essential that the former design interpretations that are an appropriate match for the patient from a cognitive-developmental stand-point. Failure to do so would result in the patient ignoring or rejecting the interpretation. Should this occur it would be a mistake to view the patient's behavior as resistance in the traditional psychodynamic sense, as the explanation would actually reside in the patient's cognitive inability to assimilate and accommodate the interpretation in its presented form.

ASSIMILATION AND ACCOMMODATION
IN PSYCHOTHERAPY

Piaget's biologically rooted model or metaphor, if you wish, of adaptation can be applied from several perspectives in exploring the field and process of psychotherapy. Adaptation consists of an equilibrated balance between assimilation and accommodation; between understanding the environment in terms of preexisting structures that provide meaning to external stimuli and the modification or invention of structures in response to the demand characteristics of that environment. Hence, adaptation simultaneously affords continuity and change, as neither assimilation nor accommodation ever occur in isolation. Yet we may examine phenomena from the standpoint of whether they lean more heavily toward one or another end of the adaptational pole. Upon considering the great diversity of psychotherapeutic schools which each therapist is faced with, we can readily appreciate that he may tend toward being assimilative or accommodative.

An assimilative therapist is one who endorses a single school of psychotherapy as true and correct, while rejecting all others as false and incorrect. Any merit seen in other approaches will be understood not in its own terms, but instead will be translated into the conceptual language of the one true school. An extreme, perhaps even a caricature, of this will be seen in the therapist who does not even accommodate to those changes and refinements in his own therapeutic school, which are seen as deviating from the immutable insights of the school's originator. Something on the order of "splitting" seems to take place with an overly assimilative therapist, so that his original belief about the only correct way to view and conduct psychotherapy is seen as absolutely good, and all other ways of doing so are seen as absolutely bad. There are many therapists who are quite bright and creative within the framework of a monolithic model to which they subscribe and which they practice. On this scale they are operating at the formal operational level. Yet on an intermodel scale they function as if at a concrete operational level only. They proceed as if their adopted model is the only possible correct one and discount evidence supporting any other approach. Some therapists will practice on a concrete operational level even within their own model. They apply only what is already familiar and known to them, generate no new therapeutic maneuvers or tactics, and do not utilize the power of combinatorial analysis in developing treatment packages or modalities. Therapists who are dysfunctionally assimilative do not engage in metacognition about their own therapeutic premises and practices, thus remaining embedded in their own model, unaware of its limitations. Yet they are so often harshly critical of alternative models, often applying rigorous criteria of judgment that they would never self-reflexively bring to bear upon their own approach.

An accommodative therapist, on the other hand, is one who tends toward eclecticism, seeking to select the best that exists from a variety of systems. While this may appear to afford greater flexibility and diversity of options, there is a risk in the direction of achieving random chaos. Without a standard for selecting procedures from across systems, how is one to avoid a mere trial and error approach, perhaps even at great cost to the patient? An equilibrated resolution may be for the therapist to maintain continuity of practice along the lines of that which has been well established as effective in his own work and from among his chosen peers, while at the same time being willing to modify his therapeutic framework by integrating or at least experimenting with new research findings that evidence empirical validation and replication. Traditional psychotherapy seems to be one of the few fields in which its practitioners are not eager to systematically incorporate the benefits of research into everyday practice. Admittedly, however, the fruits of research are rarely definitive and there remain serious methodological issues that must seek solutions adapted to the complex and unique nature of psychotherapy.

It is also possible to look at a single model of psychotherapy from the standpoint of whether it is inherently more assimilative or accommodative in relation to the patient. Both existentialism and Rogerian therapy have a strong accommodative leaning in the sense that the therapist's task is to understand the client or patient in his own terms and not through the prism of a content-based prior theory. They are process oriented rather than concept oriented. Rollo May, an outstanding existential psychotherapist, has recently stated that "the existential analysis movement is a protest against the tendency to see the patient in forms tailored to our own preconceptions or to make him over into the image of our own predilections" (1983:45). For May and the existentialists generally, the understanding of the patient which is sought is to be in terms of that individual patient's unique structure of being-in-the-world and not basically in terms of preexisting notions of instincts, forces, and dynamisms. Psychoanalysis has a strong assimilating character in that whatever the unique features of the individual patient, they will be organized and given meaning in terms of such theoretical constructs as libido, oedipal complex, superego, and resistance, to name a few. Radical behaviorism is also strongly assimilative, despite its vast differences from psychoanalysis otherwise, in that the client is expected to change behavior in conformity with preestablished criteria of personal and social adjustment. Remembering that neither assimilation nor accommodation exists without the other, a more fine-grained analysis would reveal that component not mentioned above in the exposition of each approach. For example, radical behavior therapy when properly conducted would entail a detailed behavioral analysis which is highly accommodative to the individual's unique history and life space. Psychoanalysis is certainly accommodative in its efforts to uncover the individual patient's distinctive wishes, fantasies, perceptions, thoughts, feelings, and fears. Further, existentialism is assimilative in that a successful existential analysis anticipates that ultimately the individual will assume responsibility for his own becoming, authenticicy, freedom, and choice. Lastly, despite Rogers' emphasis upon accommodating to the phenomenological meaning system of the client, observers have commented upon the fact that the individual in client-centered therapy is conditioned during the verbal interplay and, therefore, moves in the direction of talking more about those themes for which the therapist provides social reinforcement and less about themes for which he is not reinforced. Notice the reciprocal nature of the topic that has been under discussion. Where the model is assimilative, it is the patient who must do the accommodating, and vice versa.

It is possible to view the dyadic relationship between therapist and patient from the standpoint of an assimilation-accommodation model, as we have begun to see. The patient is prone to recreate in the therapeutic context the very same type of interpersonal relationship that has been so distressful to him outside the clinical office. Most of the patient's behavior may serve as a self-fulfilling prophecy. For example, anticipating rejection from other people, he may act in a cool and aloof, if not openly hostile, manner from the outset of new relationships. Potential friends, sensing this distancing behavior, do not respond warmly and back off from further contact. The patient has then reaffirmed his prediction that people tend to reject him, unaware of his own role in bringing about an event that would not have occurred were it not for his own expectation (Jones 1977). The therapist has the opportunity to resist being assimilated into the patient's interpersonal rejection schema. By not repeating the stereotypical behavior the patient is accustomed to, by sustaining warmth and continued presence in the face of the patient's aloofness, the therapist disconfirms experientially the patient's expectation. The therapist has become a benign intrusion in the patient's environment, thereby throwing the latter off balance into a state of disesquilibrium. As Block formulates it, "Cognitive disequilibration is . . . an indication to the individual that the world, or a portion of it, does not make sense or have meaning and is therefore not predictable or manageable" (1982:290). The predominance of assimilating others, at least one other, to the patient's interpersonal rejection schema has been interfered with, and the patient is faced with the necessity of revising his schema. In other words, accommodation to the new reality must take place. Even the neophyte therapist will realize that this is not a simple or automatic process, however. A predominance of assimilation does not yield readily. The patient may initially attempt to explain this new encounter by such assimilating rationalizations as "You're only being nice to me because you're getting paid for it." Eventually, however, within the matrix of a successful therapeutic alliance it becomes overwhelmingly apparent that this is not an adequate explanation, and a more adaptive balance of understanding emerges. The patient's ability to predict another's reaction to him will be regained, but based on new experiences and a modified interpersonal schema his expectations will be different.

There is also the danger that the patient in therapy will be dysfunctionally accommodative. In his effort to please the therapist and perhaps ward off rejection and retaliation, however unrealistic such an anticipation may be, the patient is sometimes overly conforming. He may accept all interpretations without question, quickly master the language of the therapist's model, and verbalize comments which seem to convincingly suggest that he is changing his views in a desired direction. The therapist must be vigilant against being reduced to thinking that this necessarily signifies genuine change. Such misleading accommodative behavior has its counterpart in Piagetian phenomena. The preconservation child can tell you that there are ten pennies spread evenly in a top row and ten pennies condensed closer together in a bottom row. Yet despite his ability to count numbers accurately, he lacks conservation structures and will tell you that there are more pennies in the top row than the bottom row. Without structural change, verbalization can be misleading. Indeed, how many students memorize words which they string alongside one another in examinations, yet do not have a true conceptual understanding of that about which they are writing?

The therapist must maintain a sound measure of equilibrium, avoiding any protracted predominance of either assimilation or accommodation, as well as be willing to risk temporary disequillibrium. If he is overly involved in the patient's phenomenological world, he may lose sight of the path to reality and become powerless to lead the way back. If he is preoccupied with his own map of the world and techniques for change, the patient will more than likely come to feel misunderstood and manipulated. If a given procedure or technique is not working, then rather than persist in attempting to assimilate the patient to it, the effective therapist had better begin to think about a modified or inventive approach that accommodates to the patient. The therapist unwilling to experience disequilibrium in the therapy will unconsciously institute behaviors that will inhibit the patient's full and appropriate expression of feeling. It is well known that some therapists have a problem expressing and encountering anger, for example. Such therapists may send to their patients subliminal messages, which are designed to avert any open expression of hostility, thereby constricting the field upon which the therapeutic game is played. The therapist who is aware of such a vulnerability in himself and willing to experience the disequilibrium of encountering powerful emotion in the other may not only facilitate therapeutic gain for his patient but may also find himself growing through the process of reequilibration. The ensuing growth is bound to feed back into the therapeutic process, thereby providing further benefit to the patient.

Piaget (1954/1981) has applied the assimilation-accommodation model to the central concept of transference in psychoanalysis. In the phenomenon of transference, "a displacement has taken place; impulses, feelings, and defenses pertaining to a person in the past have been shifted onto a person in the present. It is primarily an unconscious phenomenon, and the person reacting with transference feelings is in the main unaware of the distortion. . . . The transference reaction is unsuitable in the current context; but it was once an appropriate reaction to a past situation" (Greenson 1967:154). Transference reactions are repetitive of feelings that originated with significant care givers, such as parents, from the person's early history. In Freud's account of transference, the early nucleus of feeling involved in an object relationship somehow survives intact as originally experienced in the unconscious. Years later, the same feeling may be reactivated in a variety of contexts, triggered by someone such as an authority figure. Piaget discounts the view of an old feeling persisting in an unconscious reservoir, being periodically activated and flooding into consciousness. He proposes an alternate conceptualization, which is that "it is not feeling that is conserved but a certain scheme of interaction with other people. Feeling, properly speaking, appears, disappears, and oscillates in intensity not because it sinks into or emerges from the unconscious but because it is created, then dissipates, then is recreated. In other words, it is constructed or reconstructed on each occasion" (Piaget 1954/1981:50–51). It is the interpersonal scheme, developed from early previous experiences, that persists and evolves to which the new figure in the present is assimilated in the transference. As Piaget states, "Our hypothesis is that interpersonal schemes make the subject react to people in more or less constant fashion in analogous situations even though the persons he is interacting with may vary" (p. 51).

Wachtel (1981), continuing in his tradition as an integrator and reconciliator of disparate views (Wachtel 1977), elaborates upon Piaget's reformulation of transference in an attempt to extend the clinical utility of the concept. He argues against factionalizing the relationship between patient and therapist into that of transference, a working alliance, and the real relationship (Greenson 1967). These components of the existing relationship can be unified, yet their differences appreciated, by viewing them through the concept of an interpersonal scheme with both assimilative and accommodative functions. In effect, Wachtel is suggesting that aspects of the patient-therapist relationship be construed as existing along a continuum, with unrealistic, fantasy-bound responses to the therapist at one end and adaptive, reality-bound responses at the other end. An interpersonal schema has the potential for this range because, like all schemas, it embodies both assimilative and accommodative functions. Transference schemas have their origin in the individual's early development. When assimilation is greatly predominant, then it is the unrealistic, fantasy-bound end of the continuum which is actively distorting the situation. This excessive assimilation is what constitutes the transference reaction. Nevertheless, by invoking the schema concept, what Wachtel is seeking to highlight is that even in a schema where assimilation overwhelmingly predominates, thus producing a transference reaction, there must be some accommodation occurring, as neither function can occur in total exclusion of the other. By examining this small but certain sector of accommodation, significant aspects of the patient's interpersonal dynamics can be brought to light. Taking into account the accommodative pole of the transference schema corrects for the oversight that comes about by viewing transference reactions as purely archaic and historical feelings preserved in their pristine form and surfacing from the unconscious for each occasion. Wachtel formulates it in the following manner: "The postulation of a somewhat malleabale and responsive structure, built on the basis of prior experience, but shaped as well by new experiences that do not quite fit, would permit a reconciliation and synthesis of observations of 'distortion' in the transference and observations of accurate perceptions and of realistic, cooperative engagement in the analytic process" (1981:66). Wachtel develops the argument that since anxiety and conflict are at the root of transference reactions which will be of most interest to the analyst, it is likely that the patient will defend himself from the anxiety by conveying aspects of his relationship with the therapist obliquely. What is conveyed will seem so unrealistic and distorted that if the therapist is unattuned to the accommodative end of the pole, he will ignore what there is in the present situation that the patient is responding to, thus losing valuable information that is potentially available. Vigilance in this area permits the therapist to discern what it is in the present situation and his own being or style that is activating the transference. Such information then becomes a clue to the patient's interpersonal behavior outside the clinical office, and further use can be made of it in the therapeutic process.

PIAGETIAN PERSPECTIVES ON COGNITIVE THERAPY

Theory and Practice of Cognitive Therapy. The field of cognitive therapy is a rapidly developing one encompassing a variety of models (Beck 1976; Kendall and Hollon 1979; Mahoney 1974; Meichenbaum 1977; Spivack, Platt, and Shure 1976). Raimy (1975) has advanced the thesis that all therapeutic gains can essentially be accounted for by a cognitive change in the patient regardless of what type of therapy he has been experiencing. Two major pioneers in the field are Kelly (1955) and Ellis (1962). Although a small band of people (Adams-Webber and Mancuso 1983; Epting 1984) continue to amplify the work of Kelly, his personal construct theory has not had widespread influence. The work of Ellis, in contrast, not only remains vigorous on the contemporary American scene, but his influence has been pervasive, particularly among psychologists and nonmedical therapists generally (Ellis and Greiger 1977; Walen, Di Giuseppe, and Wessler 1980). Arieti (1980) and Bieber (1980), both psychoanalysts, have each developed a distinctive cognitive orientation which characterizes their respective psychotherapeutic approaches. Applications to cognitive therapy are being extended to children at an accelerated pace (Meyers and Craighead 1984), and new directions for the application continue to be enthusiastically explored (Emery, Hollon and Bedrosian 1981; Freeman 1984). Until recently an omission in the literature has been the imparting of a cognitive-developmental perspective to the theory and practice of cognitive therapy. There is a beginning shift in this area as can be witnessed in the recent work of Bobbitt and Keating (1983), Cohen and Schleser (1984), and Gholson and Rosenthal (1984). The emphasis in each of these works is upon children. Guidano and Liotti (1983) have begun to integrate a cognitive-developmental approach into a cognitive therapy model for work with adult populations.

The most theoretically sophisticated and heuristic model of cognitive therapy currently available for the treatment of adult populations has been evolving for more than twenty years through the efforts of Aaron Beck and his colleagues at the Center for Cognitive Therapy at the University of Pennsylvania. A profile of the model will be presented here, followed by an attempt to elaborate upon some aspects of it from a Piagetian perspective. Beck started out as a practicing psychoanalyst, gradually shifting toward a cognitive orientation as he began to reconceptualize feedback from his clinical work. He is an internationally renowned expert on the treatment and theory of depression (Beck 1967; Beck, Rush, Shaw, and Emery 1979). A good deal of the literature on applying Beck's cognitive therapy model is on the subject of treating depressed populations. Work in this area has been well researched and the results are very promising, lending considerable credibility to the cognitive therapy approach (Kovacs 1980; Kovacs, Rush, Beck, and Hollon 1981; Rush, Beck, Kovacs, and Hollon 1977; Wright and Beck 1983). Presently being conducted is a multi-million-dollar research project, sponsored by the National Institute of Mental Health, designed to investigate the comparative efficacy of cognitive therapy, interpersonal therapy, and psychopharmacological agents in the treatment of depression (Waskow, Hadley, Parloff, and Autry 1979). Although to date its greatest empirical support is derived from the research on treating depression, cognitive therapy has been extended to many other areas with apparent good results. These include the treatment of anxiety, phobias, loneliness, addiction, sexual dysfunction, and disturbed interpersonal relationships. A critical appraisal of Beck's theory has been offered by Coyne and Gotlib (1983).

The profile of Beck's cognitive therapy model as presented here is not intended to be exhaustive. It will, however, outline the basic principles and constructs that guide the therapy. Paramount to conducting cognitive therapy is socializing the patient into adopting the personal scientist metaphor. In keeping with this metaphor, the patient is encouraged to view his own unsubstantiated thoughts and feelings not as certain indicators of truth or fact, but as hypotheses to be held tentatively while subjected to rational scrutiny and behavioral experimentation. He is taught to bring logic to bear upon his dysfunctional beliefs and feelings, to seek out evidence relevant to them, and to design experiments to test them out whenever possible. Because he *feels* guilty or worthless does not mean that he *is*, by any objective standard. Because he thinks that others view him with disrespect does not prove that they actually do. Because he anticipates that he will be turned down should he apply to college or ask a pretty woman out to dinner, it does not follow that either will necessarily occur. In inviting the patient to adopt the personal scientist metaphor, the therapist dissuades the patient from maintaining his former stance of certitude, or rather pseudo-certitude, toward his own thoughts, feelings, and expectations. In this process the patient achieves distancing from his dysfunctional cognitions as opposed to being embedded in and governed by them. The objectivity acquired by distancing affords him greater leverage in attempting to change his cognitions. Similarly, greater objectivity is sought by facilitating a decentering process in which the patient moves away from conceiving of himself as the focal point of external events. He is taught to separate himself from events that occur to other people so that he does not automatically suffer vicarious anxiety, for example, when an accident occurs to a friend. Further, as he learns to decenter he discontinues interpreting neutral events as if they were somehow designed to inconvenience him, such as when there is a storm on a day he had planned to go on a picnic. The underlying spirit of the personal scientist metaphor is nicely captured by Wright and Beck in stating, "The task of therapy is to rekindle curiosity, inquiry, and rationality" (1983:1122).

At the core of the theory undergirding cognitive therapy is the postulate that cognitions[3] assume a major contributing role in the presence and maintenance of mood disorders. The acquisition of knowledge and ensuing belief systems is essential to the feelings we

3. Although this discussion will focus upon thoughts, imagery is a component of cognition which also contributes to mood changes. In particular, images of harm or danger will frequently produce anxiety.

experience. Particular feelings are not inevitable responses to events, but rather how we construe or interpret an event will greatly influence the type of feeling that will follow. For example, observing a racing ambulance accompanied by a shrill siren could lead to either sadness or anxiety at the thought of someone in distress or, alternatively, to a sense of security and relief at the thought that the public has such help and that it is on the way to assist the particular person in distress. Of course, there exist other possible constructs, as well. The depressed person has what Beck calls a negative cognitive triad, which consists of negative thoughts about the patient's own self, environmental conditions, and what the future holds for him. Themes of loss, self-deficiency, environmental deprivation, worthlessness, pessimism, and hopelessness are present in the cognitive triad. In the case of anxiety, it is more likely that a judgment of danger or threat to security has been made and the individual anticipates that physical or psychological harm will, therefore, come to him. Actions of others that are construed as unfair or a perpetration of injustice will produce a feeling of anger. The aim of cognitive therapy is not to eliminate all feelings, of course, but only those that are based on inaccurate or arbitrary interpretations *and* that are maladaptive.

Personal experiences over time lead to the acquisition of knowledge and beliefs which are stored in schemas, defined as durable cognitive structures. Schemas are described by Beck et al. as "the basis for screening out, differentiating, and coding the stimuli that confront the individual. He categorizes and evaluates his experiences through a matrix of schemas" (1979:13). Schemas, in turn, become guides for the individual's actions. Maladaptive cognitions are those that prevent a sense of well-being and overall functional behavior. They are generally founded upon distortions, spring from primitive schemas developed during early childhood experiences, and become the focus for change in the therapy. However, not all false cognitions are maladaptive, and it is not the task of the therapist to work with the patient on changing them if they are not (Kovacs and Beck 1978).

In Beck's theory of psychopathology there are essentially two levels of cognitions. The first and more fundamental level is that of the schema, which has been introduced above. The schema constitutes a deep structure of which the individual is not generally aware. It is variously referred to as a general rule, a premise, or a silent assumption. A schema is more general and abstract than a particular thought and does not rely for its existence upon an immediate context. Examples of schemas are as follows: 1) I must always be agreeable to be accepted; 2) If someone disagrees with me, it means he dislikes me; 3) When I am not being productive, I am worthless; 4) If I am not performing perfectly at whatever I am doing, then I am worthless. The second level of cognition is comprised of automatic thoughts, and thoughts of this type are either conscious or at least more readily accessible to consciousness than are schemas. An automatic thought, in contrast to schemas, is more specific, concrete, and contextualized. Something in the environment will generally trigger the automatic thought, yet it is rooted in a schema. For example, if the patient has had an encounter with someone who disagrees with him, the patient may then become sad, convinced that the other person dislikes and rejects him. It is as if he reasoned, "Jack disagreed with me [external event]. If someone disagrees with me it means he dislikes me [activated schema]. Therefore, Jack dislikes me [negative automatic thought]." The affect of sadness may then follow, particularly if the other person, Jack, is of special significance to the patient. Further negative cognitions may then follow, such as "No one will ever like me again," "I am unlikable," and "I was stupid to let Jack know what my opinions are." These in turn will produce additional and more intense negative affects.

An essential part of the therapy entails teaching the patient to identify these negative automatic thoughts which are triggered by environmental stimuli and shaped by the general pattern of the deeper structure or schemas. Clinical intervention at the point of cognition, eliminating dysfunctional automatic thoughts and revising basic distorted schemas or assumptions, leads to an improvement in specific feelings, overall emotional well-being, and behavioral performance. Schemas have been categorized into areas of work, love, approval, perfectionism, entitlement, and omnipotence (Burns 1980). Maladaptive cognitions are plausible to the patient, tend to be recurrent, cannot be easily willed away, seem at first to have no apparent antecedents, are private and specific to the individual, and are resilient in the face of contrary evidence (Kovacs and Beck 1978).

Cognitive therapy in practice tends to be relatively brief, usually lasting from about fifteen to twenty sessions. It is directive and structured, aiming toward both symptom reduction and prophylactic goals. The process is one of problem solving with an emphasis upon patient and therapist working in a collaborative relationship. The role of the therapist is a more active one than in traditional psychodynamic psychotherapy, as the therapist directly engages the patient in mutual dialogue during most of the session. Homework assignments constitute a regular feature of the therapy. Behavioral techniques form a significant part of the therapist's armamentarium, but the theoretical rationale is always to produce a cognitive shift as an outcome of the prescribed actions.

The early phase of cognitive therapy, with the exception of the severely depressed patient, focuses upon pinpointing negative automatic thoughts and promoting the patient's ability to come up with rational, adaptive responses to them. He is encouraged to ask such questions as the following: 1) "What is the evidence?" 2) "Are there other ways of looking at this?" 3) "Is it really so catastrophic even if it is true?" and 4) "What are the advantages and disadvantages of maintaining this belief?" The role of the therapist is to engage the patient in a Socratic dialogue through which the patient rationally examines and revises his negative automatic thoughts. As the therapy progresses, silent assumptions are brought to light and these also become subject to rational examination. With the severely depressed patient who may be completely inactive, behavioral techniques are employed initially to get him up and about, but this is quickly followed by the same cognitive procedures under discussion.

Encouraging the patient to design and execute a behavioral experiment to test out the patient's beliefs, premises, and expectations is a major strategy utilized by the cognitive therapist. Should the patient's negative prediction be disconfirmed, a frequent occurrence, the feedback provides a compelling basis for him to challenge and reconsider his own assumptions. If it should not be disconfirmed, the therapist then has an opportunity to review the patient's behavior during the experiment with him to see if there are deficits or flaws in his behavioral repertoire which need to be attended. This review often discloses further dysfunctional cognitions.

Observations from a Piagetian Perspective. If Jean Piaget were to have developed a model for therapeutic practice based upon his research and epistemological theories, would he have designed something on the order of Aaron Beck's approach to cognitive therapy? While we will never have a definitive answer to this question, there does seem to be a very close affinity between the two systems even though the objectives of the originators differ. Beck is informed on the subject of Piaget's work and does refer to him in some of his own literature (Beck 1967; Beck et al. 1979; Wright and Beck 1983). However, there is little in the way of elaboration on points of contact between them. In this section I shall expand upon Beck's comments on Piaget, as well as contribute some additional ones, in the belief that doing so will flesh out a complementary aspect of Beck's evolving model.

The personal scientist metaphor adopted by Beck and other cognitive therapists (Kelly 1955; Mahoney 1977) is congruent with Piaget's image of a growing person. Motivationally there is a "need to know" wired into every human organism and a "need to function" characterizing every schema. As early as the fifth stage of the sensorimotor period we find Piaget referring to the striving infant as a "little scientist" who seeks novelty and understanding of the environment through his actions upon it. Means-end behavior, essential to problem-solving activity, has its origins in the practical intelligence of the infant. Toward the end of the sensorimotor period the infant is inventing new means to solve problems by active experimentation with the environment. In defining the therapist's task as rekindling "curiosity, inquiry, and rationality," Wright and Beck (1983) are implicitly giving credence to Piaget's view on the indissociability of cognition and affect. For the therapeutic work to be effective, the cognitive activity of the patient must be "energized," to use Piaget's term, so that there is interest, commitment, and a volitional participation in the therapeutic collaboration between patient and therapist. It may be precisely when these affective aspects of cognition have not been genuinely rekindled that the therapist is faced with the bedeviling response "I know that intellectually, but I don't feel it."

The manner in which emotions are shaped by cognition in Beck's model is complemented by Kohlberg's cognitive-developmental theory. Beck emphasizes how different ways of construing a situation may produce differential emotional responses. Kohlberg's stage theory demonstrates how the same emotion may have differential cognitive-structural antecedents. Anxiety may be experienced at any moral stage by an individual transgressing the precepts governing that stage. The specific meaning of the anxiety, however, will be determined by the conception of morally correct behavior characterizing that stage. While a stage 1 person may be anxious because he fears he will be sent to jail, a stage 3 person will be anxious because he fears the disruption of a significant relationship, and a stage 4 person because he has failed to fulfill his duty properly. Hence, a developmental perspective sensitizes the clinician to seeking more specific information about the meaning of a given emotion to the individual and provides a cognitive-structural stage theory as a means for going about this with greater precision.

Kegan (1982) has demonstrated the same phenomenon in his research on depressed patients in which the emphasis is upon a sense of loss as a variable critical to the affect. In Kegan's neo-Piagetian paradigm of personality, what is lost at each stage of development is one's former self, but the individual who becomes stuck in the transition from one stage to the next has not yet regained a new self. Mourning the loss of an old self with no vision of gaining the more highly evolved self to follow, the patient has become depressed. He has lost the old balance that gave meaning and coherence to self and its relation to the world, but has not yet constructed the new balance that will impart greater meaning and coherence to the self-world relation.

Independently of Kegan, Beck (1981) has recently formulated some of his views on depression from the standpoint of a personality typology. Specifically, he has offered a classification of two personality types, the "autonomous" and the "socially dependent" or "sociotropic." The autonomous individual is less dependent upon social feedback and approval than is the sociotropic person, and the successful execution of his appropriate role in life is the source of his sense of self-worth. In contrast, the sociotropic individual is dependent upon maintaining relationships and approval from others for a sense of personal security, self-worth, and overall well-being. Beck makes the point that despite a superficial similarity of symptoms when individuals from either of these two personality types become depressed, there are actually significant differences that are predictable on the basis of which personality organization is involved. As he states it, "The specific symptoms may seem to be the same for the types of depression but on close questioning of the patient it becomes apparent that they take a different form and have a somewhat different meaning for the two groups" (1981:22). The depressed autonomous individual is preoccupied with thoughts of failure at not having lived up to role expectations and of being incompetent to achieve his goals. The depressed sociotropic individual is preoccupied with thoughts of being responsible for rupturing social bonds and of being socially undesirable. Beck recommends differential therapeutic foci following naturally from these two personality organizations and the cognitions typifying depressive symptomatology in each. In working with the depressed autonomous patient, emphasis upon the relationship, as such, is of less importance, whereas attention is given to helping him to engender a sense of personal accomplishment and competence. He should be helped to clarify and reach his goals, as well as to reevaluate and perhaps modify the assumptions from which they arise. In working with the depressed sociotropic patient, greater emphasis is placed upon a comfortable personal exchange in the relationship, and the work itself can be more introspective with less emphasis upon achieving career goals in the external world. Attention is given to the patient's cognitions regarding interpersonal relationships.

Returning now to Kegan (1982), we find that his research disclosed three types of depression of qualitatively different organizations. (Although he has elaborated two additional theoretical types, we will focus only upon those identified in his research with psychiatric patients.) Type A is characterized by a basic concern with the loss of getting one's own needs met or the expense involved in obtaining need gratification. Type B is typified by a basic concern with either having been abandoned and, hence, having lost an interpersonal relationship or suffering damage to the relationship. Type C has as its primary concern a failure to meet self-imposed standards or to maintain self-control and perform as expected. In each type, the individual equates self with that which is lost. The result, therefore, is that the loss is experienced as a loss of self without awareness that a new self will emerge. The resemblance between Kegan's types B and C to Beck's sociotropic and autonomous types, respectively, is striking. Kegan's research has gone a step beyond classification, however, and demonstrated a strong relationship between the types and Kohlbergian stages of development. He posits a relationship between stage 2 or 2–3 and the need-oriented depressive (type A), stage 3 or 3–4 and the interpersonal-oriented depressive (type B), and stage 4 or 4–5 and the role-oriented depressive (type C). The depressive types, from a cognitive-developmental viewpoint, constitute part of a stage hierarchy. Each stage is actually organized in the form of a subject-object balance.

Let us use the stage 3 interpersonal orientation as an example. Formally the stage 3 individual, while at stage 2, had been so embedded in his own needs that he could not reflect upon them to make them an object of knowledge, for he was subject to his needs, in Kegan's formulation. However, in the successful transition to stage 3, that which was subject or self, needs, now becomes object. At stage 3, needs become an object of knowledge; that which the new self is no longer embedded in can now be reflected upon. The transformation has widened the scope of the newly evolved self which, however, is now embedded in a conception of interpersonal relationship as constituting the subject or self-structure. At this stage, since the self is equated with relationship, the loss or damage of a significant relationship may be experienced as a loss of self. Each stage is organized as an equilibrated self-other or subject-object balance. The transition to the next higher stage involves a reequilibrated subject-object balance. With each successfully navigated transition the evolving self is freed from the constraints of its former structure only to take on new constraints at a higher level.

In Kegan's view, the evolving self is in a process of "meaning-making." The therapist's role is not simply to relieve the patient's pain, preserve or restore the homeostasis of a preferred stage, but rather it is to promote that very process of making meaning. It is said by Kegan that all clinical problems share a common feature: "They are all about the threat of the constructed self's collapse" (1982:275). The therapist must find a way to support the person as he navigates from the security of the old self through unchartered waters toward the construction of a new self. The patient does not know, but the therapist does, that there is land ahead upon which the construction can be founded. Only then can the old land be looked upon from a different perspective and understood with newfound freedom. Kegan cautions the cognitive-developmental therapist to avoid too narrowly construing his role as stimulating development from one stage to the next, for in doing so he may lose contact with the developing person, the meaning-maker himself. The therapist must adopt extraordinary empathic sensitivities as he assists the patient's growth through what is actually a natural developmental process. The strong empathic and phenomenological cast found in Kegan's exposition of developmental therapy is also an essential feature of cognitive therapy as formulated by Beck et al. (1979). Kegan argues against a neutral or arbitrary approach to therapeutic goal setting in favor of the natural developmental process he describes. He states, "Stages or evolutionary balances (the structure of made meanings) can be more or less better than each other; stages have a qualified validity. . . I *exercise* my judgment in my address to the experience of the new voice emerging, and I judge our mutual process according to whether or not the person is being presented the opportunity to move from a less evolved to a more evolved state"(1982:292).

The integrity of Beck's cognitive therapy model, its theory and techniques, can be maintained while at the same time imparting to it new direction and a set of meta-goals based upon Kegan's version of the Piaget-Kohlberg paradigm. It is conceivable that the strategy of fostering distancing and decentering in the patient supports movement in the direction of which Kegan speaks. Perhaps before the patient can achieve "objectivity" in certain areas of his life, he must transcend the old self and construct a new one to look back objectively upon the old. This would explain, for example, why the depressed patient with an autonomous personality organization can already exhibit distancing and objectivity with respect to interpersonal relationships, but not yet in relation to his roles and duties to which he remains subject. The process of helping him achieve objectivity may very well be that of creating a context for furthering the evolution of the patient's self.

A question that frequently arises is whether cognitive therapy is effective with people of average intelligence or is confined in its utility to people of above average intelligence only. Verbal reports from clinicians suggest that it is not necessary to be especially bright to benefit from the cognitive therapy process. A cognitive-developmental approach to the question would eschew a dichotomous phrasing of it. Two different patients may derive benefit from the same intervention, but the meaning of the intervention may vary depending upon their developmental level. For example, in a discussion of how his behavior may look from alternate perspectives (decentering), a patient who has achieved Selman's stage 4 of perspective taking would be able to adopt the viewpoint of a *generalized other* and thereby examine his behavior at a relatively abstract level, using as a standard the customs and laws of his society. A patient who has not gone beyond stage 2, although he would be able to take the view of another in the immediate environment, would not yet be able to coordinate that perspective of how his behavior would look to the other with his own perspective. The intervention could take the form of role playing or inductive questioning, both techniques being commonly employed by cognitive therapists. The point is that the general approach could be of some benefit to both patients, but their use of the intervention would be at different levels. In other instances there may be a developmental threshold below which a particular technique might be completely ineffective.

One tactic in cognitive therapy is to ask a patient, who exaggerates the significance of a minor event by repeatedly calling it terrible, to rank its "terribleness" on a scale from 1 to 100. It will usually be ranked quite high, let us say 85. The patient is then asked to rank a genuinely catastrophic event such as returning home to find his house, along with all his earthly possessions, burned to the ground. He may give this event a 90. At that point he is asked to compare the two events and their assigned ranks. The result usually is that the comparison drives home the point that the first event was comparatively inconsequential. The original ranking of the minor event is then revised downward. In utilizing this technique the therapist is invoking a seriation structure, although in a relatively weak form since only two events are being compared. The more events being ranked and compared, the more developed the structure would have to be. There is called into play here a reciprocal relation in that if event B is greater than A, then event A is less than B. A preoperational respondent would have difficulty with this technique, a concrete operational respondent should do well with it, and formal operations would simply not be necessary. However, as the technique becomes more conceptually complex, perhaps asking the patient to compare the ratio of two events in his life to two events in someone else's life, we would find formal operations necessary because of the proportionality structure called into play.

Another technique often used by cognitive therapists is to ask the patient who unnecessarily construes an event negatively to generate alternative ways of looking at the event. The concrete operational thinker will tend to cling to his original interpretation as if that were the only possible reality. He might, by extension, come up with one or two alternatives. In contrast, the formal operational thinker can not only come up with some alternatives, but as a result of possessing a combinatorial structure he can view his original interpretation as only one of the many that are possible and he can more systematically generate alternatives than less developed individuals. Of course, the more severe the pathology, the less likely even the formal operational patient will do this spontaneously. The main point is that he has the competence for doing it, as opposed to the more limited concrete operational patient. The degree to which any patient will bring to bear his fullest potential is in large measure a function of the therapist's skill.

We have previously noted the distinction between negative automatic thoughts and silent assumptions. The patient is taught to pinpoint his negative automatic thoughts, which are internal self-statements, by introspecting whenever he experiences distressing, maladaptive feelings. These thoughts tend to be specific, tied to environmental events, and relatively accessible to consciousness. Maladaptive silent assumptions are disclosed by exploring the meaning to the patient of particular automatic thoughts or by looking for fundamental themes that appear to cut across a cluster of automatic thoughts. Assumptions are abstract as in general rules or basic premises and must be inferred. While focusing upon automatic thoughts can produce fairly quick amelioration of the patient's distress, identifying and revising silent assumptions requires more time and may be necessary to achieve long-range preventive goals. Speculatively, we might consider the hypothesis that patients who are predominantly concrete operational in their thinking can work well at the level of negative automatic thoughts, but that at least some formal operational cognitive organization is a necessary, if not sufficient, condition for working at the deeper structural level of dysfunctional silent assumptions. If verified through empirical research, several clinical guidelines would be indicated. The first would be to adopt more limited and realistic goals in working with concrete operational patients. The second would be to stimulate cognitive development of such patients toward formal operations, once their initial distress has been relieved by focusing on automatic thoughts. The rationale of this strategy would be that formal operational capability would be seen as a precondition to effectively working on silent assumptions. The third guideline would be to design tactics for activating formal operational thought in those patients who would seem to have the competence (developmental attainment) of such thought, but who are not presently performing at that level in the area of concern. On the other hand, the way in which cognitive therapy is presently conducted is likely to promote the activation of dormant formal thought because it utilizes an inductive strategy, going from the known concrete reality of automatic thoughts to the abstract inferred structures of silent assumptions. In introducing new material to even a formal operational thinker, it is a sound principle derived from cognitive-developmental theory to go from the particular to the general, rather than to plunge right in at the abstract level.

In connection with the present discussion, a relevant analogy may be made to the appreciation and comprehension of poetry at its various levels and in relation to the subject's stage of cognitive development. Hardy-Brown conducted an experiment with thirty college students, each of whom were classified as being in one of three categories of cognitive development, as follows: concrete operational, transitional, and formal operational. She reported that "subject responses disclosed a range of ability to comprehend the symbolic level, and a sort of hierarchical categorizability of the responses reflecting increasing complexity of interpretation, and increasing integrative ability. The categories proceed from concrete to abstract interpretations of the poem's central figure (a jar) and from lesser to greater ability to suggest abstract, summarizing meanings for the poem" (1979:131). There was found to exist a strong positive relationship between a subject's stage of cognitive development and his ability to deal with more abstract, complex, and integrative aspects of the poem. A comparison between the cognitive ability to comprehend the text of a poem and the text of one's personal script is highly suggestive. Its applicability goes beyond that of cognitive therapy to encompass all of the psychotherapies.

Beck et al. (1979) and Burns (1980) have identified a set of cognitive distortions that are based on faulty reasoning patterns. These flawed patterns of reasoning account for maladaptive cognitions and the corresponding mood disorders. Part of the task in therapy is to familiarize the patient with these forms of distortion and lead him toward replacing them with correct reasoning strategies that will provide accurate information. Attention has been drawn by Beck to the fact that cognitive distortions are characterized by the thinking of young children as described by Piaget in his work on preoperational thought. Beck describes such thinking as "primitive" and characterizes it as "global, absolutistic, and irreversible." It is contrasted to "mature" thought which is "multidimensional, relativistic, and reversible."

A few examples from the list of cognitive distortions may be instructive. One type of cognitive error is *overgeneralization*, in which a single isolated incident gives rise to a general rule that is then rigidly and inappropriately applied to a wide and even unrelated range of phenomena. The absence of a classification structure in the young child can contribute to this. A child bitten by a dog could develop a phobia for all furry animals. There is no structure for distinguishing between furry animals that are dogs and those that are not. Transductive thinking comes into play here. The child reasons that since the furry dog Fido has bitten him and his friend's dog Dancer is furry, it follows that Dancer will also bite. *Dichotomous thinking*, another form of cognitive error, is typified by centration, which is a major feature of preoperational thought. In dichotomous thinking the individual reasons in an exclusionary manner. An action is either absolutely right or absolutely wrong. The individual centers on only one perspective to arrive at this judgment, failing to adopt alternate perspectives which might suggest a relative view of right and wrong based on historical, circumstantial, and contextual variables. *Drawing arbitrary inferences* is another form of cognitive error that abounds in the thinking of many patients. This involves jumping to firm conclusions in the absence of evidence or even drawing a conclusion that runs counter to the evidence. Several preoperational thought patterns could contribute to this. For example, the negative prediction by a patient that he is going to become ill as punishment for a misdeed could be predicated upon a lingering concept of immanent justice. Maintaining a conclusion in the face of contrary evidence can be supported by the preoperational turn of mind that makes it difficult to perceive contradictions at times. *Emotional reasoning* is a form of cognitive error that seems almost to accord objective existence to one's feelings. If I am angry, then the anger must be real beyond my phenomenological field and there is necessarily a true, objective cause external to me. This bears a resemblance to the concept of realism in which subjective entitites such as dreams and thought itself are seen by young children as having an absolute corporeal existence outside of their own minds. *Labeling* or *mislabeling* is a distortion which Burns suggests is an extreme form of overgeneralization. On the basis of one or a few failed attempts at reaching a goal, the patient labels himself as a failure. Failure is then absolutized as opposed to being seen as relative to time, available resources, demand characteristics of the task, and other related variables. The preoperational thought characteristics of irreversibility and the absence of transformation are apparent here. The patient does not reason that although he failed today he may succeed tomorrow and that the very failure itself could become a source of learning to help transform it into later success.

There are still other forms of cognitive distortions, but perhaps the link to preoperational thought has been demonstrated by now. The more severe the pathology, the more likely the patient's thought is grounded in primitive as opposed to mature forms of reasoning. It should be kept in mind that the patient may be using mature thought forms in areas of his life that fall outside the realm of what Beck calls one's personal domain. The area of personal domain includes those phenomena in which an individual has a psychological investment. This could range all the way from his self-concept and personal possessions to social causes in distant lands. Primitive thought, or at least an excess of it to a dysfunctional degree, may be confined to certain select sectors of an individual's personal domain.

The growing subject of metacognition (Flavell and Wellman 1977; Flavell 1978, 1979) within the field of cognitive development is especially relevant to working with patients' cognitive distortions. Metacognition entails thinking about thinking. It involves becoming aware of one's own reasoning strategies by reflecting upon them, and the corollary to this process is the greater potential for changing them by virtue of the awareness attained. Although he never uses the term, Beck's treatment model places strong emphasis upon teaching patients to metacognize with the aim of correcting their distorted forms of thinking. The patient is instructed to record his negative automatic thoughts and upon examining them to detect whatever cognitive distortions are present. The next step is for him to respond to each automatic thought with a rational statement that avoids any of the forms of cognitive distortion he has become familiar with. Formal operational thought has been described as the capacity to "think about thinking." However, metacognition is a developmental phenomenon and much of the work in this area has been done with children (Meichenbaum and Asarnow 1979; Borkowski and Kurtz 1984). Therefore a metacognitive treatment strategy can be employed with patients of varying developmental levels, within the constraints of each patient's predominant cognitive stage.

An analogy is made by Beck et al. (1979) between the personal paradigm of the patient, based on an incorrect and dysfunctional knowledge organization (Guidano and Liotti 1983), and the scientific paradigm described by Kuhn (1972). Kuhn, a student of the history of science, has noted that scientists subscribing to a particular paradigm tend to be conservative in the face of a growing body of evidence contradicting the beliefs comprising the paradigm. They may at first ignore contrary evidence and later attempt to assimilate further such evidence into the paradigm without fundamental change. Eventually peripheral aspects of the paradigm may change, leaving intact its core postulates (Lakatos 1974). When the burden of a current paradigm's inadequacy becomes too great there occurs a "scientific revolution," and the old paradigm is abandoned in favor of a new and more adequate one.[4] Chalmers, in writing about scientific revolutions, states, "Science should contain within it a means of breaking out of one paradigm into a better one. This is the function of revolutions. All paradigms will be inadequate to some extent as far as their match with nature is concerned. When the mismatch becomes serious, that is, when a crisis develops, the revolutionary step of replacing the entire paradigm by another becomes essential for the effective progress of science" (1982:99). Assisting the patient to undergo a personal paradigm revolution, to give up the old dysfunctional conceptual framework in order to adopt a new and more adaptive one, is the primary role of the therapist.

4. There is debate over the nature of a new paradigm following a scientific revolution in Kuhn's theory. Some critics maintain that Kuhn is a subjectivist and that, therefore, the new paradigm does not truly represent objective progress. Kuhn disavows the label of subjectivist, however (see Lakatos and Musgrave 1970 for further elaboration of this point).

The analogy between personal paradigm revolutions and scientific revolutions applies no less to the developmental process in Piagetian psychology. When interacting with the environment there is always an attempt first to assimilate events to preexisting schemes. Novelty that is too disparate from those schemes will often simply be ignored and avoided. Yet many occasions of interaction with the environment will produce a mismatch between cognitive structure and experience which in turn induces disequilibrium and leads to a process of cognitive reorganization. As Inhelder et al. state, "The source of the progress is to be sought in the disequilibrium which incites the subject to go beyond his present state in search of new solutions" (1974:264). Major reorganizations such as those from one Piagetian or Kohlbergian stage to the next represent a paradigm shift to a qualitatively different and more adaptive organization of knowledge structures.

Upon close examination of the procedures and techniques advocated by Beck we find that many of them serve to induce disequilibrium, similar to that described by Piaget, in the patient. They seem to be based on a strategy of contradiction and conflict as a means for promoting cognitive change. The literature in the field of cognitive development, most of it confined to children and adolescents, is replete with studies successful in facilitating cognitive growth through methods utilizing conflict strategies (Inhelder et al. 1974; Kuhn 1972; Smedslund 1961b; Turiel 1974, 1977; Walker 1983). Two types of contradiction found in Piaget's equilibration model are as follows: pitting one opposing scheme against another; and disconfirmation occurring when the prediction or expectation stemming from a scheme or structure does not materialize upon acting on the environment.

The first type of contradiction is exemplified in an experiment conducted by Smedslund. It involves attempting to facilitate the acquisition of substance conservation in preoperational children. The heart of the procedure was to produce a cognitive conflict by pitting one scheme against another. Smedslund pitted the addition/subtraction schema against the deformation schema. For example, he would simultaneously elongate a piece of clay (deformation) while at the same time visibly removing a section of it (addition/subtraction). The subjects, being nonconservers, were inclined to think that there would be a greater amount as a result of elongation. On the other hand, they realized that removing a piece should lead to a lesser amount. Smedslund hypothesized, "Since the addition/subtraction schema presumably has greater clarity, simplicity, and consistency, it will gradually or suddenly begin to dominate, whereas the deformation schema with its high degree of ambiguity, complexity and internal contradiction will be weakened and will eventually disappear completely even in pure deformation situations without addition/subtraction" (1961b:157). Smedslund reported comparatively good results from this experiment and viewed the outcome as supporting Piaget's theory of equilibration in which disequilibrium leads to a reorganization of cognitive structures at a higher and more adaptive level. Those children who progressed during this experiment at the completion of it were not only able to make conservation judgments but were also able to provide conceptual explanations for their new conserving beliefs. (See Inhelder et al. 1974, for many excellent examples and an extended theoretical discussion of this subject.)

Turning now to cognitive therapy we find a concise illustration in Beck el al. of Piaget's notion of playing one scheme off against another.

Arguments against a patient's belief system are more effective when they are tied in with the patient's adaptive beliefs. For example, a patient believed that others disagreeing with him meant that they disliked him. He also believed that he couldn't be all things to all people. By applying the second belief to the first, he was able to accept the "new belief" that whether others agreed with him was not a crucial concern. Thus an adaptive belief was used to counter the other beliefs. (1979:252)

In our web of beliefs many assumptions are held in isolation from one another. As with the preoperational child, contradictions are unperceived and unreconciled. The therapist induces disequilibrium by skillfully leading the patient to perceive the incompatibility and contradiction inherent in the premises he holds pertaining to the problem area. A reequilibrated resolution to the conflict moves the patient toward a more realistic and adaptive conceptualization.

The strategy of setting up a behavioral experiment to test out the patient's predictions is one of the most potent in the cognitive therapist's repertoire of options. It corresponds to the second type of contradiction cited in Piaget's equilibration model. Initially the patient maintains his expectation as an unquestioned conviction. He is encouraged to reconceptualize it as a hypothesis subject to experimental testing in order to obtain evidence that will either support or invalidate it. The assumption underlying the expectation is identified and operationalized within the context of the experiment. Beck et al. comment, "The behavioral methods can be regarded as a series of small experiments designed to test the validity of the patient's hypotheses or ideas about himself. As the negative ideas are contradicted by these 'experiments,' the patient gradually becomes less certain of their validity and he is motivated to attempt more difficult assignments" (1979:118). There are an infinite number of ways for testing out dysfunctional beliefs, limited only by the creativity of the therapist-patient collaboration. A prototype of this strategy is evidenced in Piaget's description of the infant, in the fourth stage of the sensorimotor period, who is surprised to find that an object placed alongside a cushion does not come toward him as he pulls the cushion. The surprise is an emotional response to the disconfirmation of the expectation that the object would move in his direction. The disequilibrated infant then engages in a series of heightened interactions with the environment resulting in a reequilibrated scheme which permits knowing that the object will move toward him only when placed on the cushion that he pulls. Inhelder et al. in conclusion to a report on a series of studies designed to examine the mechanism for cognitive growth state, "In the studies discussed here the constructive role to interaction with reality appears in two different forms: an awakening of the child's curiosity about new situations and his feelings of conflict when the outcome of an experimental event does not correspond to his predictions" (1974:266). The resemblance to Beck's therapeutic orientation is striking.

One of the strongest points of emphasis that came out of the studies by Inhelder and her associates is that the subjects who made the greatest gains were those who were at an intermediate level between their former stage and the stage to which the intervention of the studies moved them. In other words, for the stimulus from the environment to be effective the subjects had to be sufficiently advanced to assimilate it to their cognitive organization. Put another way from the standpoint of a clinical guideline, the stimulus or intervention should be appropriately adapted to the developmental level of the patient. This is a relational notion. The patient should never be criticized or put down for not being appropriate for the intervention.

Patient and intervention must be fit to one another and it is the therapist who must do the fine-tuning. The clinical utility of this viewpoint, grounded in developmental theory, is that as opposed to labeling the unresponsive patient as "resistant," the therapist is obliged to reexamine his own skills and knowledge base with the aim of coming up with new solutions. Being faced with a "resistant" patient can be a disequilibrating experience for the therapist. The choice for him is whether to construe this as an invitation to further his own growth, which would directly benefit the patient, or to blame the patient for either not being properly motivated or appropriate to the type of therapy being practiced.

The relevance and compatibility of Piaget's work to the theory and practice of cognitive therapy has been highlighted. Piagetian theory is seen as illuminating and deepening aspects of Beck's formulations, and it is believed that Piagetian research on the mechanism of change lends support to the therapeutic strategies and tactics devised by him. The work of Beck is a bonanza for the practicing therapist, for it offers a clearly delineated and highly specific set of strategies and tactics for collaboratively promoting change in the patient. These flow logically from a well-formulated theory of psychopathology with strong epistemological moorings.

SOCIAL-COGNITIVE DEVELOPMENTAL TRAINING

The Role of the Social Context. The past decade has witnessed an expanding interest in the area of social cognition which is certain to continue into the future. Much of the literature on social cognition training deals with efforts to promote perspective-taking abilities and this will be discussed shortly. However, a striking question of a different nature that has been receiving considerable attention lately is the extent to which the construction of knowledge about the physical world is itself contingent upon social interaction. To be sure, this question has its roots in the early work of Piaget, who emphasized the significance of peer interaction to produce confrontation and conflict in effecting decentration from one's egocentric beliefs. However, an examination of his later work could misleadingly suggest that cognitive growth is exclusively a matter between the individual and his inanimate world. Countering this notion, Bearison has written that "Cognitive development cannot be adequately explained solely in terms of children's solitary reflections upon hypothetical problems. Knowledge is not constructed independently of the social contacts in which it is shared, confirmed, and used to mediate social discourse" (1982:218).

Doise and his associates have conducted a series of experiments that are particularly relevant to the role of social interaction in the construction of knowledge (Doise and Mugny 1979; Doise, Mugny, and Perret-Clermont 1975, 1976; Mugny and Doise 1978; Perret-Clermont 1980). They demonstrated that children performing on cognitive tasks in a group did better than those acting in isolation and that the children who had performed better in the group, when observed afterward performing tasks in isolation, continued to do better than those who had not performed in the group at all. The possibility of imitation of one child by another was ruled out as none was initially superior to the others. A critical finding in their ongoing research was that intermediary preoperational children when paired with one another could progress to concrete operational judgments and explanations. It was found to be essential in training of this kind that the preoperational children participating not possess the same initial incorrect views on the task. In other words, the impetus to development came from the dialogue and conflict predicated upon a confrontation of contradictory *incorrect* centrations. It is this phenomenon that is accredited with jolting both children in each working pair out of their egocentrism. The opposing centrations which each child in the dyad had now become aware of was then coordinated to produce a resolution to the task at a higher level of cognitive organization. The same results were found when an adult would present an incorrect judgment opposite to that of the incorrect judgment being made by the child. The tasks involved in all of these experiments were those of spatial transformation and varying types of conservation.

Two clinical implications come to mind upon contemplating the work of Doise and his colleagues in Geneva. The first is that perhaps we should consider exploring the potential of structured dyadic or "couples" therapy with preschool and middle-childhood children. Criteria for selecting those who would participate in this process could be developed in advance and modified or refined through feedback from clinical results. An initial assessment might seek to identify those children who are having interpersonal problems partly due to what appears to be a level of egocentrism below what would appear to be appropriate for their age group. Children who tend to be isolated and withdrawn might also be prime candidates. The therapist might direct the therapy to dealing with issues of social cognition that have particular existential reality for the participants. The therapy could be conducted with pairs of children at the same cognitive stage and with children at different stages in order to see if developmental match versus mismatch is a significant variable.

The second implication is the hypothesis that we as therapists working with patients of any age may not need to be quite so preoccupied with the correctness or truth, in absolute terms, of our interpretations. Their value may not be so much in their accuracy as in their potential to dislodge the patient from the embeddedness of his own centration, thereby providing the impetus to revising his beliefs. This hypothesis would contribute toward explaining how it might be that patients exposed to differing psychotherapeutic systems could still find meaningful and useful the varying interpretations offered to them in the process. Viewing the presentation of an interpretation in this light would, of course, continue to require that the therapist display the customary tact and sensitivity in delivering the communication.

Perspective-Taking Training. There are three types of perspective taking. The first is visual, which is generally of no particular interest in the clinical sector. The other two are cognitive and affective perspective taking. In the former, an individual exhibits the capacity to accurately infer what another is thinking or what information that person possesses about a given situation. In the latter, an individual exhibits the capacity to accurately discern the emotional experience of another person. The defining characteristic of perspective taking is the ability to take the view of another person, when that viewpoint differs from one's own. As it progresses it also entails the recognition that the other person can reciprocally take one's own point of view. It gradually leads to the ability to coordinate multiple points of view. Perspective taking or role taking, as it has been alternately called, has been successfully increased through training programs specifically designed to promote that increase (Chandler 1973; Chandler, Greenspan, and Barenboim 1974; Ianotti 1978; Silvern, Waterman, Sobesky, and Ryan 1979). Perspective-taking training has also been reported to lead to increased altruism (Ianotti 1978), cooperation and prosocial behavior (Johnson 1975), and ability to analyze interpersonal problems (Marsh, Serafica, and Barenboim 1980). It has been found to bear a relationship of positive correlation to moral development (Jurkovic 1980) and to peer group status and classroom adjustment (Burka and Glenwick 1978). Feshbach (1978) reported a reduction of aggressive behavior in late middle childhood subsequent to role-taking training. Finally, low perspective-taking skills have been linked to learning difficulties (Burka and Glenwick 1978), delinquency (Chandler 1973; Little 1979; Kennedy, Kirchner, and Draguns 1980), high levels of aggression (Burka and Glenwick 1978), and social withdrawal (Waterman, Sobesky, Silvern, Aoki, and McCaulay 1981). The acquisition of high-level perspective-taking ability does not assure comparably high levels in such areas as empathy, prosocial behavior, and moral judgment, but is facilitative of increases in those areas. Selman (1971a) holds that each new stage of perspective taking is a necessary but not sufficient condition for the emergence of a corresponding stage of moral development. He maintains the same position with respect to empathy. In fact, perspective-taking skills can be utilized on behalf of antisocial behavior when the individual is so motivated (Waterman et al. 1981).

Perspective-taking training programs are a direct outgrowth of the cognitive-developmental field. In assessing an individual's problems with a view toward selecting an intervention, the clinician may wish to consider the patient's perspective-taking abilities and what bearing they seem to be having upon his interpersonal difficulties. It is important in conducting such an assessment to keep in mind that perspective taking is not an all-or-nothing matter, but that there is a progression of levels through which one can evolve. Equally important is the fact that an individual at a particular level may utilize it in some domains of his life and not others or that it may be inhibited from use under certain circumstances, as in a case where he has an unusually high degree of emotional involvement. For diagnostic purposes, the clinician can put to good advantage the model proposed by Flavell (1974) consisting of the following components: Existence, Need, Inference, and Application (see alos Hains and Ryan 1983). The model generates a series of questions to pinpoint the appropriate juncture of intervention. Does the patient recognize the fundamental distinction between his own and the other's thoughts and feelings? Is he aware that the thoughts and feelings which the other has may be different from those that he has? In the case of young children the absence of this awareness, based upon a structural deficit, may be primarily an issue of rate of development. In the adult patient, the failure to make the shift from egocentric to nonegocentric awareness may be more likely to be associated with pathology. If the *existence* criterion is satisfied, then the question becomes whether the patient recognizes the *need* to exercise his role-taking ability in a given situation. If both the *existence* and *need* criteria are met, the question becomes whether the patient has the appropriate strategy at his command to make an accurate inference about what the other is thinking or feeling.

The form that perspective-taking training has assumed varies from one research project to another. A significant variable influencing that form is whether emphasis is being given to cognitive or affective role taking. The setting where it is being conducted and the nature of the participating subjects are others. Authoring scripts, videotaping, and puppetry are three innovative means that have been utilized in the training. Urbain and Kendall have reviewed perspective-taking training programs across a wide range of approaches and have concluded "The interventions that emphasized training in the perspective-taking component of problem solving have generally been successful in improving performance on measures that were designed to assess perspective-taking abilities. In addition, some studies found improvement on ratings of behavioral adjustment" (1980:137). One of the major approaches utilized in this type of training is to have each member of a participating group play a role in a skit, which may even be written by the group, and then proceed to switch roles until each member has had the opportunity to enact each role in the skit. This is then followed by a series of probing questions either about the thoughts, intentions, and feelings of different characters or about what it had been like for the participants as they alternated roles and what they learned by assuming the various perspectives (Chandler et al. 1974). The ability to see the relations among the various perspectives and to coordinate them is a major goal of perspective-taking development with significant implications for social competence. The skit enacted might be especially tailored to the real-life problems of the participants, or it might have a generic aspect that would be potentially enhancing of perspective-taking abilities for anyone. One example that might be highly productive generally yet at the same time be of specific value to delinquents and adult offenders would be role-playing a court scene. Various roles that could be enacted are those of the following: juror, victim, accused, judge, spectator, lawyer for the defense, and friend or relative of the victim. A variation of the training would be to extend it to family therapy, having each member of the family rotate through everyone's role, followed by a discussion of each person's experience. The options for designing training programs are limitless and represent an invitation to call forth the creativity of the therapist. By engaging the participants in the actual designing process, the therapist will have initiated perspective-taking training from the very outset and will most likely be assuring greater involvement in the direct role-taking portion of the training to follow.

The reader should be aware that most of the training programs carried out thus far have been with nonclinical populations. We have been discussing a fledgling area of activity, and there are some exciting times ahead as we witness an increasing application of the training across a wider range of populations. Further, most of the training activities have been conducted with children and adolescents. However, there is nothing that should theoretically discourage the application of perspective-taking training with adult populations whenever clinical judgment indicates it as the treatment of choice. One interesting prospect for such an application would be to conduct a group with parents who have been identified as low in role-taking skills. This could not only benefit the participants, but it might also have a strong preventive outcome for the children of the parents. The assumption would be that low perspective-taking skills among parents would result in their children not having their needs adequately met and that an increase in the parents' perspective-taking skills would result in an enhancement of the children's well-being. In any event, having a perspective-taking training model within one's therapeutic repertoire is one of the distinctive advantages of adopting a cognitive-developmental orientation.

The Work of Robert Selman. Selman is a leading figure in pointing the way toward applying the cognitive-developmental orientation to the child therapy process. He and his colleagues intensively studied children's social-cognitive developmental process in natural settings under the auspices of the Harvard–Judge Baker Social Reasoning Project, which had its official inception in 1973. The subjects were preadolescent and adolescent youngsters. Many of them were enrolled in the Manville School operated by the Judge Baker Center. These boys and girls suffered various combinations of emotional and learning difficulties. Longitudinal studies of their social-cognitive development were compared with similar studies of children in public schools. Hence, the project encompassed a comparative assessment of both clinical and nonclinical populations. A report of the project's findings can be found in Selman (1980).

The main focus of the study was children's developing levels of social and interpersonal understanding and how these conceptions developing within the children influenced their overt behavior. Emphasis was placed upon the structural characteristics of children's developing concepts and not upon content. The reader is already familiar with Selman's perspective-taking model, which is the central undergirding component of the work. One of the contexts for conducting the study was that of the long-term dynamically oriented psychotherapy sessions that the children of the Manville School were involved in. This permitted an opportunity for a genuinely microscopic examination of the children's evolving conceptions of intrapsychic and interpersonal phenomena. It further allowed for an exploration of how these evolving conceptions affected the children's comprehension of the therapist's communications and how, in turn, the therapist adapts his communications to match the young patient's level of comprehension.

Selman (1980) elaborates upon the child's developing understanding of his own inner life and how this progression of intrapsychic comprehension affects the therapeutic process. At each of four developmental stages there are four issues explored. The issues are as follows: subjectivity, self-awareness, personality, and personality change. Let us examine the evolution of the "self-awareness" issue as explicated by Selman. Prior to the first stage the child simply has no differentiated conception between internal psychic experiences and the outside physical world as he knows it. Between ages five and seven, stage 1, children seem to have no conception that a person can say one thing about their motives, thoughts, and feelings to self or another and yet mean something else. Self deception at this stage is equated with changing one's mind or decision, such as shifting from wanting to do something to not wanting to do it. Somewhere between the ages of seven and fourteen, the child develops to stage 2. At this stage there exists an introspective capacity in which the child can take the view of a second person and from that perspective reflect upon his own internal states. Although cognitive developmentalists rarely make the connection, this new achievement may be the precursor to what existentialists refer to as "transcending" the immediate situation.[5] Observe May's comment: "The capacity to transcend the immediate situation uniquely presupposes *Eigenwelt*—that is, the mode of behavior in which a person sees himself as subject and object at once" (1983:147). The child now recognizes that it is possible for him or another to outwardly misrepresent true inner experiences. Internal states are now accorded priority, the child recognizing that external behavior reflects inner experience. Understanding that he can monitor both his own actions and thoughts is present at this stage. By stage 3 the youngster has constructed a theory of self as self-aware and as an active agent in controlling his own inner experiences and outward actions. He now has a coordinated comprehension of the self-reflexive mind, of a mind that strives to grasp its own nature; a mind that is simultaneously subject and object. We see here a move further in the direction of achieving *Eigenwelt,* essential to authentic human being in the existentialist's orientation. It is at stage 4 that a concept of the "unconscious" emerges, although the youngster may never use that term. The adolescent's theory of mind now encompasses a recognition that there is a form of self-deception that escapes conscious introspection. Selman states, "The development of the concept-in-theory of the unconscious emerges out of a need to explain observed aspects of social behavior and experience that previous conceptions of intrapsychic phenomena were inadequately structured to explain" (1980:105). This description may strike a chord in the reader, for it embodies the same principle as the hypothetical example in a previous

5. Kegan (1977) is an exception to this statement.

section, where a new and more complex concept is invented to explain a broader range of experiences for which an earlier scheme does not adequately account.

Selman and his colleagues have sought to demonstrate how knowledge of the child's developing conceptions of intrapsychic life, such as stages of self-awareness and his perspective-taking skills, will afford a framework for adaptive therapeutic interventions and communications. They cite one example, to illustrate, in which an early adolescent in treatment can understand only that he is being picked on, but not that his own behavior is provocative and responsible for inciting the other boys to belligerent actions toward him. Lacking the stage 2 capacity to observe his own behavior and make inferences about his own motives from a second person social perspective, he fails to comprehend his contribution to the problem. Selman advocates a therapeutic direction of helping such a youngster acquire or activate stage 2 skills in such a case when a social-cognitive assessment indicates that he is not performing at that level. Stage 2 self-awareness would then give the youngster the leverage he needs to work on changing his behavior. Rather than to make the psychodynamic assumptions pertaining to mechanisms of denial and projection, Selman's approach would seem to be the appropriate course of action to explore from a cognitive-developmental perspective in this case. Literally, insight here would be equated with cognitive-structural development, as in Piaget's and Tenzer's formulations on the grasp of consciousness.

In another striking illustration of a developmental approach, the same youngster reports to the therapist that he is contemplating returning to live with his father[6]. When the therapist reminds the boy that his father drinks and occasionally hits him, the boy replies that his father has "changed." Upon further inquiry, however, it is revealed that what the boy means is that his father has changed only his living quarters, having moved from one apartment to another. In this instance, the boy's functional level amounts to stage 0, at which no distinction is made between inner experiences and outer physical behavior. That the therapist should not assume a mutual understand-

6. The therapist in the case was Daniel S. Jaquette, who was being supervised by Selman from a cognitive-developmental perspective.

ing between himself and the patient about the meaning of a significant word is a point made by Bandler and Grinder (1975) in the exposition of their Meta-Model for linguistic analysis and is appreciated by many therapists. However, outside the context of a developmental framework, it often appears that the patient is using the word idiosyncratically. The developmental perspective gives the therapist a theoretical frame of reference to consider. This guides his inquiries in attempting to understand the meaning of the patient's words and, upon succeeding, gives him a specific therapeutic direction in which to move. In the case reported by Selman, once it was understood what the boy meant by "change," the therapist then posed a series of questions designed to help him differentiate between physically observable change and what can be reasonably inferred from it. Selman formulates concisely, "Social-cognitive-developmental theory may represent a useful paradigm for ordering therapist communications into a developmental hierarchy" (1980:256).

CONCLUSION

In this chapter I have presented a collage of Piagetian contributions to clinical theory and practice. Creative efforts by such developmentalists as Selman and Chandler have demonstrated distinctive and specific clinical procedures that have their origins in Piaget's work. Scholar-practitioners such as Greenspan, Tenzer, and Wachtel have led the way in exploring how Piagetian concepts can serve to enrich preexisting models and conceptions guiding practice. The germinal references in Beck's work to Piaget have been expanded to sharpen the interplay between the two systems. I have emphasized that because of the inseparable relationship between cognition and affect, to address cognitive development is inevitably to address emotional development. Implicit in what has been presented is an appealing paradox, which is that despite the universality of Piagetian structural stages in development, when the theory is applied in a clinical context, the demand is for a high degree of individualizing each patient regardless of age. It is essential to assess how the patient's structural level of development shapes his strategies of reasoning and perspective-taking skills. Certainly if there is one predominant theme in this chapter it is that the therapist's communications and intervention strategies should be designed specifically to take into account the cognitive-developmental level of the patient. Knowledge about the way in which a patient makes meaning out of self and others, his personal and impersonal worlds, the past, present, and future, is central to individualized and effective helping.

The constructive-developmental framework offers a clear set of goals for the psychotherapeutic process. It does not prescribe content, but it suggests a direction for growth with empirical and philosophical underpinnings (Kegan 1982). There have been intimations in some quarters that Piaget's psychology is elitist because it favors one stage over others. This is a mistaken ideological judgment. Piaget has articulated and demonstrated the utmost of respect for each individual person and for what Kegan refers to as that person's "meaning-making" activity. There is no implication whatsoever that special privileges should be conferred within society to people operating at the highest stage of development. *That* would be elitist! Certainly each person is entitled to equal justice, compassion, and love in the world. Nevertheless, the stages, or competencies, that are an outgrowth of each person's developmental process are not equal. Piaget's theory is based upon the concept of adaptation. Each succeeding stage or period of development represents a higher level of adaptation, liberating the individual from embeddedness in the prior stage, while imparting a wider perspective and greater autonomy to the evolving individual. Embedded in a spaceship constructed of concrete operations, we simply would not make it to the moon. To achieve that, we would need to reconstruct the spaceship into formal operations. Coming down to earth, progression to a higher stage affords the individual greater ego flexibility, a wider range of applicaton of his new structural organization, and an increased capacity to handle new and previously unfamiliar problems (Greenspan 1979). The choice of what to do with his newly developed powers remains with the individual.

The Piagetian paradigm does not require of the clinician that he abandon what he already believes and practices, in favor of the cognitive-structural developmental perspective. It does, however, beckon him to coordinate this perspective with his current orientation in order to reequilibrate toward a higher level of equilibrium. Through a judicious process of assimilation and accommodation, the clinician can emerge with an enlarged vision of his patients and a significantly increased range of therapeutic options.

References

Adams-Webber, J. and J.C. Mancuso. 1983. *Applications of Personal Construct Theory*. New York: Academic Press.

Alvy, K.T. 1968. Realation of age to children's egocentric and cooperative communications. *Journal of Genetic Psychology*, 112:275 – 286.

Anthony, E.J. 1956. The significance of Jean Piaget for child psychiatry. *British Journal of Medical Psychology*, 29:20 – 34.

Anthony, E.J. 1957. The ststem makers: Piaget and Freud. *British Journal of Medical Psychology*, 30:255 – 269.

Anthony, E.J. 1976. Freud, Piaget, and human knowledge: Some comparisons and contrasts. In the Chicago Institute for Psychoanalysis, ed., *The Annual of Psychoanalysis*, vol. 4. New York: International Universities Press.

Arieti, S. 1955. *Interpretation of Schizophrenia*. New York: Robert Brunner.

Arieti, S. 1980. Cognition in psychoanalysis. *Journal of the American Academy of Psychoanalysis*, 8:3 – 23.

Asher, S. R. and A. Wigfield. 1981. Training referential communication skills. In W. P Dickson, ed., *Children's Oral Communication Skills*. New York: Academic Press.

Bandler, R. and J. Grinder. 1975. *The Structure of Magic*. Palo Alto, Calif.: Science & Behavior Books.

Basch, M. F. 1977. Development of psychology and explanatory theory in psychoanalysis. In the Chicago Institute for Psychoanalysis, ed., *The Annual of Psychoanalysis*, vol. 5. New York: International Universities Press.

Basch, M. F. 1981. Psychoanalytic interpretation and cognitive transformation. *International Journal of Psychoanalysis*, 62:151 – 175.

Bearison, D. J. 1982. New directions in studies of social interaction and cognitive growth. In F. C. Serafica, ed., *Social-Cognitive Development in Context*. New York: Guilford Press.

Beck, A. T. 1967. *Depression: Clinical, Experimental, and Theoretical Aspects*. New York: Harper & Row.

Beck, A. T. 1976. *Cognitive Therapy and the Emotional Disorders*. New York: International Universities Press.

Beck, A. T. 1981. Cognitive theory of depression. Paper presented at APPA.

Beck, A. T. and G. Emery. In press. *Anxiety and phobias: A Cognitive Approach.* New York: Basic Books.

Beck, A. T., A. J. Rush, B. F. Shaw, and G. Emery. 1979. *Cognitive Therapy of Depression.* New York: Guilford Press.

Beilin, H. 1981. Language and thought. In I. Sigel, D. M. Brodzinsky, and R. M. Golinkoff, eds., *New Directions in Piagetian Theory and Practice.* Hillsdale, N.J.: Lawrence Erlbaum.

Bell, S. M. 1970. The development of the concept of object as related to infant-mother attachment. *Child Development,* 41:292–311.

Bettelheim, B. 1967. *The Empty Fortress.* New York: Free Press.

Beutler, L. E. 1983. *Eclectic Psychotherapy: A Systematic Approach.* New York: Pergamon Press.

Bieber, I. 1980. Psychoanalysis—a cognitive process. *Journal of the American Academy of Psychoanalysis,* 8:25–38.

Blasi, A. 1980. Bridging moral cognition and moral action: A critical review of the literature. *Psychological Bulletin,* 88:1–45.

Blatt, S. J. 1974. Levels of object representation in anaclitic and introjective depression. *Psychoanalytic Study of the Child,* 29:107–157.

Blatt, S. J. and C. M. Wild. 1976. *Schizophrenia: A Developmental Analysis.* New York: Academic Press.

Bleuler, E. 1951. The basic components of schizophrenia. In D. Rapaport, ed., *Organization and Pathology of Thought,* P.P. New York: Columbia University Press. 581–649.

Block, J. 1982. Assimilation, accommodation, and the dynamics of personality. *Child Development,* 53:281–295.

Bloom, L. 1970. *Language Development: Form and Function in Emerging Grammars.* Cambridge, Mass.: MIT Press.

Bloom, L. 1973. *One Word at a Time: The Use of Single-Word Utterances Before Syntax.* The Hague: Mouton.

Bobbit, B. L. and D. P. Keating, 1983. A cognitive-developmental perspective for clinical research and practice. In P. C. Kendall, ed., *Advances in Cognitive-Behavioral Research and Therapy.* New York: Academic Press.

Borke, H. 1971. Interpersonal perception of young children: Egocentrism or empathy. *Developmental Psychology,* 4:263–269.

Borke, H. 1973. The development of empathy in Chinese and American children between three and six years of age: A cross cultural study. *Developmental Psychology,* 9:102–108.

Borkowski, J. G. and B. E. Kurtz. 1984. Metacognition and special children. In B. Gholson and T. L. Rosenthal, eds., *Applications of Cognitive-Developmental Theory.* New York: Academic Press.

Brainerd, C. J. 1978a. *Piaget's Theory of Intelligence.* Englewood Cliffs, N.J.: Prentice-Hall.

Brainerd, C. J. 1978b. Learning research and Piagetian theory. In L. S. Siegel and C. J. Brainerd, eds., *Alternatives to Piaget.* New York: Academic Press.

Breger, L. 1974. *From Instinct to Identity: The Development of Personality.* Englewood Cliffs, N.J.: Prentice-Hall.

Brossard, M. D. 1974. The infant's conception of object permanence and his reactions to strangers. In T. G. Décarie, ed., *The Infant's Reaction to Strangers*. New York: International Universities Press.

Brown, G. and C. Desforges. 1979. *Piaget's Theory: A Psychological Critique*. Boston: Routledge & Kegan Paul.

Bryant, P. E. 1974. *Perception and Understanding in Young Children*. New York: Basic Books.

Burka, A. A. and D. S. Glenwick. 1978. Egocentrism and classroom adjustment. *Journal of Abnormal Child Psychology*, 6:61–70.

Burns, D. D. 1980. *Feeling Good: The New Mood Therapy*. New York: New American Library.

Byrne, D. 1975. Role-taking in adolescence and adulthood. Ph.D. dissertation, Harvard University.

Cameron, N. 1938. Reasoning, regression and communication in schizophrenia. *Psychological Monograph*, 50:1–34.

Cameron, N. 1939a. Deterioration and regression in schizophrenic thinking. *Journal of Abnormal Social Psychology*, 34:265–270.

Cameron, N. 1939b. Schizophrenic thinking in a problem-solving situation. *Journal of Mental Science*, 85:1012–1035.

Cameron, N. 1944. Experimental analysis of schizophrenic thinking, In J. Kasamin, ed., *Language and Thought in Schizophrenia*. Berkeley: University of California Press.

Cameron, N. 1951. Perceptual organization and behavior pathology, In R. R. Blake and G. V. Ramsey, eds., *Perception: An Approach to Personality*. New York: Ronald Press.

Carter, R. E. 1980. What is Lawrence Kohlberg doing? *Journal of Moral Education*, 9:88–100.

Case, R. 1978. Intellectual development from birth to adulthood: A neo-Piagetian interpretation. In R. Siegler, ed., *Children's Thinking: What Develops?* Hillsdale, N.J.: Lawrence Erlbaum.

Casey, E. S. 1980. Piaget and Freud on childhood memory. In H. J. Silverman, ed., *Piaget, Philosophy, and the Human Sciences*. Atlantic Highlands, N.J.: Humanities Press.

Chalmers, A. F. 1982. *What Is This Thing Called Science?* 2d ed. St. Lucia, Queensland: University of Queensland Press.

Chandler, M. J. 1973. Egocentrism and anti-social behavior: The assessment and training of social perspective-taking skills. *Developmental Psychology*, 9:326–332.

Chandler, M. J. 1982. Social cognition and social structure. In F. C. Serafica, ed., *Social-Cognitive Development in Context*. New York: Guilford Press.

Chandler, M. J. and S. Greenspan. 1972. Ersatz egocentrism: A reply to H. Borke. *Developmental Psychology*, 7:104–106.

Chandler, M. J., S. Greenspan, and C. Barenboim. 1974. Assessment and training of role-taking and referential communication skills in institutionalized emotionally disturbed children. *Developmental psychology*, 10:456–553.

Chandler, M. J., K. F. Paget and D. A. Koch. 1978. The child's demystification of psychological defense mechanisms: A structural and developmental analysis. *Developmental Psychology*, 14:197–205.

Chazan, S. E. 1981. Development of object permanence as a correlate of dimensions of maternal care. *Developmental Psychology*, 17:79–81.

Cicchetti, D. 1984. The emergence of developmental psychopathology. *Child Development*, 55:1–7.

Cicchetti, D. and P. Hesse, eds. 1982. *New Directions for Child Development: Emotional Development*, no. 16. San Francisco: Jossey-Bass.

Clarke, J. 1969. The concept of "aliveness" in chronic schizophrenia. *British Journal of Medical Psychology*, 42:59–66

Clarke-Stewart, K. A. 1973. Interactions between mothers and their young school children: Characteristics and consequences. *Monograph of the Society of Research in Child Development*, No. 38.

Cohen, B. D. and J. F. Klein. 1968. Referential communication in school age children. *Child Development*, 39:597–609.

Cohen, R. and R. Scheleser. 1984. Clinical development and clinical interventions. In A. W. Meyers and W. E. Craighead, eds., *Cognitive Behavior Therapy with Children*. New York: Plenum Press.

Colbiner, W. G. 1967. Psychoanalysis and the Geneva School of Genetic Psychology: Parallels and counterparts. *International Journal of Psychiatry*, 3:82–129.

Colby, A. 1978. Evolution of a moral-developmental theory. In W. Damon, ed., *New Directions for Child Development: Moral Development*, no. 2. San Francisco: Jossey-Bass.

Colby, A. and W. Damon. 1983. Listening to a different voice: A review of Gilligan's *In a Different Voice*. *Merrill-Palmer Quarterly*, 29:473–481.

Corsini, R. J. ed., 1981. *Handbook of Innovative Psychotherapies*. New York: Wiley.

Corsini, R. J., ed. 1984. *Current Psychotherapies* 3d ed. Itasco, Ill.: F. E. Peacock.

Cowan, P. A. 1978. *Piaget with Feeling*. New York: Holt, Rinehart & Winston.

Cowan, P. A. 1982. The relationship between emotional and cognitive development. In D. Cicchetti and P. Hesse, eds., *New Directions for Child Development: Emotional Development*, no. 16. San Francisco: Jossey-Bass.

Cox, M. V., ed. 1980. *Are Young Children Egocentric?* New York: St. Martin's Press.

Coyne, J. C. and I. H. Gotlib. 1983. The role of cognition in depression: A critical appraisal. *Psychological Bulletin*, 94:472–505.

Cromer, R. F. 1974. The development of language and cognition: The cognitive hypotheses. In B. Foss, ed., *New Perspectives in Child Development*. Baltimore: Penguin Books.

Damon, W. 1977. *The Social World of the Child*. San Francisco: Jossey-Bass.

Damon, W. 1980. Patterns of change in children's social reasoning: A two-year longitudinal study. *Child Development*, 51:1010–1017.

Damon, W. 1981. The development of justice and self-interest during childhood. In M. Lerner and S. Lerner, eds., *The Justice Motive in Social Behavior*. New York: Plenum Press.

Damon, W. 1983a. *Social and Personality Development*. New York: Norton.

Damon, W. 1983b. The nature of social-cognitive change. In W. F. Overton, ed., *The Relationship Between Social and Cognitive Development*. Hillsdale, N.J.: Lawrence Erlbaum.

Damon, W. and M. Killen. 1982. Peer interaction and the process of change in children's moral reasoning. *Merrill-Palmer Quarterly,* 28:347–367.

Décarie, T. G. 1965. *Intelligence and Affectivity in Early Childhood.* New York: International Universities Press.

Décarie, T. G. 1974. *The Infant's Reaction to Strangers.* New York: International Universities Press.

De Lisi, R. 1979. Genetic epistemology: The missing link in "Piagetian Psychology." *The Genetic Epistemologist,* vol. 8, no. 3, July.

Dickson, W. P. 1981. *Children's Oral Communication Skills.* New York: Academic Press.

Doise, W. and G. Mugny. 1979. Individual and collective conflicts of centrations in cognitive development. *European Journal of Social Psychology,* 9:105–108.

Doise, W., G. Mugny and A. Perret-Clermont. 1975. Social interaction and the development of cognitive operations. *European Journal of Social Psychology.* 5:367–383.

Doise, W., G. Mugny and A. Perret-Clermont. 1976. Social interaction and cognitive development: Further evidence. *European Journal of Social Psychology.* 6:245–247.

Driscoll, R. 1984. *Pragmatic Psychotherapy.* New York: Van Nostrand Reinhold.

Elkind, D. 1974. *Children and Adolescents: Interpretive Essays on Jean Piaget.* New York: Oxford University Press.

Ellis, A. 1962. *Reason and Emotion in Psychotherapy.* New York: Lyle Stuart.

Ellis, A. and R. Grieger, eds., 1977. *Handbook of Rational-Emotive Therapy.* New York: Springer.

Emery, G., S. D. Hollon, and R. C. Bedrosian, eds., 1981. *New Directions in Cognitive Therapy.* New York: Guilford Press.

Epting, F. R. 1984. Personal Construct Counseling and Psychotherapy. New York: Wiley.

Escalona, S. K. 1968. *The Roots of Individuality.* Chicago: Aldine.

Evans, R. J. 1973. *Jean Piaget: The Man and His Ideas.* New York: E. P. Dutton.

Feffer, M. H. 1959. The cognitive implications of role-taking behavior. *Journal of Personality,* 27:152–167.

Feffer, M. H. 1967. Symptom expression as a form of primitive decentering. *Psychological Review,* 74:16–28.

Feffer, M. H. 1970. Developmental analysis of interpersonal behavior. *Psychological Review,* 77:197–214.

Feffer, M. H. 1982. *The Structure of Freudian Thought.* New York: International Universities Press.

Feffer, M. H. and V. Gourevitch. 1960. Cognitive aspects of role-taking in children. *Journal of Personality,* 28:384–396.

Feffer, M. H. and L. Suchotliff. 1966. Decentering implications of social interactions. *Journal of Personality and Social Psychology,* 4:415–422.

Feshbach, N. D. 1978. Empathy training: A field study in affective education. Paper presented at the American Educational Research Association meeting, Toronto, March 1978.

Feshbach, N. D. and K. Roe. 1968. Empathy in six and seven years olds. *Child Development*, 39:133–145.

Fischer, K. W. 1980. A theory of congitive development: The control of hierarchies of skill. *Psychological Review*, 87:477–531.

Fishbein, H. D., S. Lewis, and K. Keiffer. 1972. Children's understanding of spatial relations: Co-ordination of perspectives. *Developmental Psychology*, 7:21–23.

Fishbein, H. D. and M. Osborne. 1971. The effects of feedback variations on referential communication of children. *Merrill-Palmer Quarterly*, 17:243–250.

Flavell, J. H. 1963. *The Developmental Psychology of Jean Piaget*. Princeton, N.J.: D. Van Nostrand.

Flavell, J. H. 1974. The development of inferences about others. In T. Mischel, ed., *Understanding Persons*. Great Britain: Blackwell.

Flavell, J. H. 1977. *Cognitive Development*. Englewood Cliffs, N.J.: Prentice-Hall.

Flavell, J. H. 1978. Metacognitive development. In J. M. Scandura and C. J. Brainerd, eds. *Structural/Process Theories of Complex Human Behavior* Alphen ad Rign, the Netherlands: Sijtoff & Noordhuff.

Flavell, J. H. 1979. Metacognition and cognitive monotoring. *American Psychologist*, 34:906–911.

Flavell, J. H., P. T. Botkin, C. L. Fry, J. W. Wright, and P. E. Jarvis. 1968. *The Development of Role-Taking and Communication Skills in Children*. New York: Wiley.

Flavell, J. H. and H. M. Wellman. 1977. Metamemory. In R. V. Kail, Jr., and J. W. Hagen, eds., *Perspectives on the Development of Memory and Cognition*. Hillsdale, N.J.: Lawrence Erlbaum.

Forman, G. E. and I. E. Sigel. 1979. *Cognitive Development: A Life-Span View*. Monterey, Calif.: Brooks/Cole.

Fraiberg, S. 1969. Libidinal object constancy and mental representation. *Psychoanalytic Study of the Child*, 24:9–47.

Frank, J. D. 1961. Persuasion and Healing. Baltimore: Johns Hopkins University Press.

Franks, C. M. and G. T. Wilson. 1976. *Annual Review of Behavior Therapy: Theory and Practice*. New York: Brunner/Mazel.

Freeman, A., ed. 1984. *Cognitive Therpy with Couples and Groups*. New York: Plenum Press.

Freeman, T. and A. McGhie. 1957. The relevance of genetic psychology for the psychopathology of schizophrenia. *British Journal of Medical Psychology*, 30:176–187.

Fry, C. L. 1966. Training children to communicate to listeners. *Child Development*, 37:674–685.

Fry, C. L. 1969. Training children to communicate to listeners who have varying listener requirements. *Journal of Genetic Psychology*, 114:153–166.

Furth, H. G. 1964. Research with the deaf: Implications for language and cognition. *Psychological Bulletin*, 62:145–164.

Furth, H. G. 1966. *Thinking Without Language*. New York: Free Press.

Furth, H. G. 1969. *Piaget and Knowledge.* Englewood Cliffs, N.J.: Prentice-Hall.

Furth, H. G. 1970. On language and knowing in Piaget's developmental theory. *Human Development,* 13:241–257.

Furth, H. G. 1971. Linguistic deficiency and thinking: Research with deaf subjects 1964–1969. *Psychological Bulletin,* 74:191–211.

Furth, H. G. 1973. *Deafness and Learning: A Psychosocial Process.* Belmont, Calif.: Wadsworth.

Furth, H. G. 1980. *The World of Grown-Ups: Children's Conceptions of Society.* New York: Elsevier.

Furth, H. G. and J. Youniss. 1965. The influence of language and experience on discovery and use of logical symbols. *British Journal of Psychology,* 56:381–390.

Gardner, H. 1972. *The Quest for Mind.* New York: Knopf.

Garfield, S. L. 1980. *Psychotherapy: An Eclectic Approach.* New York: Wiley.

Gelman, R. and C. R. Gallistel. 1978. *The Child's Understanding of Numbers.* Cambridge: Harvard University Press.

Gholson, B. and T. L. Rosenthal., eds., 1984. *Applications of Cognitive-Developmental Theory.* New York: Academic Press.

Gibbs, J. C. 1977. Kohlberg's stages of moral judgment: A constructive critique. *Harvard Educational Review,* 47:43–59.

Gilligan, C. 1977. In a different voice: Women's conception of self and morality. *Harvard Educational Review,* 47:481–517.

Gilligan, C. 1982a. *In a Different Voice: Psychological Theory and Women's Development.* Cambridge, Mass.: Harvard University Press.

Gilligan, C. 1982b. New maps of development: New visions of maturity. *American Journal of Orthopsychiatry,* 52:199–212.

Glucksberg, S. and R. M. Krauss. 1967. What do people say after they have learned how to talk? Studies of the development of referential communication. *Merrill-Palmer Quarterly,* 13:309–316.

Glucksberg, S., R. M. Krauss, and T. Higgins. 1975. The development of communication skills in children. In F. Horowitz, ed., *Review of Child Development Research,* vol. 4. Chicago: University of Chicago Press.

Goldfried, M. R., ed. 1982. *Converging Themes in Psychotherapy,* New York: Springer.

Goldstein, A. P., M. Lopez, and D. O. Greenleaf, 1979. Introduction. In A. P. Goldstein and F. H. Kanfer, eds. *Maximizing Treatment Gains: Transfer Enhancement in Psychotherapy.* New York: Academic Press.

Goldstein, K. 1936. The modification of behavior consequent to cerebral lesions. *Psychiatric Quarterly,* 10:586–610.

Goldstein, K. 1944. Methodological approach to the study of schizophrenic thought disorder. In J. S. Kasamin ed., *Language and Thought in Schizophrenia.* Berkeley Calif.: University of California Press.

Goldstein, K. 1959. Concerning the concreteness in schizophrenia. *Journal of Abnormal Social Psychology,* 59:146–148.

Goulet, J. 1974. The infant's conception of causality and his reactions to strangers. In T. D. Décarie, ed., *The Infant's Reaction to Strangers*. New York: International Universities Press.

Greenson, R. R. 1967. *The Technique and Practice of Psychoanalysis*, vol. 1. New York: International Universities Press.

Greenspan, S. I. 1979. *Intelligence and Adaptation*. New York: International Universities Press.

Gruber, H. and J. Vonèche, eds. 1977. *The Essential Piaget*. New York: Basic Books.

Guidano, V. F. and G. Liotti. 1983. *Cognitive Processes and Emotional Disorders*. New York: Guilford Press.

Haan, N. 1977. *Coping and Defending*. New York: Academic Press.

Haan, N., B. Simth, and J. Block. 1968. Moral reasoning of young adults: Political social behavior, family background, and personality correlates. *Journal of Personality and Social Psychology*, 10:183–201.

Hains, A. A. and E. B. Ryan. 1983. The development of social cognitive processes among juvenile delinquents and non-deliquent peers. *Child Development*, 54:1536–1544.

Hardy-Brown, K. 1979. Formal operations and the issue of generalizability: The analysis of poetry by college students. *Human Development*, 22:127–136.

Hart, J. 1983. *Modern Eclectic Therapy*. New York: Plenum Press.

Hartmann, H. 1964. The mutual influences in the development of ego and id. *Essays on Ego Psychology*, pp. 155–182. New York: International Universities Press.

Henggeler, S. W. and R. Cohen. 1984. The Role of cognitive development in the family-ecological systems approach to childhood psychopathology. In B. Gholson and T.L. Rosenthal, eds., *Applications of Cognitive-Developmental Theory*. New York: Academic Press.

Hickey, J. E. 1972. Stimulation of moral reasoning in delinquents. Ph.D. dissertation, Boston University.

Hickey, J. E. and P. L. Scharf, 1980. *Toward a Just Correctional System*. San Francisco: Jossey-Bass.

Hoffman, M. L. 1970. Moral Development. In P. H. Mussen ed., *Carmichael's Manual of Child Psychology*, vol. 2, New York: Wiley.

Hoffman, M. L. 1983. Empathy, guilt, and social cognition. In W. F. Overton, ed., *The Relationship Between Social and Cognitive Development*. Hillsdale, N. J. Lawrence Erlbaum.

Ianotti, R. J. 1978. Effects of role-taking experiences on role-taking, empathy, altruism and aggression. *Developmental Psychology*, 14:119–124.

Inhelder, B. 1966. Cognitive development and its contribution to the diagnosis of some phenomena of mental deficiency. *Merrill-Palmer Quarterly*, 12:299–321.

Inhelder, B. 1968. *The Diagnosis of Reasoning in the Mentally Retarded*. W. B. Stephens et al., trans. New York: Chandler. (Originally published 1943.)

Inhelder, B. 1971. Developmental theory and diagnostic procedures. In D. R. Green, M. P. Ford, and G. B. Flamer, eds., *Measurement and Piaget*, pp. 148-171. New York: McGraw-Hill.

Inhelder, B. and H. H. Chipman, eds. 1976. *Piaget and His School*. New York: Springer.

Inhelder, B. and J. Piaget. 1958. *The Growth of Logical Thinking from Childhood to Adolescence*. A. Parsons and S. Milgram, trans. New York: Basic Books. (Originally published 1955.)

Inhelder, B. and J. Piaget. 1969. *The Early Growth of Logic in the Child*, E. A. Lunzer and D. Papert, trans. New York: Norton. (Originally published 1959.)

Inhelder, B. and H. Sinclair. 1969. Learning cognitive structures. In P. H. Mussen, J. Lunzer, and M. Covington, eds., *Trends and Issues in Developmental Psychology*. New York: Holt, Rinehart & Winston.

Inhelder, B., H. Sinclair, and M. Bovet. 1974. *Learning and the Development of Cognition*. S. Wedgwood, trans. Cambridge, Mass.: Harvard University Press. (Originally published 1974.)

Johnson, D. W. 1975. Affective prospective taking and cooperative disposition. *Developmental Psychology*, 11:869–870.

Jones, R. A. 1977. *Self-Fulfilling Prophecies*. New York: Wiley.

Jurkovic, G. J. 1980. The juvenile delinquent as a moral philosopher: A structural-developmental perspective. *Psychological Bulletin*, 88:709–727.

Kaplan, L. J. 1972. Object constancy in the light of Piaget's vertical décalage. *Bulletin of the Menninger Clinic*, 36:322–334.

Kazdin, A. 1978. *History of Behavior Modification: Experimental Foundations of Contemporary Research*. Baltimore: University Park Press.

Kazdin, A. E. and L. A. Wilcoxon. 1976. Systematic desensitization and nonspecific treatment effects: A methodological evaluation. *Psychological Bulletin*, 23:729.

Kazdin, A. E. and G. T. Wilson. 1978. *Evaluation of Behavior Therapy: Issues, Evidence, and Research Strategies*. Lincoln: University of Nebraska Press.

Kegan, R. 1977. Ego and truth: Personality and the Piaget paradigm. Ph.D. dissertation, Harvard University.

Kegan, R. 1982. *The Evolving Self*. Cambridge, Mass.: Harvard University Press.

Kelly, G. A. 1955. *The Psychology of Personal Constructs*. New York: Norton.

Kendall, P. C. and S. D. Hollon, eds. 1979. *Cognitive-Behavioral Interventions: Theory, Research, and Procedures*. New York: Academic Press.

Kendall, P. C. and L. E. Wilcox. 1980. Cognitive-behavioral treatment for impulsivity: concrete versus conceptual training and non-self-controlled problem children. *Journal of Consulting and Clinical Psychology*, 48:80–91.

Kennedy, R. E., E. P. Kirchner, and J. G. Draguns, 1980. Perspective-taking, socialization, and moral judgement in adult criminals and non-criminal controls. Manuscript, Pennsylvania State University.

Kilburg, R. R. and A. W. Siegel. 1976. Formal operations in reactive and process schizophrenics. In R. Cancro, ed., *Annual Review of the Schizophrenic Syndrome*. New York: Brunner/Mazel.

Klerman, G. L., M. M. Weissman, B. J. Rounsaville, and E. S. Chevron. 1984. *Interpersonal Psychotherapy of Depression*. New York: Harper & Row.

Koch, D., D. Harder, M. J. Chandler, and K. Paget. 1979. Parental defense style and child competence: A match-mismatch hypothesis. Paper presented at the biennial meeting of the Society for Research in Child Development. San Francisco, March 1979.

Kohlberg, L. 1963a. Moral development and identification. In H. Stevenson, ed., *Child Psychology, 62nd–Yearbook of the National Society for the Study of Education,* pp. 277–332. Chicago: University of Chicago Press.

Kohlberg, L. 1963b. The development of children's orientations toward a moral order. 1. Sequence in the development of moral thought. *Vita Humana,* 6:11–33.

Kohlberg, L. 1969. Stage and sequence: The cognitive developmental approach to socialization. In D.A. Goslin, ed., *Handbook of Socialization Theory and Research.* Chicago: Rand McNally.

Kohlberg, L. 1971a. From is to ought: How to commit the naturalistic fallacy and get away with it in the study of moral development. In T. Mischel, ed., *Cognitive Development and Epistemology.* New York: Academic Press.

Kohlberg, L. 1971b. Stages of moral development as a basis for moral education. In C. M. Beck, B. S. Crittenden, and E. V. Sullivan, eds. *Moral Education.* New York: Lewman Press.

Kohlberg, L. 1973. Continuities and discontinuities in childhood and adult moral development revisited. In L. Kohlberg, *Collected Papers on Moral Development and Moral Education.*

Kohlberg, L. 1978. Revisions in the theory and practive of moral development. In W. Damon, ed., *New Directions for Child Development: Moral Development,* no. 2. San Francisco: Jossey-Bass.

Kohlberg, L. 1981. *Essays on Moral Development,* vol. 1, *The Philosophy of Moral Development.* New York: Harper & Row.

Kohlberg, L. and D. Elfenbein. 1975. The development of moral judgements concerning capital punishment. *American Journal of Orthopsychiatry,* 45:614–640.

Kovacs, M. 1980. The efficacy of cognitive and behavior therapies for depression. *American Journal of Psychiatry,* 137:1495–1501.

Kovacs, M. and A. T. Beck, 1978. Maladaptive cognitive structures in depression. *American Journal of Psychiatry,* 135:525–533.

Kovacs, M., J. Rush, A. T. Beck, and S. D. Hollon. 1981. Depressed outpatients treated with cognitive therapy or pharmacotherapy. *Archives of General Psychiatry,* 38:33–39.

Krebs, D. and A. Rosenwald. 1977. Moral reasoning and moral behavior in conventional adults. *Merrill-Palmer Quarterly,* 23:77-87.

Kuhn, D. 1972. Mechanisms of change in the development of cognitive structures. *Child Development,* 43:833–844.

Kuhn, D., J. Langer, L. Kohlberg, and N. S. Haan. 1977. The development of formal operations in logical and moral judgment. *Genetic Psychology Monographs,* 95:97–188.

Kuhn, T. S. 1972. *The Structure of Scientific Revolutions,* 2d ed. Chicago: University of Chicago Press.

Kurtines, W. and E. B. Grief. 1974. The development of moral thought: Review and evaluation of Kohlberg's approach. *Psychological Bulletin,* 81:453–470.

Lakatos, I. 1974. Falsification and the methodology of scientific programs. In I. Lakatos and A. Musgrave, eds., *Criticism and the Growth of Knowledge*. London: Cambridge University Press.

Lakatos, I. and A. Musgrave, eds. 1970. *Criticism and the Growth of Knowledge*. New York: Cambridge University Press.

Langer, J. 1969. Disequilibrium as a source of development. In P. H. Mussen, J. Langer, and M. Covington, eds., *Trends and Issues in Developmental Psychology*. New York: Holt, Rinehart & Winston.

Laurendeau, M. and A. Pinard. 1970. *The Development of the Concept of Space in the Child*. New York: International Universities Press.

Lee, L. C. 1971. The concomitant development of cognitive and moral modes of thought: A test of selected deductions from Piaget's theory *Genetic Psychology Monographs*, 83:93–146.

Lerner, S., I. Bie, and P. Lehrer. 1972. Concrete operational thinking in metally ill adolecesnts. *Merrill-Palmer Quarterly*, 18:287–291.

Levick, M. F. 1983. *They Could Not Talk and so They Drew*. Springfield, Ill.: Charles C. Thomas.

Lewis, M. M. 1963. *Language, Thought, and Personality*. New York: Basic Books.

Liben, L. S. 1977. Memory from a cognitive-developmental perspective: A theoretical and empirical review. In W. F. Overton and J. McGallager, eds., *Knowledge and Development*, vol. 1. New York: Plenum.

Lickona, T. 1976. Research on Piaget's theory of moral development. In T. Lickona, ed., *Moral Development and Behavior: Theory, Research and Social Issues*. New York: Holt, Rinehart & Winston.

Lidz, T. 1973. *The Origin and Treatment of Schizophrenic Disorders*. New York: Basic Books.

Little, V. L. 1979. The relationship of role-taking ability to self control in institutionalized juvenile offenders. Doctoral dissertation, Virginia Commonwealth University. Dissertation Abstracts International, 39 2992B. University Microfilms no. 78–22, 701.

Locke, D. 1980. The illusion of stage six. *Journal of Moral Education*, 9:103–109.

Loevinger, J. 1976. *Ego Development*. San Francisco: Jossey-Bass.

Looft, W. R. 1972. Egocentrism and social interaction across the life span. *Psychological Bulletin*, 78:73–92.

Lowenherz, L. and M. Feffer. 1969. Cognitive level as a function of defensive isolation. *Journal of Abnormal Psychology*, 74:352–357.

Luborsky, L. 1984. *Principles of Psychoanalytic Psychotherapy*. New York: Basic Books.

Luborsky, L., B. Singer, and L. Luborsky. 1975. Comparative studies of psychotherapies: Is it true that "Everybody has won and all must have prizes?" *Archives of General Psychiatry*, 32:995–1008.

Mahler, B. 1966. *Principles of Psychopathology*. New York: McGraw-Hill.

Mahler, M., F. Pine, and A. Bergman. 1975. *The Psychological Birth of the Child*. New York: Basic Books.

Mahoney, M. 1974. *Cognitive and Behavior Modification.* Cambridge, Mass.: Ballinger.

Mahoney, M. J. 1977. Personal science: A cognitive learning therapy. In A. Ellis and R. Grieger eds, *Handbook of Rational Emotive Therapy.* New York: Springer.

Malerstein, A. J. and M. Ahern. 1979. Piaget's stages of cognitive development and adult character structure. *American Jounal of Psychotherapy,* 33:107–118.

Malerstein, A. J. and M. Ahern. 1982. *A Piagetian Model of Character Structure.* New York: Human Sciences Press.

Maratsos, M. P. 1973. Nonegocentric communication abilities in pre-school children. *Child Development,* 44:697–701.

Marks, I. 1981. *Cure and Care of Neuroses: Theory and Practice of Behavioral Psychotherapy.* New York: Wiley.

Marmor, J. and S. M. Woods, eds. 1980. *The Interface Between the Psychodynamic and Behavioral Therapies.* New York: Plenum Press.

Marsh, D. T., F. C. Serafica, and C. Barenboim. 1980. Effect of perspective-taking training on interpersonal problem solving. *Child Development,* 51:140–145.

Masangkay, Z. S., K. A. McCluskey, C.W. McIntyre, J. Sims-Knight, B. E. Vaughan, and J. H. Flavell. 1974. The early development of inferences about the visual percepts of others. *Child Development,* 45:357–366.

May, R. 1983. *The Discovery of Being.* New York: Norton.

Meichenbaum, D. 1977. *Cognitive-Behavior Therapy: An Integrative Approach.* New York: Plenum Press.

Meichenbaum, D. and J. Asarnow. 1979. Cognitive-behavioral modification and metacognitive development: Implications for the classroom. In P. C. Kendall and S. D. Hollon, eds., *Cognitive-Behavioral Interventions: Theory, Research, and Procedures.* New York: Academic Press.

Meltzoff, J. and M. Kornreich, 1970. *Research in Psychotherapy.* New York: Atherton.

Menig-Peterson, C. L. 1975. The modification of communicative behavior in pre-school-aged children as a function of the listener's perspective. *Child Development,* 46:1015–1018.

Meyers, A. W. and W. E. Craighead, eds. 1984. *Cognitive Behavior Therapy with children.* New York: Plenum Press.

Miller, P. H., F. Kessel, and J. H. Flavell. 1970. Thinking about people thinking about . . . : A study of social cognitive development. *Child Development,* 41:613–623.

Mosher, R. L. 1979. *Adolescents' Development and Education.* Berkeley, Calif.: McCutchan.

Mugny, G. and W. Doise, 1978. Socio-cognitive conflict and structure of individual and collective performances. *European Journal of Social Psychology,* 8:181–192.

Neale, J. M. 1966. Egocentrism in institutionalized and noninstitutionalized children. *Child Development,* 37:97–101.

Odier, C. 1956. *Anxiety and Magic Thinking.* New York: International Universities Press.

Patterson, C. H. 1980. *Theories of Counseling and Psychotherapy,* 3d ed. New York: Harper & Row.

Patterson, C. J. and M. C. Kister, 1981. The development of listener skills for referential communication. In W. P. Dickson, ed., *Children's Oral Communication Skills.* New York: Academic Press.

Perret-Clermont, A. 1980. Social interaction and cognitive development in children. *European Monographs in Social Psychology,* vol. 19. London: Academic Press.

Piaget, J. 1955. *The Language and Thought of the Child* M. Gabain, trans. Cleveland: Meridan Books. (Originally published 1923.)

Piaget, J. 1960a. *The Child's Conception of the World.* J. and A. Tomilson, trans. Totowa, N.J.: Littlefield, Adams. (Originally published 1926.)

Piaget, J. 1960b. The general problems of the psychobiological development of the child. In J. M. Tanner and B. Inhelder, eds., *Discussions on Child Development.* vol. 4. *The Proceedings of the Fourth Meeting of the World Health Organization Study Group of the Psychobiological Development of the Child.* New York: International Universities Press.

Piaget, J. 1962a. *Play, Dreams, and Imitation in Childhood.* H. Gattegano and F. M. Hodgson, trans. New York: Norton. (Originally published 1946.)

Piaget, J. 1962b. Three lectures (The stages of the intellectual development in the child; The relation of affectivity to intelligence in the mental development; Will and action). *Bulletin of the Menninger Clinic,* 26:120-145.

Piaget, J. 1963. *The Origins of Intelligence in the Child.* M. Cook, trans. New York: Norton. (Originally published 1936.)

Piaget, J. 1964. Development and learning. In R. E. Ripple and V. N. Rockcastle, eds., *Piaget Rediscovered.* Ithaca, N.Y.: School of Education, Cornell University.

Piaget, J. 1965a. *The Child's Conception of Number* C. Gattegno and F. M. Hodgson, trans. New York: Norton. (Originally published, 1941.)

Piaget, J. 1965b. *The Moral Judgment of the Child* M. Gabain, trans. New York: Free Press. (Originally published 1932.)

Piaget, J. 1966. *Psychology of Intelligence.* M. Piercy and D. E. Berlyne, trans. Totowa, N.J.; Littlefield, Adams. (Originally published 1947.)

Piaget, J. 1968. *Six Psychological Studies.* A. Tenzer, trans. New York: Vintage Books. (Originally published 1964.)

Piaget, J. 1969a. *Judgment and Reasoning in the Child.* M. Warden, trans. Totowa, N.J.: Littlefield, Adams. (Originally published 1924.)

Piaget, J. 1969b. *The Child's Conception of Physical Causality.* M. Gabain, trans. Totowa, N.J.: Littlefield, Adams. (Originally published 1927.)

Piaget, J. 1969c. *The Mechanisms of Perception.* New York: Basic Books. (Originally published 1961.)

Piaget, J. 1971a. *The Construction of Reality in the Child.* M. Cook, trans. New York: Ballantine. (Originally published 1936.)

Piaget, J. 1971b. *The Child's Conception of Time.* (A. J. Pomerans, trans. New York: Ballantine. (Originally published 1927.)

Piaget, J. 1971c. *The Child's Conception of Movement and Speed.* G. E. T. Holloway and J. J. Mackenzie, trans. New York: Ballantine. (Originally published 1946.)

Piaget, J. 1971d. Preface. In E. Ferreiro, *Les relations temporelles dans le langage de l'enfant.* Geneva: Droz.

Piaget, J. 1972a. Intellectual evolution from adolescence to adulthood. *Human Development,* 15:1–12.

Piaget, J. 1972b. Physical world of the child. *Physics Today,* 25:23–27.

Piaget, J. 1973. Affective unconscious and cognitive unconscious. In *The Child and Reality.* New York: Grossman.

Piaget, J. 1975. Foreword. In E. J. Anthony, ed., *Explorations in Child Psychiatry.* New York: Plenum.

Piaget, J. 1976a. *The Grasp of Consciousness.* S. W. Wedgwood, trans. Cambridge; Harvard University Press. (Originally published 1974.)

Piaget, J. 1976b. Identity and conservation. In B. Inhelder and H. H. Chipman, eds., *Piaget and His School.* New York: Springer.

Piaget, J. 1976c. Autobiography. In S. Campbell, ed., *Piaget Sampler.* New York: Wiley.

Piaget, J. 1977. *The Development of Thought.* A. Rosin, trans. New York: Viking. (Originally published 1975.)

Piaget, J. 1978. *Success and Understanding.* A. J. Pomerans, trans. Cambridge: Harvard University Press. (Originally published 1974.)

Piaget, J. 1980a. *Adaptation and Intellilgence.* S. Eames, trans. Chicago: University of Chicago Press. (Originally published 1974.)

Piaget, J. 1980b. *Experiments in Contradiction.* D. Coltman, trans. Chicago: University of Chicago Press. (Originally published 1974.)

Piaget, J. 1981. *Intelligence and Affectivity: Their Relationship During Child Development.* T. A. Brown and C. E. Kaegi, trans. and eds. Palo Alto, Calif.: Annual Reviews Monograph. (Originally published 1954, in outline form.)

Piaget, J. with R. Garcia. 1974. *Understanding Causality.* D. Miles and M. Miles, trans. New York: Norton. (Originally published 1971.)

Piaget, J. and B. Inhelder. 1967. *The Child's Conception of Space.* F. J. Langdon and J. L. Lunzer, trans. New York: Norton. (Originally published 1948.)

Piaget, J. and B. Inhelder. 1969. *The Psychology of the Child.* H. Weaver, trans. New York: Basic Books. (Originally published 1966.)

Piaget, J. and B. Inhelder. 1971. *Mental Imagery in the Child.* P. A. Chilton, trans. New York: Basic Books. (Originally published 1966.)

Piaget, J. and B. Inhelder. 1973. *Memory and Intelligence.* A. J. Pomerans, trans. New York: Basic Books. (Originally published 1968.)

Piaget, J. and B. Inhelder. 1975. *The Origin of the Idea of Chance in Children.* L. Leake, Jr., P. Burrell, and H. D. Fishbein, trans. New York: Norton. (Originally published 1951.)

Piaget, J., B. Inhelder, and A. Szeminska. 1960. *The Child's Conception of Geometry.* G. A. Lunzer, trans. New York: Harper & Row. (Originally published 1948.)

Pimm, J. B. 1975. The clinical use of Piagetian tasks with emotionally disturbed children. In G. I. Lubin, J. F. Magary, and M. K. Poulsen, eds., *Proceedings of the Fourth Annual U.A.P. Conference on Piagetian Theory and the Helping Professions.* Los Angeles, February, 199–213.

Pine, F. 1974. Libidinal object constancy: A theoretical note. In L. Goldberger and V. H. Rosen, eds., *Psychoanalysis and Contemporary Science*, vol. 3. New York: International Universities Press, 307–313.

Pulaski, M. A. S. 1971. *Understanding Piaget*. New York: Harper & Row.

Raimy, V. 1975. *Misunderstandings of the Self*. San Francisco: Jossey-Bass.

Rappaport, D. 1954. On the psychoanalytic theory of thinking. In R. R. Knight, ed., *Psychoanalytic Psychiatry and Psychology*, vol. 1. New York: International Universities Press, 259–273.

Rawls, J. 1971. *A Theory of Justice*. Cambridge: Belknap Press of Harvard University Press.

Rest, J. In press. Morality. In J. H. Flavell and E. Markmas, eds., *Cognitive Development*. New York: Wiley.

Roberts, R. J. and C. J. Patterson. 1983. Perspective taking and referential communication: The question of correspondence reconsidered. *Child Development*, 54:1005–1014.

Rosen, H. 1980. *The Development of Sociomoral Knowledge*. New York: Columbia University Press.

Rush, A. J., A. T. Beck, M. Kovacs, and S. Hollon. 1977. Comparative efficacy of cognitive therapy and pharmacotherapy in the treatment of depressed outpatients. *Cognitive Therapy and Research*, vol. 1, no. 1:17–37.

Saint-Pierre, J. 1962. Etude des differences entre la recherche active de la personne humaine et celle de l'object inanime. Master's dissertation, University of Montreal.

Schmid-Kitsikis, E. 1973. Piagetian theory and its approach to psychopatology. *American Journal of Mental Deficiency*, 77:694–705.

Selman, R. L. 1971a. The relation of role-taking to the development of moral judgments in children. *Child Development*, 42:79–91.

Selman, R. L. 1971b. Taking another's perspective: Role-taking development in early childhood. *Child Development*, 42:1721–1734.

Selman, R. L. 1976. Social-cognitive understanding: A guide to educational and clinical practice. In T. Lickona, ed., *Moral Development and Behavior*, pp. 299–316 New York: Holt, Rinehart & Winston.

Selman, R. L. 1980. *The Growth of Interpersonal Understanding*. New York: Academic Press.

Selman, R. L. and D. F. Byrne. 1974. A structural-developmental analysis of levels of role-taking in middle childhood. *Child Development*, 45:803–806.

Selman, R. L., M. Z. Schorin, C. R. Stone, and E. Phelps. 1983. A naturalistic study of children's social understanding. *Developmental Psychology*, 19:82–102.

Serban, G. 1982. *The Tyranny of Magical Thinking*. New York: Dutton.

Shantz, C. U. 1975. The development of social cognition. In E. M. Hetherington, ed., *Review of Child Development Research*, vol. 5. Chicago: University of Chicago Press.

Shantz, C. U. 1981. The role of role-taking in children's referential communication. In W. P. Dickson, ed., *Children's Oral Communication Skills*. New York: Academic Press.

Shantz, C. U. and K. Wilson. 1972. Training communication skills in young children. *Child Development*, 43:693–698.

Shatz, M. and R. Gelman. 1973. The development of communication skills. *Monograph of the Society for Research in Child Development*, 38 (5 serial no. 152).

Shimkunas, A. M. 1972. Conceptual deficit in schizophrenia: A reappraisal. *British Journal of Medical Psychology*, 45:149–157.

Siegel, L. S. and C. J. Brainerd, eds. 1978. *Alternatives to Piaget*. New York: Academic Press.

Silvern, L. E., J. M. Waterman, W. Sobesky, and V. L. Ryan. 1979. Effects of a developmental model of perspective taking training. *Child Development*, 50:243–246.

Simpson, E. E. L. 1974. Moral development research: A case study of scientific cultural bias. *Human Development*, 17:81–106.

Sinclair, H. 1971. Piaget's theory and language acquisition. In M. F. Rossokopf, L. P. Steffe, and S. Taback, eds., *Cognitive-Developmental Research and Mathematical Education*. Washington, D.C.: National Council of Teachers of Mathematics.

Sinclair-de-Zwart, H. 1969. Developmental psycholinguistics. In D. Elkind and J. H. Flavell, eds., *Studies in Cognitive Development*. New York: Oxford University Press.

Siomopoulos, V. 1983. *The Structure of Psychopathological Experience*. New York: Brunner/Mazel.

Sloane, R. B., F. R. Staples, A. H. Cristol, N. J. Yorkston, and K. Whipple. 1975. *Psychotherapy Versus Behavior Therapy*. Cambridge: Harvard University Press.

Smedslund, J. 1961a. The acquisition of conservation of substance and weight in children. I. Introduction. *Scandinavian Journal of Psychology*, 2:11–20.

Smedslund, J. 1961b. The acquisition of conservation of substance and weight in children. II. External reinforcement of conservation of weight and of the operations of addition and subtraction. *Scandinavian Journal of Psychology*, 2:71–84.

Smedslund, J. 1961c. The acquisition of conservation of substance and weight in children. III. Extinction of conservation of weight acquired "normally" and by means of empirical controls on a balance scale. *Scandinavian Journal of Psychology*, 2:85–87.

Smedslund, J. 1961d. The acquisition of conservation of substance and weight in children. IV. An attempt at extinction of the visual components of the weight concept. *Scandinavian Journal of Psychology*, 2:153–155.

Smedslund, J. 1961e. The acquisition of conservation of substance and weight in children. V. Practice in conflict situations without external reinforcement. *Scandinavian Journal of Psychology*, 2:155–160.

Smedslund, J. 1961f. The acquisition of conservation of substance and weight in children. VI. Practice on continuous versus discontinuous material in conflict situations without external reinforcement. *Scandinavian Journal of Psychology*, 2:203–210.

Smith, M. L. and G. V. Glass. 1977. Meta-analysis of psychotherapy outcome studies. *American Psychologist*. 132:752–760.

Spitz, R. A. 1957. *No and Yes: On the Genesis of Human Communication.* New York: International Universities Press.

Spitz, R. A. 1965. *The First Year of Life.* New York: International Universities Press.

Spivack, G., J. J. Platt and M. D. Shure. 1976. *The Problem-Solving Approach to Adjustment.* San Francisco: Jossey-Bass.

Steinfeld, G. J. 1975. Piaget's concept of decentering in relation to family process and therapy. In G. I. Lubin, J. F. Magary, and M. K. Poulsen, eds., *Proceedings of the Fourth Annual U.A.P. Conference on Piagetian Theory and the Helping Professions.* Los Angeles, February, 280–287.

Strauss, J. 1967. The classification of schizophrenic concreteness. *Psychiatry,* 30:294–301.

Strupp, H. H. 1978. Psychotherapy research and practice: An overview. In S. L. Garfield and E. Bergin eds., *Handbook of Psychotherapy and Behavior Change,* 2d ed. New York: Wiley.

Strupp, H. H. and J. L. Binder. 1984. *Psychotherapy in a New Key.* New York: Basic Books.

Suchotliff, L. C. 1970. Relation of formal thought disorder to the communication deficit in schizophrenics. *Journal of Abnormal Psychology,* 76:250–257.

Sullivan, H. S. 1953. *The Interpersonal Theory of Psychiatry.* New York: Norton.

Tenzer, A. 1983. Piaget and psychoanalysis. Some reflections on insight. *Contemporary Psychoanalysis,* 19:319–339.

Trunnell, T. 1964. Thought disturbances in schizophrenia: Pilot study utilizing Piaget's theories. *Archives of General Psychiatry,* 11:126–136.

Trunnel, T. 1965. Thought disturbances in schizophrenia: Replication study utilizing Piaget's theories. *Archives of General Psychiatry,* 13:1–18.

Turiel, E. 1974. Conflict and transition in adolescent moral development. *Child Development,* 45:14–29.

Turiel, E. 1977. Conflict and transition in adolescent moral development. II. The resolution of disequilibrium through structural reorganization. *Child Development,* 48:634–637.

Turiel, E. 1983. *The Development of Social Knowledge.* New York: Cambridge University Press.

Urbain, E. S. and P. C. Kendall. 1980. Review of social-cognitive problem-solving interventions with children. *Psychological Bulletin,* 88:109–143.

Von Domarus, E. 1944. The specific laws of logic in schizophrenia. In J. Kasanin, ed., *Language and Thought in Schizophrenics.* Berkeley: University of California Press.

Voyat, G. E. 1980. Piaget on schizophrenia. *Journal of the American Academy of Psychoanalysis,* 8:93–113.

Voyat, G. E. 1982. *Piaget Systematized.* Hillsdale, N.J.: Lawrence Erlbaum.

Voyat, G. E. 1983. Conscious and unconscious. *Contemporary Psychoanalysis,* 19:348–358.

Vuyk, R. 1981. *Overview and Critique of Piaget's Genetic Epistemology 1965–1980,* vol. 1. New York: Academic Press.

Wachtel, P. L. 1977. *Psychoanalysis and Behavior Therapy: Toward an Integration.* New York: Basic Books.

Wachtel, P. L. 1980. Transference, schema, and assimilation: The relevance of Piaget to the psychoanalytic theory of transference. *The Quarterly of Psychoanalysis,* 8:59–76.

Wachtel, P. L. 1981. Transference, schema, and assimilation: The relevance of Piaget to the psychoanalytic theory of transference. *The Annual of Psychoanalysis,* vol. 8. New York: International Universities Press.

Walen, S., R. Di Giuseppe, and R. L. Wessler. 1980. *A Practitioner's Guide to Rational Emotive Therapy.* Oxford: Oxford University Press.

Walker, L. J. 1982. The sequentiality of Kohlberg's stages of moral development. *Child Development,* 53:1330–1336.

Walker, L. J. 1983. Sources of cognitive conflict for stage transition in moral development. *Developmental Psychology,* 19:103–110.

Walker, L. J. In press. Sex differences in the development of moral reasoning: A critical review of the literature. *Child Development.*

Waskow, I. E., S. Hadley, M. Parloff, and J. Autry. 1979. Psychotherapy of depression. Collaborative Research Program. Unpublished intern research proposal. National Institute of Mental Health.

Waterman, J. M., W. E. Sobesky, L. Silvern, B. Aoki, and M. McCaulay. 1981. Social perspective-taking and adjustment in emotionally disturbed, learning-disabled, and normal children. *Journal of Abnormal Child Psychology,* 9:133–148.

Watzlawick, P., J. Weakland, and R. Fisch. 1974. *Change: Principles of Problem Formation and Problem Resolution.* New York: Norton.

Weiner, M. L. 1975. *The Cognitive Unconscious: A Piagetian Approach to Psychotherapy.* Davis, Calif.: Psychological Press.

Whitehurst, G. J. and S. Sonnenschein. 1981. The development of informative messages in referential communication: Knowing when versus knowing how. In W. P. Dickson, ed., *Children's Oral Communication Skills.* New York: Academic Press.

Wilson, G. T. and K. D. O'Leary. 1980. *Principles of Behavior Therapy.* Englewood Cliffs, N.J.: Prentice-Hall.

Wolff, P. H. 1960. The developmental psychologies of Jean Piaget and psychoanalysis. *Psychological Issues,* 2, monograph 5, New York: International Universities Press.

Wolpe, J. 1958. *Psychotherapy by Reciprocal Inhibition.* Stanford, Calif.: Stanford University Press.

Wolpe, J. 1982. *The Practice of Behavior Therapy.* 3d ed. New York: Pergamon Press.

Wright, J. H. and A. T. Beck. 1983. Cognitive therapy of depression. *Hospital and Community Psychiatry,* 34:1119–1127.

Youniss, J. 1980. *Parents and Peers in Social Development.* Chicago: University of Chicago Press.

Name Index

Subject Index